Evaluation Fundamentals

SECOND EDITION

This book is dedicated to the ones I love:
John C. Beck and, of course, Astrid and Daniella

Evaluation Fundamentals

Insights into the Outcomes, Effectiveness, and Quality of Health Programs

SECOND EDITION

Arlene Fink

SAGE Publications
International Educational and Professional Publisher
Thousand Oaks ■ London ■ New Delhi

For information:

Sage Publications, Inc.
2455 Teller Road
Thousand Oaks, California 91320
E-mail: order@sagepub.com

Sage Publications Ltd.
1 Oliver's Yard
55 City Road
London EC1Y 1SP
United Kingdom

Sage Publications India Pvt. Ltd.
B-42, Panchsheel Enclave
Post Box 4109
New Delhi 110 017 India

Printed in the United States of America

Library of Congress Cataloging-in-Publication Data

Fink, Arlene.
Evaluation fundamentals: Insights into the outcomes, effectiveness,
and quality of health programs / Arlene Fink.
p. cm.
Includes bibliographical references and index.
ISBN 0-7619-8868-8 (pbk.)
1. Medical care—Evaluation. 2. Public health—Evaluation. 3. Medical care—Quality control. 4. Public health—Planning. 5. Outcome assessment (Medical care) I. Title.
RA399.A1F563 2005
362.1′068—dc22 2004004551

This book is printed on acid-free paper.

06 07 10 9 8 7 6 5 4 3 2

Acquisitions Editor: Lisa Cuevas Shaw
Editorial Assistant: Margo Crouppen
Production Editor: Diane S. Foster
Copy Editor: Judy Selhorst
Typesetter: C&M Digitals (P) Ltd.
Proofreader: Libby Larson
Indexer: Molly Hall
Cover Designer: Janet Foulger

Contents

Preface

Over the past decade, program evaluation has made important contributions to health care practice, policy, administration, education, and research. This book explains the evaluator's goals and methods so as to provide readers with the skills they need to review and participate in program evaluations in health care settings.

This book's nine chapters are specifically organized to facilitate learning. In addition to the textual material, the chapters contain the following elements:

- Brief reader's guides to the topics to be covered
- Examples illustrating all major concepts discussed
- Separate guidelines for conducting key evaluation activities
- Examples of forms to use in completing evaluation tasks
- Checklists highlighting key concepts
- Summaries of the main ideas and topics covered
- Exercises
- Lists of suggested readings and online resources that cover the health field (e.g., public health, health services and policy, epidemiology, medicine, nursing)

The book also provides readers with a special scoring guide for reviewing the quality of their own and other evaluations.

The chapters presented here are organized according to the main tasks involved in conducting an evaluation: posing evaluation questions, setting standards of effectiveness, designing the evaluation, sampling participants, selecting information sources, ensuring reliable and valid measurement, managing data, analyzing data, and reporting the results in written and oral form. Among the special topics covered are the following:

- The origins and purposes of evaluation questions and hypotheses
- The evaluation of program outcomes and effectiveness
- Reliability and validity
- True experiments and quasi-experiments
- Sample size

- Effect size
- Qualitative evaluation methods, including participatory evaluation
- Community-based evaluation
- Evaluation questions and issues of program cost-benefit and cost-effectiveness
- Data management and computers
- Confidence intervals
- Statistical and practical significance
- Meta-analysis
- Evaluation frameworks and models
- Ethical evaluation and institutional review boards
- Informed consent forms
- Research misconduct
- Evaluation reports online
- Evaluation models online
- Economic evaluations: cost-effectiveness, cost-benefit, cost utility
- Factorial designs
- Codebooks
- Data entry
- Computerized presentations of evaluation findings

This book is recommended for program evaluators in health and education; students and faculty in courses including content in public health, public policy, health services research, and program evaluation; health program planners and administrators; health policy makers; funders of health programs; medical educators; and patient educators. It is designed to cover the health care field and to respect the needs of students in public health and the health professions as well as doctors and nurses, welfare workers, patient educators, and hospital administrators. The examples presented in the chapters that follow are taken from programs that include both younger and older patients and cover the costs and quality of care as well as issues ranging from prevention and well-being to the care of the terminally ill.

Purpose of This Chapter

The goal of this text is to provide you with the tools and skills you need to be a perceptive participant in and consumer of program evaluations. This chapter defines evaluation and discusses its purposes and methods.

1 Program Evaluation: A Prelude

A Reader's Guide to Chapter 1

What Is Program Evaluation?
- How to Evaluate: The Methods
- The Program or Intervention
- Program Merits or Standards of Effectiveness
- Program Objectives and Activities
- Program Outcomes
- Program Impact
- Program Expenses and Costs

Users and Doers of Evaluations

The Composition of Program Evaluation

Posing evaluation questions, setting standards of effectiveness, designing the study, selecting participants, collecting data, managing and analyzing data, and reporting the results

Baseline Data, Interim Data (Formative Evaluation), and Process Evaluations

Qualitative Evaluation

Participatory and Community-Based Evaluations

Evaluation Frameworks and Models

PRECEDE-PROCEED, RE-AIM, and practical evaluation (Centers for Disease Control)

Ethical Evaluations

Evaluations that need institutional review board approval and evaluations that are exempt from IRB approval, what the IRB reviews, and informed consent

Research Misconduct

A note about the Health Insurance Portability and Accountability Act

What Is Program Evaluation?

Program evaluation is the diligent investigation of a program's characteristics and merits. In the context of health care, the purpose of program evaluation is to provide information on the *effectiveness* of *programs,* or *interventions,* so as to optimize the *outcomes, efficiency,* and *quality* of health care. An evaluation may analyze a program's structure, activities, and organization as well as its political and social environment. It may also appraise the achievement of a program's goals and objectives and the extent of the program's impact and costs.

How to Evaluate: The Methods

Health program evaluators use many of the same methods that health investigators (including clinical and health services researchers, medical sociologists, and epidemiologists) rely on to gather reliable and valid evidence. Program evaluations require diligence in the choice and application of methods. These consist of formulating study questions, setting standards for establishing a program's merits, designing the evaluation, selecting participants, collecting data, and analyzing, interpreting, and reporting the results.

The Program or Intervention

At the core of an evaluation is an experimental project or *program,* sometimes called an *intervention.* Programs are systematic efforts to achieve particular planned purposes, such as the improvement of health, knowledge, attitudes, behavior, and practice. A program may be relatively small (for instance, a health education course for seniors in two high schools, a new community health center for persons over 75 years of age, or a campaign to vaccinate all children in a school district) or relatively large (such as Medicare, an experiment in the regionalization of perinatal services, or a national strategy to increase public awareness of the safety of blood transfusions). Programs can take place in differing geographic and political climates and health care settings, and they vary in their purposes, structures, organization, and constituents.

Program Merits or Standards of Effectiveness

One of the major tasks of an evaluation is to judge a program's merits. A meritorious program has worthy goals, achieves its standards of *effectiveness,* provides benefits to its participants, fully informs its participants of the potential risks of participation, and does no harm. Evaluation is often distinguished from other types of health research by its identification of convincing evidence of program merit, measurement of merit, and description of the aspects of the program that are most meritorious. A program's merit is often equated with its effectiveness.

Program Objectives and Activities

A program's objectives are its planned purposes—for example, to improve health and optimize the efficiency of the health care system. A primary function of program evaluation is to provide data on the extent to which a program's objectives are achieved. When program leaders require assistance in clarifying objectives or in establishing priorities among objectives, they might call on an evaluator to conduct a needs assessment. For example, the director of a new family practice medical residency program in a low-income urban area asked an evaluator to conduct a systematic examination of that community's health care needs so that the program designers could create a curriculum that would meet the needs of residents.

Evaluations also answer questions about a program's activities and offer insight into a program's implementation and management. When an evaluation focuses on program activities, it is termed a *process evaluation.* Process evaluations help evaluators to develop insights and to form hypotheses for later testing as to the reasons for the achievement (or lack of achievement) of the program's objectives. Suppose, for example, that an evaluation found no differences between patient-reminder and physician-reminder programs in the number of women over 50 years of age who return each year for a mammogram. A wary evaluator would make certain to measure the extent to which each program was accomplished according to its prespecified plan. Among the questions the evaluator could ask are these: Did all eligible patients receive reminders? Did all eligible physicians receive reminders? How timely were the reminders?

Program Outcomes

The ultimate, hoped-for outcomes of health care programs include optimum health and well-being and high-quality, efficient care. These outcomes are sometimes difficult to measure because of lack of consensus concerning their definitions and because evaluators only rarely have sufficient time to observe them accurately. As a result, many evaluations focus on the extent to which programs achieve more easily measured goals and objectives, such as improvement in knowledge, attitudes, skills, behavior, and practice. The idea is that if programs can foster the achievement of these objectives, accomplishment of the more remote outcomes becomes possible. The good news is that major improvements are constantly being made in the definition and measurement of health care outcomes.

Program Impact

Evaluators often examine a program's impact—that is, the scope of its effects, the duration of its outcomes, and the extent of its influence in other health care settings and among different types of practitioners and practices. For example, consider the evaluations of two programs to improve health status. Evaluation A concluded that Program A improved health status and that the gains were sustained for at least 3 years; moreover, when Program A was tried out in another country, participants in that country uniformly improved. Evaluation B concluded that Program B also improved health status and sustained the improvement for 3 years, but for fewer participants; when the program was tested in another country, the evaluators found there were few gains. The evaluators of Programs A and B agreed that Program A had greater impact because its benefits reached more people over a longer period of time.

Program Expenses and Costs

Evaluations are also concerned with the costs of programs and the relationship of costs to effects and benefits. The following are some typical questions about costs: How efficiently is the clinic (hospital, health center) run? What are the costs of shifting care from the inpatient to the outpatient setting? For each dollar spent on a monthly home visit by a nurse practitioner, how much is saved in terms of future hospitalizations and visits to a physician?

Users and Doers of Evaluations

At least six different groups use the information that results from health care program evaluations:

- Federal, state, and local government (for example, a city, county, or state department of health or the National Institutes of Health)
- Program developers (for example, a director of a community health clinic or a nursing school's curriculum committee)
- Communities (for example, geographically intact areas, such as a city's "skid row"; people with a shared health-related problem, such as HIV/AIDS; or individuals with a common culture, such as Armenians or Latinos).
- Health policy makers (for example, a subcommittee on the health of the state or a group of people who make decisions regarding how much to reimburse physicians for services)
- Program funders (for example, the various institutes of the National Institutes of Health and philanthropic foundations)
- Health researchers (for example, in government agencies, business, public agencies, and universities)

Evaluations are sometimes conducted by teams of individuals, each of whom contributes particular expertise. Consider the evaluations described in Example 1.1.

Example 1.1 Program Evaluation as an Interdisciplinary Discipline

- A 4-year evaluation of a new program in ambulatory care was conducted by a team made up of two professional evaluators, a sociologist, a survey researcher, and two physicians. The evaluation team also consulted a nurse and an economist and employed trained data collectors.
- A 3-year evaluation of a 35-project program to improve access to and use of prenatal care for low-income women relied on a professional evaluator, an epidemiologist, a nurse practitioner, and an economist.
- An evaluation of a newly developed questionnaire for physicians to use in measuring patients' social, psychological, and physical functioning relied on four physicians, a professional evaluator, a psychometrician, and an occupational therapist.
- An evaluation of a program using nurses to screen community-dwelling elderly individuals for hypertension, vision, and hearing disorders relied on two physicians and a professional evaluator.

The Composition of Program Evaluation

Program evaluations typically consist of the following activities:

1. Posing questions about the program
2. Setting standards of effectiveness
3. Designing the evaluation
4. Selecting participants
5. Collecting data
6. Managing data
7. Analyzing data
8. Reporting and disseminating the results

Posing Evaluation Questions

The combined answers to evaluation questions are a primary basis for judging a program's merits. The following are some typical evaluation questions:

- To what extent did the program achieve its goals and objectives?
- What are the characteristics of the individuals and groups who participated in the program?
- For which individuals or groups was the program most effective?
- How enduring were the program's effects?

- Which features (e.g., activities, settings, management strategies) of the program were most effective?
- How applicable are the program's objectives and activities to other participants in other settings?
- What are the relationships among the costs of the program and its effects?
- To what extent did social, political, and financial support influence the program's outcomes and acceptability?

Setting Standards of Effectiveness

Setting standards means deciding what information is needed to provide convincing evidence of a program's effectiveness, an important component of an evaluator's appraisal of merit. For example, consider these possible standards for the objective "to improve children's dietary and other health habits":

- Testimony from children in the program (and/or from their parents and teachers) that their habits had improved
- The evaluator's observations of improved health habits (e.g., through studies of children's choices of snacks during and between meals)
- Evidence of children's improved health status found in physical examinations by a nurse practitioner
- The evaluator's finding of a difference in habits and health status favoring children who are in the program compared with children who are not

The challenge to the evaluator is to identify standards that are appropriate for the program, possible to measure, and credible.

Designing the Study

Evaluation design refers to the manner in which the environment is structured so that any documented effects that seem to have resulted from the program can be conclusively linked to it. Standard evaluation designs include comparing one group's performance over time and comparing two groups at one or many times. For example, suppose five universities plan to participate in an evaluation of a new program to teach the basic principles of evaluation research to Health Corps trainees. In designing the study, the evaluator will have to decide on such issues as whether some or all universities should receive the program, how many times Health Corps trainees should be tested to determine the extent of learning, and when they should be tested (Before and after each lesson? Before and after the program? How long after the program?).

Among the general questions that an evaluator asks when considering the design of a study are these:

- How many observations or measurements should I take?
- When should I take the measurements?

- How many groups do I need to observe or compare?
- Which criteria should I use to include institutions, groups, or persons?
- Which criteria should I use to exclude institutions, groups, or persons?

Selecting the Participants

Suppose you were asked to evaluate a program to provide school-based mental health services to children who have witnessed or been victims of violence in their communities. Here are some questions you would need to ask:

- Who should be included in the evaluation? (For example, Which grades should be included? How much exposure to violence should eligible children have?)
- Who should be excluded? (For example, Should children be excluded if, in the opinion of the mental health clinician, they are probably too disruptive to participate in the program's required group therapy sessions?)
- How many children should be included? (That is, what is a sufficient number of participants to allow the evaluation to detect change if the program is effective?)

Collecting Data

The activity of collecting evaluation information includes the following tasks:

- Identifying the variables to measure (e.g., the specific knowledge, performance, attitudes, or behaviors that are the focus of the program's objectives)
- Selecting, adapting, or creating measures
- Demonstrating the reliability (consistency) and validity (accuracy) of the measures
- Administering the measures
- Scoring and interpreting the results

Some common sources of evaluation data are as follows:

- Literature reviews
- Performance tests (including "standardized patients")
- Medical record reviews
- Existing data sets such as those maintained by local, state, and federal governments and other evaluators
- Self-administered questionnaires (including mailed and online surveys)
- Interviews (in person and on the telephone)
- Achievement tests
- Direct observations
- Physical examinations
- Clinical scenarios

Managing Data

Data management includes the following activities:

- Drafting an analysis plan that defines the variables to be analyzed
- Creating a codebook
- Establishing the reliability of the coders
- Reviewing data collection instruments for incomplete or missing data
- Entering data into a database and validating the accuracy of the entry
- Cleaning the data to check for missing data and outliers
- Creating the final data set for analysis
- Storing and archiving the data set and its operations manual

Analyzing Data

Data analysis consists of the descriptive and statistical methods used to summarize information about a program's merits. The choice of which method of analysis to use is dependent on several considerations:

- The characteristics of the evaluation question and standards (Do they ask about differences or associations over time among groups? About costs and effects? About use of services?)
- How the variables are expressed, whether nominally (e.g., qualitative or categorical, such as "did or did not receive a flu shot"), ordinally (e.g., Stage I, II, or III of a disease), or numerically (e.g., scores on a physical functioning scale ranging from 1 = *very poor function* to 5 = *very good function*)
- The number of measures
- The reliability and validity of the data

Reporting the Results

An evaluation report consists of descriptions of the program's characteristics and explanations as well as judgments of the program's merits. The report describes the purposes of the evaluation, presents information on the methods used (including the standard-setting process, the research design, the sampling process, data collection, and analysis), describes the results, and discusses the program and the implications of the results. Evaluation reports may be oral or may be presented in written form, as books, monographs, or articles.

Baseline Data, Interim Data (Formative Evaluation), and Process Evaluations

Health program evaluations are conducted to find out the extent to which particular interventions or programs are effective and efficient in influencing health outcomes and the organization and quality of care. Evaluators typically assume that the programs they examine are needed and that program protocols have been prepared to meet the participants' needs. If these assumptions are erroneous, the evaluation results will necessarily be invalid.

The need for a program is demonstrated through the collection of data to show that the participants start out with one or more difficulties that are in need of an intervention. These baseline data show the participants' condition before the program. Interim data, which are collected during the course of the program, show the program's progress in meeting the needs of the participants.

Baseline Data

Baseline data are collected before the start of the program. Suppose you are to evaluate a program that is being planned to instruct physicians in the use of a new set of guidelines for treating problems such as depression and hypertension. A review of a sample of patients' medical records can assist you in determining the extent to which physicians are already using the guidelines. If you find evidence that all physicians are already using the guidelines, you can assume that the program is not needed.

Baseline data are often collected to describe the characteristics of participants (such as their health status and demographic features), information that is important later on, when the evaluator is interpreting the effects of the program. Example 1.2 illustrates some of the reasons program evaluators collect baseline data.

Example 1.2 Baseline Data and Program Evaluation

The Agency for Health Care has published extensive guidelines for identifying and treating hypertensive patients. An evaluation of the effectiveness of the guidelines is being conducted nationally. Before the evaluators begin the formal process of evaluation, they will collect baseline data on the extent to which the physicians in different kinds of health care settings (such as health maintenance organizations and private group practices) already follow the practices recommended by the guidelines, the prevalence of hypertension in the communities of interest, and the number of hypertensive patients physicians in the study sample are likely to see in the evaluation's proposed duration of 3 years.

Interim Data and Formative Evaluation

In what is sometimes called *formative evaluation*, interim data are collected after the start of a program but before its conclusion—for example, 12 months after the beginning of a 3-year intervention. An evaluator collects interim data to describe the progress of the program and of the evaluation.

Because interim data are always preliminary, they require cautious interpretation. Example 1.3 illustrates why evaluators need to take care in interpreting preliminary, formative findings.

Example 1.3 Formative Evaluation and Interim Data: Proceed With Caution

In a 3-year study of access to prenatal care, the results of a 14-month formative evaluation found that three of six community clinics had opened on schedule and were providing health services to needy women exactly as planned. Preliminary data also revealed that 200 women had been served in the clinics and that the proportion of babies born weighing less than 2,500 grams (5.5 pounds) was 4%, well below the state's average of 6%. The evaluators concluded that progress was definitely being made toward improving access to prenatal care. After 3 years, however, the evaluation results were quite different. The remaining three planned clinics had never opened, and one of the original three had closed. Many fewer women were served than had been anticipated, and the proportion of low-birth-weight babies was 6.6%.

As this example shows, although formative evaluations may sometimes appear to be useful, they also may be misleading; further, they are extremely expensive to conduct. With programs of relatively short duration—say, 2 years or less—the collection of interim data is probably not very useful at all. Some evaluators will not participate in studies of interventions that are not carefully defined and standardized (and therefore not in need of formative evaluation), suggesting that such analyses belong to the program developers. Consider the evaluation described in Example 1.4.

Example 1.4 Questions Asked in a Formative Evaluation of a Program for Critically Ill Children

Many experts agree that the emergency medical services needed by critically ill and injured children differ in important ways from those needed by adults. As a result, a number of states have attempted to reorganize their emergency services to provide better care to children. One state commissioned a 3-year evaluation of its program. It was specifically concerned with the characteristics and effectiveness of an about-to-be implemented intervention to prevent transfers from adult inpatient or intensive care units and to maximize quality of care for children with cardiopulmonary arrest in hospital emergency departments and intensive care units.

In planning the evaluation, the evaluators decided to check a sample of medical records in 15 of the state's 56 counties to see whether sufficient information was available for them to use the records as a main source of data. Also, the evaluators planned to release preliminary findings after 12 months. This would involve reviews of records as well as interviews with physicians, hospital administrators, paramedics, and patients' families. An expert's review of the evaluation's design raised these questions for the evaluators:

1. Does the description of this evaluation as a "3-year evaluation" mean that there will be 3 years of data collection? How much time will you need to plan the evaluation?
2. Interim data have been promised in a year. Can you develop and validate medical record review forms in time to collect enough information to present meaningful findings?
3. Can you develop, validate, and administer the survey forms in the time available?
4. To what extent will the interim and preliminary analyses answer the same or similar questions? If they are very different, will you have sufficient time and money to do both well?
5. Will a written or oral interim report be required?

Process or Implementation Evaluation

A process evaluation is concerned with the extent to which planned activities are implemented, and its findings may be reported at any time. Process evaluations are nearly always useful. For example, in a randomized trial of three interventions to increase the rates at which women returned to follow up on abnormal Pap smears, a process evaluation concluded that implementation of the intervention protocols was less than perfect and thus introduced a conservative bias into the results of the outcome evaluation. This study is the subject of Example 1.5.

Example 1.5 Process or Implementation Evaluation: Follow-Up of Abnormal Pap Smears

During the course of a 2-year evaluation, all women were to be surveyed at least once regarding whether they had received the program and the extent to which they understood its purposes and adhered to its requirements. Telephone interviews after 18 months revealed that 74 of 100 women (74%) in the slide-tape intervention had seen the entire 25-minute presentation, 70 of 111 (63%) had received mailed reminders from their physicians' offices to come back for another

Pap smear, and 32 of 101 (about 32%) had received phone calls from their physicians' offices. These findings helped explain the apparent failure of the third intervention to achieve positive results when compared with the other two.

Qualitative Evaluation

Qualitative evaluations collect data through in-person interviews, direct observations, and review of written documents (such as private diaries). These evaluations aim to provide personalized information on the dynamics of a program and on participants' perceptions of the program's outcomes and impact.

Qualitative evaluation is useful for examining programs for which the goals are in the process of being defined and for testing out the workability of particular evaluation methods. Because they are "personalized," qualitative methods may add emotion to otherwise purely statistical findings and provide a means of gauging outcomes when reliable and valid measures of those outcomes are unlikely to be available in time for inclusion in the evaluation report.

Qualitative methods are employed in program evaluations to complement the usual sources of data (such as standardized surveys and medical record reviews, physical examinations, and achievement tests). Example 1.6 illustrates some of the uses of qualitative methods in program evaluation.

Example 1.6 Uses of Qualitative Methods in Program Evaluation

- To evaluate the effectiveness of a campaign to get heroin addicts to clean their needles with bleach, the evaluators spend time in a heroin "shooting gallery." Although they bring a tape recorder with them, they rarely use it. They find that, although needles are being cleaned, the addicts use a common dish to rinse needles and dilute the drug before shooting. The evaluators recommend that the community's program be altered to take into account the dangers of this practice.
  Comment: The evaluators are observers of the participants at the shooting gallery. They do not conduct systematic surveys of these individuals.

- To evaluate the effectiveness of an education-counseling program for mentally ill adults, the evaluation team lives for 3 months in each of five different residential communities. After taping more than 250 counseling sessions, the evaluators conclude that the quality of the counseling varies greatly both within and among the communities; this helps to explain the overall program's inconsistent results.
  Comment: The evaluators tape the sessions and then interpret the results. The interpretations come after the data are collected; the evaluators make no effort to postulate hypotheses in advance of data collection.

- To evaluate the impact of a school-based health program for homeless children, the evaluators teach a cohort of children to keep diaries over a 3-year period. The evaluation finds that children in the program are much more willing to attend to the dangers of smoking and other drug use than are children in schools without the program. The diaries reveal that children in the program are especially pleased to participate. The evaluators conclude that the children's enjoyment may be related to the program's positive outcomes.
  Comment: The use of diaries is a primary qualitative tool. It allows participants to say how they feel in their own words.

- An evaluation of the impact on the county of a program to improve access to and use of prenatal care services asks "opinion leaders" to give their views. These people are known in the county to have expertise in providing, financing, and evaluating prenatal care. The interviewers encourage the leaders to bring up any issues that concern them. The leaders share their belief that any improvements in prenatal care are probably due to medical advances rather than to enhanced access to services. After the interviews are completed, the evaluators conclude that major barriers to access and use continue to exist even though statistical registries reveal a decline in infant mortality rates for some groups of women.
  Comment: The experts are invited to give their own views; the evaluators make little attempt to oblige the opinion leaders to adhere to certain topics.

Participatory and Community-Based Evaluations

A participatory evaluation invites representatives of the organizations and communities that will be affected by the evaluation's findings to join the evaluation team as partners in some or all evaluation activities. Proponents of community-based evaluations believe that when such participation is encouraged, evaluations' findings are particularly useful in helping to reduce health disparities based on characteristics such as race, ethnicity, age, sexual orientation, socioeconomic status, and geography, for at least four reasons:

1. Participation helps to improve the quality and validity of research by giving it a basis in local knowledge, culture, and history. In participatory evaluations, health concerns are viewed *ecologically*—that is, in their political and social context as well as in their clinical setting.

2. Including the expertise of community members enhances the relevance of the evaluation questions, the quality and quantity of data gathered, and the use of the data. Community members as well as researchers "own" the data and will want to see them used.

3. Participatory evaluation projects can assist in providing community members with resources and possible employment opportunities. For example, community members can help evaluators in translating data collection instruments and conducting interviews.

4. Participatory evaluations can lead to improvements in the health and well-being of communities by studying and addressing important community needs and increasing community members' power and control over the research process. The community can keep the evaluators on track, preventing them from taking an approach that is too academic or theoretical.

To be effective, participatory evaluators must be skilled in working with diverse groups of individuals. They must learn how to lead meetings, encourage consensus, and inform participants about the objectives and purposes of evaluation studies in general and their own evaluations in particular. At the same time, participatory evaluators must lead the process of collecting unbiased data and interpreting those data objectively. Not all programs—no matter how well-intentioned—are effective, and even those that have positive effects may not be cost-effective. The participatory evaluator must be prepared to be the bearer of bad news. Participatory evaluations also tend to be extremely costly because they are labor-intensive: They require many individuals from the evaluation team and the community to spend time on such evaluation activities as setting standards of program merit and assisting with technical activities, including research design, data collection, and report writing. Example 1.7 provides illustrations of participatory evaluation in action.

Example 1.7 Participatory Evaluation in Action

- An evaluation of a cancer control program involves the community in all phases of the project, from the development of the grant proposal through to interpretation of the data. The purpose of the project is to evaluate the effectiveness of a culturally appropriate intervention as a means of increasing breast and cervical cancer screening practice among the community's women. The results show a community-wide impact on cancer-related knowledge, attitudes, and behaviors; increased research capabilities; and improvements to the health systems and services given to the community.
  Comment: Members of the community are actively included in all phases of the evaluation study, including the writing of the proposal for funding and the interpretation of the data.

- A mental health intervention is designed to diminish symptoms of depression in urban schoolchildren who have witnessed or participated in community violence. A group of parents assist the evaluators in developing evaluation questions, translating some of the data collection measures into Spanish and Russian, and collecting data from other parents. They also review the evaluation's findings and comment on them. The comments are incorporated into the final report of the intervention's effectiveness.
  Comment: Parents work with the evaluators on many activities, including the formulation of evaluation questions, data collection, and reporting. They are not necessarily involved in designing the evaluation (e.g., determining which children are eligible for participation and the characteristics of the control or comparative intervention) or in the data analysis.

- The directors of a health care clinic, interested in improving patient education, intend to organize a series of seminars for staff and then evaluate whether patient education improves after all staff have attended the seminars. As part of the evaluation, the evaluation team convenes a series of four noon meetings with clinic staff to identify the nature and extent of current problems in the clinic's education for patients and to examine alternative solutions. The clinic staff members agree to form a committee to work with the evaluators to set standards for determining whether the seminars are effective; they also agree to advise the evaluators on questions to ask patients about their experiences at the clinic and to review and comment on the report of the evaluation's findings. *Comment:* This is a participatory evaluation in that the evaluators work with the health clinic's staff to set standards, identify appropriate questions to ask patients about their experiences, and report on the study's findings.

Evaluation Frameworks and Models

Evaluation frameworks provide guidance for evaluators, helping them to be certain that their evaluations' overall designs consider the origins and contexts of the programs they examine. Example 1.8 provides an overview of three evaluation models.

Example 1.8 Three Evaluation Models

PRECEDE-PROCEED

The acronym PRECEDE stands for *predisposing, reinforcing, and enabling constructs in education/environmental diagnosis and evaluation.* The acronym PROCEED stands for *policy, regulatory, and organizational constructs in educational and environmental development.* PRECEDE-PROCEED is a framework for program planning and evaluation that entails the following nine factors:

1. *Social assessment* to determine perceptions of people's needs and quality of life using community organization theories. For instance, evaluators use focus groups to find out which health problems are most important among children in the community's elementary school.

2. *Epidemiological assessment* to identify the health problems that are most important in the community. For instance, evaluators conduct interviews with providers at local clinics to find out why neighborhood children visit the clinics; evaluators review county records to study inoculation rates.

3. *Behavioral and environmental assessment* to uncover factors that contribute to the occurrence and severity of a health problem. Behavioral factors include the lifestyles of individuals at risk. Environmental factors include resources for health care in the workplace and community. For instance, to

conduct a behavioral assessment to help understand why so many children are overweight, evaluators survey parents concerning their views of their children's nutritional habits. The evaluators also study school resources to determine how to improve food service to make it more nutritious and conduct focus groups with local leaders to find out about the availability of health insurance and health education programs in the workplace.

4. *Educational and ecological assessment* to identify the factors that might be needed to foster changes in health behaviors. These may include assessments of health-related knowledge, beliefs, and self-efficacy (referred to as *predisposing factors*); social support (*reinforcing factors*); and programs and services necessary for good outcomes to be realized (*enabling factors*).

5. *Administrative and policy assessment* to review policies and resources that facilitate or hinder program implementation.

6–9. *Implementation and evaluation of process, impact, and outcomes.* Using the assessments as a guide, communities implement programs and evaluators study the programs' activities and immediate and longer-term outcomes.

RE-AIM

The acronym RE-AIM stands for *reach, efficacy* (or *effectiveness*), *adoption, implementation, and maintenance. Reach* refers to the percentage of potential participants who are exposed to an intervention and how representative they are of others who might benefit from the program. *Efficacy,* or *effectiveness,* concerns both the intended effects of a program and the possible unintended outcomes. *Adoption* refers to the participation rate of eligible subjects and how well the setting and the people who deliver the intervention reflect future participants. *Implementation* denotes the extent to which various components of the program are delivered as intended. *Maintenance* is related to two questions: What are the program's long-term effects? To what extent is the program continued after the completion of the evaluation? All five of these dimensions are considered equally important in the RE-AIM framework.

The Centers for Disease Control's Framework for Planning and Implementing Practical Program Evaluation

Figure 1.1 illustrates the framework for planning and implementing practical program evaluation used by the Centers for Disease Control (CDC). This framework consists of six steps for accomplishing the evaluation (e.g., beginning with engaging stakeholders) and includes four standards for evaluating the evaluation: accuracy, utility, feasibility, and propriety.

The three frameworks described above share several important features. First, they are all more precisely described as frameworks rather than models. That is, their purpose is to provide guidance in program planning and evaluation. Strictly speaking, models "predict" behavior or outcomes and are based on theoretical

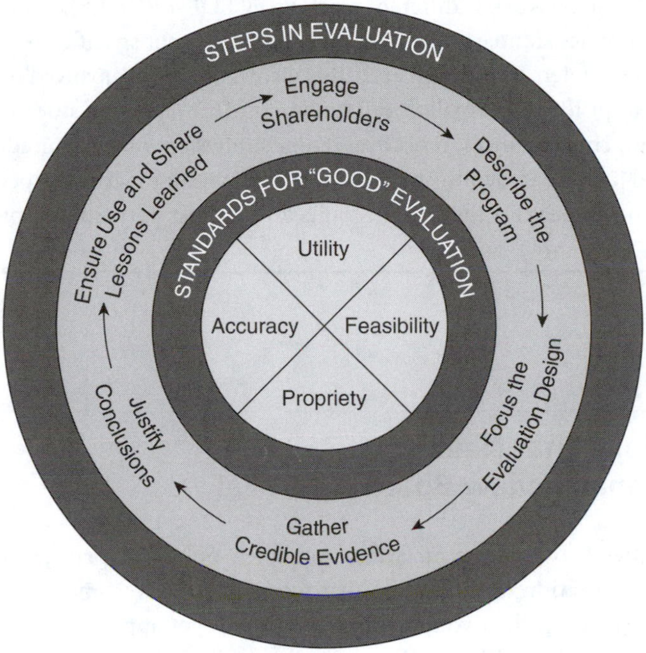

Figure 1.1 The CDC's Framework for Planning and Implementing Practical Program Evaluation

expectations or empirical evidence gained through experience and experiment. Frameworks leave the theories and methods of implementation to the evaluator.

These three frameworks are all-inclusive. PRECEDE-PROCEED, for example, contains a comprehensive set of factors that should be considered in program planning and evaluation. It is unlikely, however, that evaluators will ever find themselves involved in all aspects of program development and evaluation as characterized in this framework. In many cases, evaluators are called in to appraise the merits and effectiveness of existing programs. In others, evaluators are asked to be part of research teams that are developing interventions. No one really expects an individual evaluator to be *the* expert in the planning process or in the development of a program. The evaluator's primary domain is collecting and interpreting valid data on the implementation of the program and its effectiveness.

Frameworks such as PRECEDE-PROCEED, RE-AIM, and the CDC's approach to practical evaluation may be useful in encouraging evaluators to pay attention to the origins and development of the programs they examine (even if they had little to do with establishing the need for the programs or with implementing them). The knowledge they gain may help them to design more realistic and relevant studies.

RE-AIM is also comprehensive because it is a public health model. This framework may be especially useful for an evaluator in that it can provide a "score" that can be applied to a program and its evaluation. For instance, a program that beneficially affects all eligible individuals and achieves many positive outcomes may be scored higher than one that is similar but has many negative unintended outcomes.

The CDC's framework is different from PRECEDE-PROCEED and RE-AIM in that it incorporates standards for a "good" evaluation that specifically include propriety. *Propriety* refers to the legal and ethical considerations involved in evaluation research. Except for very small, local studies, and some larger studies conducted under certain circumstances, most evaluation studies are now required by law and institutional practice to demonstrate their ethical nature in writing, specifying how they will show respect for their participants and protect participants' privacy.

Ethical Evaluations

Evaluations That Need Institutional Review Board Approval

If you intend to conduct an evaluation for a public or private nonprofit or for-profit organization or institution that receives U.S. government support (even if you are a student), then you are likely to have to get approval from an institutional review board, or IRB, before you can begin. The IRB is in charge of reviewing the design of your evaluation study to guarantee that it is structured in a way that will protect each participant's privacy and other rights. If the IRB approves, you can proceed with the evaluation. If it does not, you will not be allowed to collect data. Although various state and local institutional review boards may differ in their specific requirements, nearly all major social, health, and welfare agencies have standards in place for the protection of human research subjects.

An IRB is an administrative body whose purpose is to protect the rights and welfare of individuals who are recruited to participate in research activities. According to the U.S. government, all IRB activities related to human research subjects should be guided by the ethical principles published in *The Belmont Report: Ethical Principles and Guidelines for the Protection of Human Subjects of Research* (see the Web site for the U.S. Government Office of Human Subject Protections at http://www.ohrp.osophs.dhhs.gov). This report, which was prepared by the National Commission for the Protection of Human Subjects of Biomedical and Behavioral Research in 1979, is the foundation for ethical standards in all research involving human subjects, including evaluation. Three major principles come from *The Belmont Report:*

- *Respect for persons:* This principle incorporates at least two ethical convictions: first, that individuals should be treated as autonomous agents; and second, that persons with diminished autonomy (for example, very young children or people with dementing illnesses) are entitled to protection.
- *Beneficence:* This principle holds that researchers must treat research participants in an ethical manner, not only by respecting their decisions and protecting them from harm, but also by actively making efforts to secure their well-being.

- *Justice:* This principle concerns the balance for research participants between receiving the benefits of research and bearing its burdens. For example, to ensure justice, researchers need to examine their selection of research subjects in order to determine whether they are systematically choosing persons from some classes (e.g., welfare recipients, persons in institutions) simply because of those individuals' easy availability rather than for reasons directly related to the problems being studied.

U.S. government policy mandates that an IRB must have at least five members and that the members must have varied backgrounds. When selecting IRB members, an institution must take into account the racial and cultural heritage of potential members and must be sensitive to community attitudes. In addition to possessing the professional competence necessary to review specific research activities, IRB members must be able to ascertain the acceptability of proposed research in terms of institutional commitments and regulations, applicable law, and standards of professional conduct and practice.

U.S. government policy also requires that if an IRB regularly reviews research that involves subjects within vulnerable categories (such as children, prisoners, pregnant women, or handicapped or mentally disabled persons), the institution must consider including among the IRB's members one or more individuals who are knowledgeable about and experienced in working with such subjects. Also, the institution must make every effort to ensure that its IRB consists of a mix of male and female members.

Evaluations That Are Exempt From IRB Approval

A program evaluation is considered to be *research* (and thus needs IRB approval) when the evaluator intends to create generalizable knowledge that will be shared outside of the program being evaluated, whether in professional presentations, reports, or published articles. Process and implementation evaluations are less likely to require IRB approval because the data gathered in such evaluations are typically used only to assess progress and to identify areas for improvement *within* programs. Example 1.9 describes such an evaluation.

Example 1.9 An Evaluation for Which IRB Approval Is Not Required

A community health center wants to improve its rate of vaccination to prevent pneumonia in the elderly. An e-mail system is set up to remind physicians which of their patients are due for the vaccination. The health center conducts an evaluation of the effectiveness of the e-mail reminder system, collecting data each year for 2 years. Information from the evaluation is not shared outside the health center.

Comment: This evaluation is not considered to be research because the findings are used only by the health center. Evaluations of this type (which focus on the progress of an intervention—here the e-mail reminder system) are called *quality improvement evaluations* because their purpose is to improve deficiencies in health care quality. In this case, the inadequacy is the poor rate of delivery of a vaccination that is recommended for the elderly by many national and international agencies.

What the IRB Will Review

When determining whether an evaluation can be implemented, an IRB will consider all of the elements listed below.

Criteria Used by the Institutional Review Board

✓ **Study design:** Many experts agree that the IRB should approve only research that is both valid and of value. Poorly designed studies necessarily produce misleading results. Study design includes how subjects are recruited, selected, and assigned to groups; the reliability and validity of measures or instruments; and the method of data analysis.

✓ **Risks and benefits:** The IRB evaluates whether the risks to subjects are reasonable in relation to the anticipated benefits, if any, to the subjects, as well as the importance of the knowledge reasonably expected to result from the evaluation research.

✓ **Equitable selection of subjects:** The IRB usually considers the purpose of the research and the setting of the evaluation and closely examines any proposed study involving vulnerable subject populations, such as children, prisoners, persons with cognitive disorders, or economically or educationally disadvantaged persons.

✓ **Identification of subjects and confidentiality:** The IRB reviews the researcher's planned methods for prospective identification of subjects, for identifying and contacting potential subjects, and for ensuring subjects' privacy and confidentiality.

✓ **Qualifications:** The IRB examines the qualifications of the evaluator and the evaluation team. In addition, the IRB considers the adequacy of the facilities and equipment to be used in conducting the research and maintaining the rights and welfare of the subjects.

✓ **Informed consent:** The process of obtaining subjects' informed consent to be included in the evaluation study goes to the heart of the matter of ethical research. The IRB often focuses a great deal of attention on the issue of informed consent.

If your evaluation is considered research, the IRB will ask to review the following documents:

- *Advance letters:* Are you sending letters or e-mails from physicians or members of the community supporting the evaluation and recommending participation? If so, the IRB will need to review the contents.
- *Posters or flyers:* Are you planning to post notices inviting participation? Are you going to prepare flyers to hand out at clinics or health fairs? If so, the IRB will need to review the contents.
- *Screening scripts:* Will you be screening potential participants to determine if they meet the criteria for inclusion in the evaluation? Will you be asking people to give their ages or describe their health behaviors? Regardless of how you approach people (e.g., in person, on the phone), the IRB will need to review the details of your planned approach, including any scripts used for screening.
- *Informed consent forms:* Once you have determined that a potential participant is eligible, willing, and able to participate, you must give him or her an opportunity to decide freely whether or not to participate. To do this, you must provide the potential subject with complete information about the research through an informed consent form. The IRB will need to review this form.

Informed Consent

Purpose

When subjects give their *informed consent* to participate in a program evaluation, this means that they are knowledgeable about the risks and benefits of participation and the activities that participating entails. They also agree to the terms of participation and are knowledgeable about their rights as research subjects.

Participants are usually required to acknowledge their informed consent to participate in writing. If you cannot obtain a participant's signature on an informed consent form (for instance, if your only contact with the participant is over the telephone), then you must be able to provide evidence that the contents of the form were explained to the participant and that he or she understood them. Informed consent forms are designed to protect all parties: the subject, the evaluator, and the institution. Therefore, it is important that such forms present information in a well-organized and easily understood format.

If your evaluation includes children, you may have to design separate informed consent forms for their parents and assent (verbal) forms for the children. If your evaluation does not include children, the IRB may ask you to justify their exclusion.

Contents of an Informed Consent Form to Participate in an Evaluation

The required contents of informed consent forms vary from institution to institution, but the principles do not. Program evaluators should include all of the elements shown in Example 1.10 in their informed consent forms.

Example 1.10 An Informed Consent Form for Participants in a Study of Alcohol Use and Health

Dear Participant,

The Medical Foundation Clinic is taking part in an important research project conducted by university professors and sponsored by the National Institutes of Health. You have been asked to participate in this project because you told us over the phone that you are at least 65 years old, that you are planning to stay in the area and live in the community during the next 12 months, and that you have had at least one drink with alcohol in it during the past 3 months.

Your participation in the project is completely voluntary. If you decide not to participate, or if you agree and then change your mind before finishing, the care you receive at the Medical Foundation Clinic will not be affected in any way.

What is the project about?

Older adults become more sensitive to alcohol, and alcohol also interacts with medications used by older persons. The aim of the project is to see if educational reports can help you and your doctor understand more about alcohol use and its influence on health, medications, and physical and mental functioning among people 65 years of age and older.

What am I being asked to do?

The study has two parts. Today, you are being asked to participate in the first part of the study. For this part of the study, we would like you to complete a written questionnaire about your alcohol use, health, and use of health care. Please complete the questionnaire, sign this consent form, and mail both forms back to us in the accompanying stamped envelope. The information you provide in this questionnaire will be analyzed for research purposes.

Some of the patients who participate in the first part of the study will be chosen for the second part of the study as well. If you are chosen for this next stage, we will be contacting you for more information over the next year.

At intervals 3 months, 6 months, and 12 months from now, we will ask you to complete questionnaires and mail them back to us. It will take you about 30–40 minutes to complete today's questionnaire, about 15–25 minutes to complete the second questionnaire, about 5–10 minutes to complete the third questionnaire, and about 25–30 minutes to complete the fourth questionnaire.

We also ask for your consent to give your personalized report of alcohol-related risks and problems to your doctor and to consult the administrative records to find out which medical services (if any) you used during the time period being studied.

If you are asked and agree to participate in this second part of the study, you will be assigned to one of two groups of patients. The first group of patients will receive a booklet about alcohol use in older adults at the beginning of the study and will also receive periodic reports of their questionnaire results during the course of the study. Patients assigned to the first group will be asked to read the reports and the booklet and will be called by a health educator to answer questions about the materials. The second group of patients will receive the same materials, but not until the end of the study. Whether you are assigned to the first or the second group will depend on which group your doctor was randomly assigned to, and not on any decision made by the researchers or your physician.

Are there any risks or discomforts of participating in this project?

The only risks of participating in the project are the inconvenience of taking the time to answer the questions and review the report and the possibility that some of the questions on the questionnaire may worry or embarrass you. You are not required to answer any questions you may feel uncomfortable about answering. There are no medical procedures involved, and there is no financial cost to you associated with this study in any way, shape, or form.

What are the possible benefits?

The benefits of the study are the chance to learn about the possible risks of alcohol use and the possibility of improving the health education of other older adults. However, you might not benefit from participation in the study.

Will I be paid for my participation in the study?

To partially compensate you for your time, we will mail you $5 in cash after you complete the first questionnaire. If you are chosen for the second part of the study, you will be paid $15 for the second questionnaire, $10 for the third questionnaire, and $20 for the fourth questionnaire, for a total of $50 if you complete all of the questionnaires.

How will my privacy be protected?

All the information you report is highly confidential and will be used only for study purposes. The consent form you sign will be filed in a locked storage cabinet during the project and shredded after completion of the project. Only the study's principal investigator, project manager, and the Medical Foundation Clinic data coordinators will have access to these files. All reports of information gained from your answers to the questionnaire will be shown as summaries of all participants' answers. No individual results will ever be used by the project team. All members of the team will be educated about the importance of protecting the privacy of patients and physicians.

Whom do I contact if I have any further questions?

You may call Dr. Lida Swan, the principal investigator, at 31X-794-ABCD, or e-mail her at lswan@med.edu. Dr. Swan is Professor of Medicine and Public Health at the University of Eastwich. You may also contact Dr. Samuel Wygand, Professor of Medicine and Public Health, at 31X-459-DEFG, or Dr. John Tsai, Professor of Medicine, at 31X-459-UVWX. The project office is located in the Department of Medicine, Division of General Medicine and Evaluation, Box ABC, Eastwich, CA 90000.

What are my rights as a research subject?

You may withdraw your consent at any time and discontinue participation without penalty. You are not waiving any legal claims, rights, or remedies because of your participation in this research study. If you have questions regarding your rights as a research subject, contact the Office for Protection of Research Subjects, 832222 Humanities and Science Building, Box DEF, Eastwich, CA 90000; 31X-825-XYZA.

What if I agree to be in the study and then change my mind?

You can leave the project at any time. Again, the care you receive at the Medical Foundation Clinic will not be affected in any way if you decide to withdraw from the study.

How do I sign up?

If you want to join the project, please sign below on the line marked "Signature of Research Subject," write down the date next to your signature, and mail this form together with your completed questionnaire in the prepaid envelope provided. We will mail you a copy of the signed consent form.

Thank you very much for your interest in this research study!

SIGNATURE OF RESEARCH SUBJECT

Date of preparation:
IRB number:
Expiration date:

__________________________ __________________________

Signature of Research Subject Date

SIGNATURE OF INVESTIGATOR

__________________________ __________________________

Signature of Investigator Date

Notice that the participant is given a copy of the consent form. In mailed surveys (whether conducted through e-mail or conventional mail), a completed and returned questionnaire may be considered evidence of informed consent, but this depends on the rules laid down by the IRB and the purpose of the survey.

Participants in mailed surveys sometimes neglect to include their informed consent forms when they return their questionnaires.

Limits to Confidentiality

Depending on the subject matter of your evaluation, there may be limits to your promise of confidentiality to your subjects. For example, if a subject reveals information about child or elder abuse, you may be required by law to report this information to authorities.

Confidentiality of Audio-/Videotapes and Photographs

If you use photographs, videotapes, or audiotapes in the course of conducting your evaluation, you need to be sure to discuss in the consent form how these materials will be used (e.g., for classroom presentations, for presentations at professional conventions, or possibly for release to news or advertising media). The consent form should also indicate when the tapes/photographs will be destroyed as well as detail the provisions you have made for masking the subjects' identity. Such a statement might read as follows:

> In the process of the study, you will be videotaped [and/or photographed and/or audiotaped]. The tapes [and/or photographs] will be used for teaching and/or research purposes only, and your identity will not be disclosed. The tapes [and/or photographs] will be destroyed at the study's conclusion or no later than April 200X, whichever comes first.

Research Misconduct

Research misconduct is becoming an increasingly important concern throughout the world. Documenting such misconduct (if it occurs) is currently an issue for evaluators who work in academic institutions and in organizations that receive funding from the U.S. government. Table 1.1 lists and defines some of the problematic research behaviors that may occur in many situations in which evaluations are conducted.

Faking the data is a clear example of research misconduct. Subtler examples include the following:

- Exaggerating an evaluation's findings to support the evaluator's point of view
- Changing the evaluation protocol or method of implementation without informing the IRB before doing so
- Failing to maintain adequate documentation of the evaluation's methods (such as by preparing a codebook or operations manual)
- Releasing participant information without permission to do so
- Having insufficient resources to complete the evaluation as promised
- Having financial or other interests in common with the funders or supporters of the evaluation (conflict of interest)

Table 1.1 Problematic Research Behaviors

Problematic Behavior	*Definition*
Misconduct	Fabrication, falsification, or plagiarism
Questionable research practices	Actions that violate values of research and may be detrimental to the research process but do not directly threaten the integrity of the research record; examples include failing to retain research records for a reasonable period and using inappropriate statistics to enhance findings
Other misconduct, not pertaining to scientific integrity	Unacceptable behaviors that are subject to generally applicable legal and social penalties but are not unique to research; examples include sexual harassment, misuse of funds, and violations of federal regulations
Other misconduct, pertaining to scientific integrity	Unacceptable behavior that does not directly affect the integrity of the research process but is nevertheless directly associated with misconduct in science; examples include cover-ups of scientific misconduct and reprisals against whistle-blowers
Sloppiness	Negligent or irregular research practices that risk distortion of the research record but lack the intent to do so

A Note About the Health Insurance Portability and Accountability Act

The federal Health Insurance Portability and Accountability Act of 1996 (HIPAA) safeguards the health information of individuals obtaining health care in the United States. Because they may create, use, or exchange individually identifiable health information when conducting health-related research, investigators, including evaluators, must ensure that their studies are in compliance with HIPAA.

HIPAA contains provisions that protect the confidentiality and security of individually identifiable health information, which is defined as any information created, used, or received by a health care provider that relates to (a) the past, present, or future physical or mental health or condition of an individual; (b) the provision of health care to an individual; or (c) the past, present, or future payment for the provision of health care to an individual with respect to which there is a reasonable basis to believe the information can be used to identify the individual. Any research in which individually identifiable health information is collected is automatically considered to be human subjects research.

Protected Health Information

HIPAA defines protected health information (PHI) as any individually identifiable health information collected or created as a consequence of the provision of health care by a covered entity, in any form, including verbal communications. This definition of PHI includes the following:

1. Names
2. Dates of birth, death, admission, and discharge (except year)
3. Postal address (including city, state, and zip code)
4. Telephone number
5. Fax number
6. E-mail address
7. Social Security number
8. Medical record number
9. Health plan identification number
10. Account number
11. Certificate/license number
12. Vehicle identifier
13. Device identifiers and serial numbers
14. URLs
15. IP address
16. Biometric identifiers, including fingerprints
17. Full-face photos and other comparable images
18. Any other unique identifying number, characteristic, or code

HIPAA covers two types of research that are germane to evaluation studies: research that includes the review of medical records and research that results in the addition of new information to a medical record (e.g., research in which a health care service is performed, such as testing a new diagnostic method or creating new information in a medical record).

The IRB acts as a privacy board (required by HIPAA) to review the research use or disclosure of PHI and determine whether research participants should sign a "HIPAA authorization" in addition to the informed consent form. Alternatively, a waiver of authorization (roughly analogous to a waiver of informed consent) may be granted. All investigators (including program evaluators and research staff) should probably take a course to receive HIPAA research certification, especially if they plan to work in large institutions.

It is no longer possible for evaluators in the United States to receive funding from federal agencies or from many other granting agencies without proving that they have been trained in human subjects protection principles and that they understand the basics of HIPAA regulations.

Summary and Transition to the Next Chapter on Evaluation Questions and Standards of Effectiveness

Program evaluation is the diligent investigation of a program's characteristics and merits. Its purpose is to provide information on a program's objectives, activities, outcomes, impact, and cost. To conduct evaluations, researchers pose questions and set standards for effectiveness, make decisions regarding study design and sampling, and collect, analyze, interpret, and report information. Increasingly, evaluators are finding that they must submit their study plans to formal boards for review. These institutional review boards focus on the integrity of research designs and on researchers' proposed procedures for respecting the privacy and other rights of study participants.

The information produced by health program evaluations is used by the financial supporters of the programs as well as by program developers, policy makers, and other evaluators and health researchers.

Collecting and analyzing interim or formative evaluation data is expensive and may produce misleading results; researchers who choose to collect interim data should proceed with caution. Process evaluations, in contrast, are usually useful.

Before evaluators can decide on the types of data to collect and the design for collecting them, they must decide on the evaluation questions and the standards by which they will appraise program effectiveness. The next chapter discusses both the sources and the statement of evaluation questions and standards. The chapter also explains where standards of program effectiveness come from and describes the principles behind the use of expert panels, a common method of coming to agreement on standards when statistical methods alone are insufficient.

Exercises

EXERCISE 1

Directions

Read the example below and, using only the information offered, answer these questions:

1. What are the evaluation questions?
2. What are the standards?
3. What is the design?
4. What data collection measures are being used?
5. What additional information do you need to perform the evaluation?

An Evaluation of a Geriatrics Education Program

Huntington-Ball University's Medical School is concerned with improving its education in geriatrics and gerontology and is planning to revise its entire curriculum in that area, starting with geriatric medicine. The improvements are to take place over a 3-year period. The evaluation team convenes a panel of nurses, physicians, pharmacists, and social workers to help identify the key curriculum objectives that should be evaluated. Based on the panel's suggestions as well as reviews of the current and proposed curriculum and the published literature, the evaluation team decides on a plan of action. Each year, the evaluators will test all third- and fourth-year medical students and survey all residents and a sample of faculty physicians to ascertain their knowledge. The evaluation team also plans to conduct medical record reviews to determine the quality of care delivered to patients between 65 and 75 years of age, ages 76 to 85, and over 85. Team members will monitor student achievement and quality of care over time. The evaluators will also investigate whether the curriculum is equally successful for students, residents, and faculty and whether any observed improvements are sustained over time. The evaluators will produce report on their findings 6 months after the conclusion of the program.

EXERCISE 2

Directions

The following is an informed consent form for a hypothetical diabetes self-care program. Parts of the form are completed, but others are not. Using the descriptions provided, complete the form by writing in the needed content.

Informed Consent Form for the Diabetes Self-Care Program

You are asked to take part in three telephone interviews and three self-administered questionnaires on your general health, your quality of life since being diagnosed with diabetes, and the quality of health care you have received while in the program. Robert Fung, MD, MPH, is directing the project. Dr. Fung works in the Department of Medicine at the University of East Hampton. You are being asked to take part in the interviews and questionnaires because you are enrolled in the Diabetes Self-Care Program.

1. **Tell eligible subjects that participation is voluntary, they can leave whenever they choose, and their health care will not be affected.**

____

____

____

____

Disclosure Statement

Your health care provider may be an investigator in this study protocol. As an investigator, he/she is interested in both your clinical welfare and your responses to the interview questions. Before entering this study or at any time during the study, you may ask for a second opinion about your care from another doctor who is in no way associated with the Diabetes Self-Care Program. You are not under any obligation to take part in any research project offered by your physician.

Reason for the Telephone Interviews and Self-Administered Questionnaires

The interviews and the questionnaires are being done for the following reason: to find out if the Diabetes Self-Care Program is meeting the needs of the patients enrolled in the program.

During the telephone interview, a trained member of the Diabetes Self-Care Program staff will ask you a series of questions about

Your health,

Your quality of life since being diagnosed with diabetes, and

The quality of the health care you have received while in the Diabetes Self-Care Program.

The self-administered survey questions will cover the same topics, but you will be able to answer them on your own and in any place that is convenient for you.

2. Tell participants that the program will use their answers (and answers from others) to find out about the appropriateness of services and any needed changes.

____

____

____

____

What You Will Be Asked to Do

If you agree to take part in this study, you will be asked to do the following things:

1. Answer three short (20-minute) telephone interviews. The telephone interviewer will ask you general questions about your health, your quality of life since you were diagnosed with diabetes, and the quality of health care you have received while in the Diabetes Self-Care Program. You will be called to complete an interview when you first enroll in the program, 6 months after your enrollment, and when you leave the program. The interviews will be completed at whatever times are best for you.

Sample questions:

How confident are you in your ability to know what questions to ask a doctor?

During the PAST 4 WEEKS, how much did diabetes interfere with your normal work (including both work outside the home and housework)?

Would you say not at all, a little bit, moderately, quite a bit, or extremely?

2. Answer three short (20-minute) self-administered questionnaires. The self-administered questionnaires will ask you general questions about your health, your quality of life since you were diagnosed with diabetes, and the quality of health care you have received while in the Diabetes Self-Care Program. The self-administered questionnaires will be mailed to you when you first enroll in the program, 6 months after your enrollment, and when you leave the program. You can complete the self-administered questionnaires at whatever times are best for you. You will be provided with a prepaid envelope in which to return each questionnaire.

Sample questions:

How many drinks of alcohol did you usually drink each day during the past four weeks? (None, one, two, three, or four or more)

On a scale of 1 (very confident) to 6 (not at all confident), how confident are you in your ability to know what questions to ask a doctor?

3. If you do not understand a question or have a problem with a self-administered questionnaire, you will be asked to call Ms. Estella Ruiz at the Diabetes Self-Care Program office at **1-800-000-0000.** She will be able to assist you.

Possible Risks and Discomforts

3. **Tell respondents that the surveys may include questions about their physical or emotional health or their experience with the program that they may feel sensitive about answering, and that they do not have to answer questions that bother them.**

____

____

____

____

Potential Benefits to Subjects and/or to Society

The purpose of the telephone interviews and self-administered questionnaires is to improve the services that the Diabetes Self-Care Program provides to the patients enrolled in the program. Your responses might lead to changes in the program that would improve the services that the Diabetes Self-Care Program provides.

Payment for Taking Part

4. **Tell participants that they will not be paid for their time.**

____

____

____

____

Confidentiality

Any information that is collected from you and that can be identified with you will remain confidential. Your identity will not be revealed to anyone outside the research team unless we have your permission or as required by law. You will not be identified in any reports or presentations. Confidentiality will be maintained in the following ways:

- All of your interviews and questionnaires will be coded with a number that identifies you. Your name will not be on any of these materials.
- A master list of names and code numbers will be kept in a completely separate, confidential, password-protected computer database.
- All copies of the self-administered questionnaires will be kept in a locked file cabinet in a locked research office.

- All telephone interviews will be recorded in a confidential computer database.
- When analysis of the data is conducted, your name will not be associated with your data in any way.
- Only research staff will have access to these files.

Taking Part and Choosing Not to Take Part in Telephone Interviews and Self-Administered Questionnaires

5. **Tell participants that it is up to them whether or not they want to take part and that, if they do, they can stop at any time and their health care will not be affected.**

____

____

____

____

Identification of Investigators

If you have concerns or questions about this study, please contact Robert Funk, MD, MPH, by mailing inquiries to Box 000, Los Angeles, CA 90000–9990. Dr. Funk can also be reached by telephone at 1-800-000-0000 or by e-mail at rfunk@medmail.edu.

Rights of Participants

You may choose to end your agreement to take part in the telephone interviews and self-administered questionnaires at any time. You may stop taking part without penalty. You are not giving up any legal claims, rights, or remedies because you take part in the telephone interviews and self-administered questionnaires. If you have questions about your rights as a research subject, contact the Office for Protection of Research Subjects, 2107 QQQ Building, Box 951694, East Hampton, CA 90273, 1-800-123-XYZZ.

I understand the events described above. My questions have been answered to my satisfaction, and I agree to take part in this study. I have been given a copy of this form.______________________________________

____

____

____

____

Name of Subject (Please Print)

______________________ ______________________

Signature of Subject Date

Suggested Readings

Evaluations

The evaluation reports listed below are available in their entirety online. They have been selected for inclusion here because they provide accessible examples of published peer-reviewed evaluations that deal with a variety of topics in health and health care. They also include an assortment of approaches to determining program merit and effectiveness and provide illustrations of the use of experimental, qualitative, and participatory methods. All of these articles are available online through MEDLINE, the bibliographic database of the National Library of Medicine. To get to MEDLINE, go to the National Institutes of Health's Web site at http://www.nih.gov.

Chernoff, R. G., Ireys, H. T., DeVet, K. A., & Kim, Y. J. (2002). A randomized, controlled trial of a community-based support program for families of children with chronic illness: Pediatric outcomes. *Archives of Pediatric and Adolescent Medicine, 156,* 533–539.

Objective: To develop, implement, and evaluate child outcomes of a 15-month, community-based, family-support intervention designed to reduce risk for poor adjustment and mental health problems in children with one of four chronic illnesses (diabetes mellitus, sickle-cell anemia, cystic fibrosis, or moderate to severe asthma) and their mothers.

Diamant, A. L., Brook, R. H., Fink, A., & Gelberg, L. (2001). Assessing use of primary health care services by very low-income adults in a managed care program. *Archives of Internal Medicine, 161,* 1222–1227.

Objective: To assess the effects of providing free health care services to low-income adults.

Eisen, M., Zellman, G. L., & Murray, D. M. (2003). Evaluating the Lions-Quest "Skills for Adolescence" drug education program. *Addictive Behavior, 28,* 883–897.

Objective: To test the hypothesis that the Skills for Adolescence training curriculum with a dedicated drug education unit is more effective than standard care in deterring and delaying substance use in children through middle school.

Fishbein, M., Hall-Jamieson, K., Zimmer, E., von Haeften, I., & Nabi, R. (2002). Avoiding the boomerang: Testing the relative effectiveness of antidrug public service announcements before a national campaign. *American Journal of Public Health, 92,* 238–245.

Objective: To examine the relative perceived effectiveness of 30 antidrug public service announcements and assess the extent to which judgments of effectiveness are related to judgments of realism, amount learned, and positive and negative emotional responses.

Hay, J., LaBree, L., Luo, R., Clark, F., Carlson, M., Mandel, D., Zemke, R., Jackson, J., & Azen, S. P. (2002). Cost-effectiveness of preventive occupational therapy for independent-living older adults. *Journal of the American Geriatrics Society, 50,* 1381–1388.

Objective: To evaluate the cost-effectiveness of a 9-month preventive occupational therapy (OT) program in the Well-Elderly Study, a randomized trial in independent-living older adults that found significant health, function, and quality-of-life benefits attributable to preventive OT.

Jha, A. K., Perlin, J. B., Kizer, K. W., & Dudley, R. A. (2003). Effect of the transformation of the Veterans Affairs health care system on the quality of care. *New England Journal of Medicine, 348,* 2218–2227.

Objective: To determine the change in the quality of health care for veterans resulting from a mid-1990s systemwide reengineering of the VA health care system to improve quality of care and to compare the quality of care in the VA system with that of the Medicare fee-for-service program.

Katoaka, S. H., Stein, B. C., Jaycox, L. H., Wong, M., Escudero, P., Tu, W., Zaragoza, C., & Fink, A. (2003). A school-based mental health program for traumatized Latino immigrant children. *Journal of the American Academy of Child and Adolescent Psychiatry, 42,* 311–318.

Objective: To pilot-test a school mental health program for Latino immigrant students who have been exposed to community violence.

Keyserling, T. C., Samuel-Hodge, C. D., Ammerman, A. S., Ainsworth, B. E., Henriquez-Roldan, C. F., Elasy, T. A., Skelly, A. H., Johnston, L. F., & Bangdiwala, S. I. (2002). A randomized trial of an intervention to improve self-care behaviors of African-American women with type 2 diabetes: Impact on physical activity. *Diabetes Care, 25,* 1576–1583.

Objective: To determine whether a culturally appropriate clinic- and community-based intervention for African American women with type 2 diabetes will increase moderate-intensity physical activity.

Malouin, R., Winch, P., Leontsini, E., Glass, G., Simon, D., Hayes, E. B., & Schwartz, B. S. (2003). Longitudinal evaluation of an educational intervention for preventing tick bites in an area with endemic Lyme disease in Baltimore County, Maryland. *American Journal of Epidemiology, 157,* 1039–1051.

Objective: To determine whether a targeted educational intervention in an area with endemic Lyme disease could increase knowledge, positive attitudes, and reported behaviors related to tick bite prevention and consequently decrease tick bites, as measured by a biomarker of tick bites.

Sheeran, P., & Silverman, M. (2003). Evaluation of three interventions to promote workplace health and safety: Evidence for the utility of implementation intentions. *Social Science & Medicine, 56,* 2153–2163.

Objective: To evaluate a motivational intervention based on the theory of planned behavior, a volitional intervention based on implementation intentions, and a combined motivational plus volitional intervention in promoting attendance at workplace health and safety training courses in the United Kingdom.

Simon, G. E., Von Korff, M., Ludman, E. J., Katon, W. J., Rutter, C., Unutzer, J., Lin, E. H., Bush, T., & Walker, E. (2002). Cost-effectiveness of a program to prevent depression relapse in primary care. *Medical Care, 40,* 941–950.

Objective: To evaluate the incremental cost-effectiveness of a depression relapse prevention program in primary care.

Stevens, M. M., Olson, A. L., Gaffney, C. A., Tosteson, T. D., Mott, L. A., & Starr, P. (2002). A pediatric, practice-based, randomized trial of drinking and smoking prevention and bicycle helmet, gun, and seatbelt safety promotion. *Pediatrics, 109,* 490–497.

Objective: To compare the effects of two interventions (based on an office systems' approach), delivered through pediatric primary care practices, on early adolescent health risk behaviors and the maintenance or improvement of safety behaviors.

Taylor, J. A., Kwan-Gett, T. S., & McMahon, E. M., Jr. (2003). Effectiveness of an educational intervention in modifying parental attitudes about antibiotic usage in children. *Pediatrics, 111,* 548–554.

Objective: To determine the effectiveness of educational materials in improving the attitudes of parents of young children about the judicious use of antibiotics.

Washington, D. L., Stevens, C. D., Shekelle, P. G., Baker, D. W., Fink, A., & Brook, R. H. (2000). Safely directing patients to appropriate levels of care: Guideline-driven triage in the emergency service. *Annals of Emergency Medicine, 36,* 15–22.

Objective: To develop and validate standardized clinical criteria to identify patients presenting to the emergency department whose care may be safely deferred to a later date in a nonemergency setting.

Werch, C. E., Owen, D. M., Carlson, J. M., DiClemente, C. C., Edgemon, P., & Moore, M. (2003). One-year follow-up results of the STARS for Families alcohol prevention program. *Health Education Research, 18,* 74–87.

Objective: To examine the 1-year follow-up effects of the STARS (Start Taking Alcohol Risks Seriously) for Families program, a 2-year preventive intervention based on a stage-of-acquisition model and consisting of nurse consultations and parent materials.

Wight, D., Raab, G. M., Henderson, M., Abraham, C., Buston, K., Hart, G., & Scott, S. (2002). Limits of teacher delivered sex education: Interim behavioural outcomes from randomized trial. *British Medical Journal, 324,* 1430. (Erratum in *British Medical Journal* [2002], *325,* 435)

Objective: To determine whether a theoretically based sex education program for adolescents (SHARE) delivered by teachers reduced unsafe sexual intercourse compared with current practice.

You can find other examples of evaluation reports on the Institute of Medicine's Web site at http://www.iom.edu (click on "reports") and on the RAND Web site at http://rand.org (click on "health"). (RAND is one of the most prestigious think tanks in the United States.) For other evaluations of program costs, see the "Suggested Readings" section in Chapter 2.

Evaluation Models

PRECEDE-PROCEED

Green, L. W., & Kreuter, M. W. (1991). *Health promotion planning: An educational and ecological approach* (2nd ed.). Mountain View, CA: Mayfield.

Green, L. W., & Kreuter, M. W. (1999). *Health promotion planning: An educational and environmental approach* (3rd ed.). Mountain View, CA: Mayfield.

RE-AIM

Glasgow, R. E., McKay, H. G., Piette, J. D., & Reynolds, K. D. (2001). The RE-AIM framework for evaluating interventions: What can it tell us about approaches to chronic illness management? *Patient Education and Counseling, 44,* 119–127.

Glasgow, R. E., Vogt, T. M., & Boles, S. M. (1999). Evaluating the public health impact of health promotion interventions: The RE-AIM framework. *American Journal of Public Health, 89,* 1322–1327.

CDC's Practical Evaluation

For details on applying the CDC's framework, see the information on the CDC's Evaluation Working Group on the CDC Web site at http://www.cdc.gov/eval.

Purpose of This Chapter

This chapter explains the characteristics of evaluation questions and discusses how to set standards. It explains the major purpose of evaluation questions, which is to provide data on the characteristics and merits of programs. Standards of effectiveness are the criteria against which evaluators appraise program effectiveness. They can be set statistically, but evaluators must be careful to check them for practical meaning or clinical significance. This chapter also reviews the special roles of experts and consumers, or users, in setting standards. Experts and users can provide insights into the practical and clinical meanings of standards when data are unavailable or the data alone are insufficient. Two additional primary sources for meaningful evaluation standards are large, community-based data sets and the research literature. The relationships among evaluation questions and standards and the independent and dependent variables are also examined here and are illustrated by a special reporting form that depicts their connections.

2 Evaluation Questions and Standards of Effectiveness

A Reader's Guide to Chapter 2

Evaluation Questions

Goals and objectives; participants and effectiveness; program activities, organization, and effectiveness; economics and costs; program environment

Setting Standards: What They Are and How to Set Them

How to Set Standards

Setting standards using comparisons with other programs, experts, community data sets, and the literature; evaluation standards and economic evaluations

Evaluation Questions and Standards: Establishing a Healthy Relationship

When to Set Standards

The QSV Report: Questions, Standards, Variables

Evaluation Questions

Goals and Objectives

Evaluators use evaluation questions to guide them in gathering and analyzing data on the characteristics and merits of programs. In most evaluations, one of the evaluator's main concerns is to find out whether the program's goals and objectives have been met. The goals are usually meant to be relatively general and long-term, as shown in Example 2.1.

Example 2.1 Typical Program Goals

- For the public or the community at large
  Optimize health status
  Improve quality of life
  Foster improved physical, social, and psychological functioning
  Support new knowledge about health care
  Enhance satisfaction with health care
- For health care practitioners
  Promote research
  Enhance knowledge
  Support access to new technology and practices
  Improve the quality of care delivered
  Improve education
  Foster the delivery of efficient care
- For institutions
  Improve institutional organization, structure, and efficiency
  Optimize institutional ability to deliver accessible high-quality care and superior education
- For the health care system
  Expand capacity to provide high-quality care
  Support the efficient provision of care
  Ensure respect for the health care needs of all citizens

The term *objectives* refers to the specific goals of a program—what the program planners intend to achieve. Consider the excerpts from the description of a new health-related graduate-level course given in Example 2.2.

Example 2.2 The Objectives of a New Course

Course Description

The new two-semester course is designed to teach first- and second-year graduate students to conduct evaluations of health programs. Among the primary aims of the course is the development of a handbook on evaluation that teaches students the basic principles of evaluation and offers an annotated bibliography so that readers can obtain more information when they need it. At the end of the two semesters, each student will be expected to plan the evaluation of a program. The plan is to include evaluation questions, standards, study design and sampling methods, and data collection measures.

Based on this excerpt, the objectives of this course are as follows:

- For the curriculum developer:
  To produce an evaluation handbook with an annotated bibliography
- For the student:
  To prepare an evaluation plan that includes questions, standards, research design, sampling methods, and data collection measures

---

Objectives can involve any of the users or participants in the evaluation: patients, students, health care practitioners, the health care system, and so on. The evaluation questions for the health program evaluation course described in Example 2.2 might include the following:

1. Was a health program evaluation handbook produced?
2. Did each student prepare an evaluation plan with questions, standards, study design, sampling, and data collection measures?

The identification of these two questions immediately raises some additional questions: By when should the handbook be produced? How will we determine if it is any good? What are the characteristics of a satisfactory evaluation plan, and who will judge the students' plans? These questions must be answered in subsequent evaluation activities. In the next step of the evaluation, for example, we will consider ways of setting standards for determining achievement of objectives as well as program effectiveness and efficiency.

When identifying evaluation questions based on goals and objectives, evaluators must be certain that they have identified all of the important goals and objectives, that the evaluation questions cover all of the important objectives, and that all of the questions can be answered with the resources available.

Participants and Effectiveness

In health program evaluation, evaluation questions often aim to describe the demographic and health characteristics of participants in a program and to link effective outcomes to specific participants. An evaluator might be asked, for example, to find out whether a diabetes education program was effective for all patients or only for a portion—say, patients under 18 years of age. Returning to the new health program evaluation course discussed above, consider the questions about the program's participants shown in Example 2.3.

Example 2.3 Evaluation Questions, Participants, and Program Effectiveness

The developer of the new health program evaluation course for first- and second-year graduate students was concerned with finding out whether the program was effective for all types of students. One measure of effectiveness for a student who has completed the course is the student's ability to prepare a satisfactory evaluation plan. The evaluator asked the following evaluation questions:

- What are the demographic characteristics of each year's students?
- Is the program equally effective for differing students (for example, males and females)?
- Do first- and second-year students differ in their learning?
- At the end of their second year, do the current first-year students maintain their learning?

As noted previously, evaluation questions should be answerable with the resources available. Suppose that the evaluation described in Example 2.3 is only a one-year study. In that case, the evaluator cannot answer the question regarding whether this year's first-year students maintained their learning over the next year. Practical considerations often temper the ambitions of an evaluation.

Program Activities, Organization, and Effectiveness

Evaluators often find that learning about a program's specific activities and its organization is important to their understanding of its success or failure and whether it is applicable to other settings. The following are some typical questions evaluators ask when focusing on program activities:

- What were the key activities?
- To what extent were the activities implemented as planned?
- How well was the program administered?
- Did the program's influence carry over to other programs, institutions, or consumers?
- Was the effectiveness of the program influenced by changes in the social, political, or financial circumstances under which it was conducted?

Consider the case study in Example 2.4, in which specific questions are posed about program activities and organization.

Example 2.4 Evaluation Questions About Program Activities and Organization

A nine-member panel of experts in public health, nursing, health services research, and evaluation met to define the kinds of learning that are appropriate for a course in health program evaluation. The course's evaluation is to take place over a 4-year period so as to enlist two groups of first- and second-year students. Several of the graduate school's best instructors were selected to help design the curriculum and the handbook and to teach the course. The evaluator asks:

- To what extent is the selection of the best teachers responsible for the quality of student learning and of the handbook?
- Does the new course affect students' subsequent education activities?
- Over the 4-year period of the evaluation, do any changes occur in the school's support for the program or the number and types of faculty members who were willing to participate?

Economics and Costs

Program evaluations can be designed to answer questions about the resources that are consumed to produce program outcomes. The resources used, or the program costs, include any expenditures, whether in the form of money, personnel, time, and facilities (e.g., office equipment and buildings). The outcomes may be monetary (e.g., numbers of dollars saved) or substantive (e.g., years of life saved). When questions focus on the relationship between costs and monetary outcomes, the evaluation is termed a *cost-benefit analysis.* When questions are asked about the relationship between costs and substantive outcomes, the evaluation is called a *cost-effectiveness analysis.* The distinction between evaluations concerned with cost-effectiveness and those addressing cost-benefit is illustrated by these two examples:

- *Cost-effectiveness evaluation:* What are the comparative costs of Programs A and B in providing the means for pregnant women to obtain prenatal care during the first trimester?
- *Cost-benefit evaluation:* For every $100 spent on prenatal care, how much is saved on neonatal intensive care?

In the past, health program evaluators have asked questions about costs relatively infrequently, for a number of reasons. Among these are the difficulties inherent in defining costs and measuring benefits in the area of health care. Also, adding the complexities of an economic analysis to an already complex evaluation design may not be a good idea. After all, why study the costs of an intervention of (as yet) unproven effectiveness? To conduct cost studies, evaluators require knowledge of economics and statistics. It is often wise to include a health economist on the evaluation team if you plan to analyze costs.

Example 2.5 illustrates the types of questions that program evaluators pose about the costs, effects, benefits, and efficiency of health care programs.

Example 2.5 Evaluation Questions: Costs

- What is the relationship between the cost and the effectiveness of three prenatal clinic staffing models: physician based, mixed staffing, and clinical nurse specialists with physicians available for consultation? Costs include number of personnel, hourly wages, number of prenatal appointments made and kept, and number of hours spent delivering prenatal care. Outcomes (effectiveness) include maternal health (such as complications at the time of delivery), neonatal health (such as birth weight), and patient satisfaction.
- How efficient are a health care center's ambulatory clinics? Efficiency is defined as the relationship between the use of practitioner time and the size of a clinic, waiting times for appointments, time spent by faculty in the clinic, and time spent supervising house staff.
- How do the most profitable private medical practices differ from the least profitable in terms of types of ownership, collection rates, no-show rates, percentage of patients without insurance coverage, charge for a typical follow-up visit, space occupancy rates, and practitioner costs?
- To what extent does each of three programs to control hypertension produce an annual savings in reduced health care claims that is greater than the annual cost of operating the program? The benefits are costs per hypertensive client (the costs of operating the program in each year, divided by the number of hypertensive employees being monitored and counseled that year). Because estimates of program costs are produced over a given 2-year period but estimates of savings are produced in a different (later) period, benefits have to be adjusted to a standard year. To do this, one must adjust the total claims paid in each calendar year by the consumer price index for medical care costs to a standard 2003 dollar. The costs of operating the programs are similarly adjusted to 2003 dollars, using the same index.

As these questions illustrate, evaluators must define costs and effectiveness or benefits and, when appropriate, must describe the value of the monetary costs. Evaluators who answer questions about the costs of health programs sometimes perform a "sensitivity analysis" when measures are not precise or the estimates are uncertain. For example, in a study of the comparative cost-effectiveness of two state-funded school-based health care programs, the evaluators might analyze the influence of increasing each program's funding first by 5% and then by 10% to test the "sensitivity" of the program's effectiveness to changes in funding level. Through this analysis, the evaluators will be able to tell whether or not increases in measures of effectiveness keep pace with increases in costs.

Program Environment

All programs take place in particular institutional, social, and political environments. For instance, Program A, which aims to improve the preventive health care practices of children under age 14, takes place in rural schools and is funded by the federal government and the state. Program B has the same aim, but it takes place in a large city and is supported by the city and a private foundation.

When an evaluation takes place over several years (say, 3 years or longer), the social and/or political environment in which the program exists can change. New people and policies may emerge, and these may influence the program and the evaluation. Among the environmental changes that have affected programs in health care are alterations in reimbursement policies for hospitals and physicians, the development of new technologies, and advances in medical science. For example, the decrease in the infant mortality rate seen in the United States in recent decades is generally conceded to be the result of programs in prenatal care as well as increases in Medicaid spending for prenatal care, medical advances in treating the underdeveloped lungs of premature infants in their first hours of life, and other improvements in neonatal intensive care.

When evaluators are investigating a program's environment, they will often consider the program's setting and funding as well, as illustrated in Figure 2.1. In addition to asking questions about a program's setting and funding, questions about program management and politics are also relevant:

- *The managerial structure:* Who is responsible for the program's outcomes? How effective is the managerial structure? If the individuals or groups who are running the program were to leave, would the program continue to be effective?
- *The political context:* Is the political environment (meaning within and/or outside the institution) supportive of the success of the program? Is the program well funded?

Program/Intervention Settings

Type of setting(s):
(check all that apply)

[ ] Community hospital clinic
[ ] Community freestanding clinic
[ ] Community physicians' office
[ ] Academic hospital clinic
[ ] Residential treatment facility
[ ] Private residence
[ ] Other facility type not shown above, specify:

____

____

Geographic location(s):

A. Country:

[ ] U.S.
[ ] European
[ ] Other, specify:
____
____

B. State(s):

1. ________
2. ________
3. ________
4. ________
5. ________

(enter up to five different state codes or abbreviations)

[ ] CHECK HERE IF STUDY USED >5 STATES

C. Local (e.g., county/city)

1. ________
2. ________
3. ________
4. ________
5. ________

[ ] CHECK HERE IF STUDY USED >5 CITIES/COUNTIES

Funding source(s):
(check all that apply)

[ ] Federal government, specify: ______________

[ ] State government, specify: ______________

[ ] Local government (county/city), specify: ______________

[ ] Private foundation, specify: ______________

[ ] Other, specify: ______________

[ ] None stated

Figure 2.1. A Form to Use in Surveying the Program's Environment

Setting Standards of Effectiveness: What They Are and How to State Them

Program evaluations aim to provide convincing evidence of programs' effectiveness. Evaluators measure program effectiveness against particular standards, or specific criteria. Consider the following evaluation questions and their associated standards:

- *Evaluation question:* Did students learn to formulate evaluation questions?
- *Standard:* Of all students in the new program, 90% will learn to formulate evaluation questions. Learning to formulate questions means identifying

and justifying program goals, objectives, and benefits and stating the questions in a comprehensible manner. Evidence that the questions are comprehensible will come from review by at least three potential users of the evaluation.

And:

- *Evaluation question:* Did the current group of first-year students maintain their learning by the end of their second year?
- *Standard:* No decreases in learning will be found between students' second and first years.

In this case, unless 90% of students learn to formulate questions by the end of the first year *and* first-year students maintain their learning over time, the evaluator cannot say the program is effective.

The standards are the key to the evaluation's credibility. The more specific they are, the easier they are to measure. To get at specificity, evaluators must clearly define all potentially ambiguous terms in the evaluation questions and standards. Ambiguity arises when uniformly accepted definitions or levels of performance are unavailable. For example, in the evaluation question "Has the Obstetrical Access and Utilization Initiative improved access to prenatal care for high-risk women?" the terms *improved access to prenatal care* and *high-risk women* are potentially ambiguous. To clarify these terms and thus eliminate ambiguity, the evaluators might find it helpful to engage in a dialogue like the one presented in Example 2.6.

Example 2.6 Clarifying Terms and Setting Standards: A Dialogue Between Evaluators

Evaluator 1: "Improved" means bettered or corrected.

Evaluator 2: For how many women and over what duration of time must care be bettered? Will all women be included? Or 90% of all women, but 100% of teens?

Evaluator 1: "Improved access" means more available and convenient care.

Evaluator 2: What might render care more available and convenient? Care can be made more available and convenient if some or all the following occur: changes in the health care system to include the provision of services relatively close to clients' homes; shorter waiting times at clinics; for some women, financial help, assistance with transportation to care, and aid with child care; and education regarding the benefits of prenatal care and compliance with nutrition advice.

Evaluator 1: "High-risk women" are women whose health and birth outcomes have a higher-than-average chance of being poor.

Evaluator 2: Which, if not all, of the following women will you include? Teens? Users of drugs or alcohol? Smokers? Low-income women? Women with health problems such as gestational diabetes or hypertension?

After they have clarified the terms of the question "Has the Obstetrical Access and Utilization Initiative improved access to prenatal care for high-risk women?" the evaluators might develop standards such as those listed in Example 2.7.

Example 2.7 Standards for Access to and Use of Prenatal Care Services

- At least four classes in nutrition and "how to be a parent" will be implemented, especially for teenagers.
- All clinics will provide translation assistance in English, Spanish, Hmong, and Vietnamese.
- Over a 5-year period, 80% of all pregnant women without transportation to clinics and community health centers will receive it.

Notice that these three standards refer to changes in the structure of health care provision: specially designed education, translation assistance, and transportation. A useful way to think about standards is to decide whether you want to measure the program's effectiveness in terms of the structure, process, or outcomes of health care. Health program evaluators often conceptualize the quality of care in these terms.

The *structure of care* refers to the environment in which health care is given as well as the characteristics of the health care practitioners (including the number of practitioners and their educational and demographic backgrounds), the setting (a fee-for-service program or managed care, for example), and the organization of care (for example, how departments and teams are run).

The *process of care* refers to what is done to and for patients and includes the technical and humanistic aspects of care. The processes of care include the procedures and tests used by the health care team in prevention, diagnosis, treatment, and rehabilitation.

The *outcomes of care* are the results, or the consequences for the patient, of the health care systems, settings, and processes. These include measures of morbidity and mortality; social, psychological, and physical functioning; satisfaction with care; and quality of life.

Example 2.8 presents illustrative standards for the evaluation question "Has the Obstetrical Access and Utilization Initiative improved access to care for high-risk women?"

Example 2.8 Structure, Process, and Outcome Standards for an Evaluation Question About Access to Prenatal Care

- *Structure standard:* All waiting rooms will have special play areas for patients' children.
- *Process standard:* All physicians will justify and apply the guidelines prepared by the College of Obstetrics and Gynecology for the number and timing of prenatal care visits to all women.
- *Outcome standard:* Significantly fewer low-birth-weight babies will be born in the experimental group than in the control group, and the difference favoring the experimental group will be at least as large as the most recent findings reported in the literature.

Standards must be purposeful; arbitrary standards may doom a program. Suppose the Obstetrical Access and Utilization Initiative aims to reduce the no-show rate for obstetrical clinic appointments from 30% to 20%. If the rate actually decreases by only 5% rather than 10%, will the program be considered a failure? What about if the rate decreases by 7%? The evaluators should justify their answers to these questions by using data from other evaluations, the views and ideals of experts, and statistical comparisons.

In addition to being meaningful, standards of effectiveness should be realistic and measurable. Consider the following evaluation question and standard:

- *Evaluation question:* How do students in our medical center compare with students in other medical centers in their knowledge of the content of appropriate prenatal care for high-risk women?
- *Standard:* A statistically significant difference in knowledge will be obtained that favors our institution.

Unless the evaluators have access to students in other medical centers and can test or observe them in the time allotted for the evaluation, this standard, although perhaps desirable, is unrealistic and cannot be used.

How to Set Standards

To establish standards, program evaluators often review other programs, rely on the consensus of experts regarding what is clinically meaningful, use data from community-based data sets, and analyze the research literature.

Setting Standards Using Comparisons With Other Programs

Evaluators can make comparisons using one group's performance over time, several groups' performance at one time, or several groups' performance over time. It is sometimes difficult, however, to constitute similar comparison groups, engage their cooperation, and also have enough time to collect data to measure and observe meaningful differences (assuming they exist). It is extremely important to note that, just because an evaluation seems to find that one group is different from another and the difference favors the new program, this does not automatically mean that an effective program is at work. At least two questions must be asked before any such judgment is possible:

1. Were the groups comparable to begin with? (After all, by coincidence, the individuals in one group might be smarter, healthier, more cooperative, or otherwise different from those in another.)

2. Is the magnitude of the difference large enough to be meaningful? With very large samples, small differences (in scores on a standardized test of achievement, for example) can be statistically, but not clinically, significant. (That is, when the evaluation data are analyzed using standard statistical methods, the groups are found not to be the same on some important health-related outcome, but this statistically significant difference means little at the clinical level.)

Consider an evaluator who is asked to study the effectiveness of an 8-week cognitive-behavioral therapy program for children with measurable symptoms of depression. The evaluation design consists of an *experimental group* of children who receive the program and a *control group* of children who do not. In such a study design, the participants in the control group may get an alternative program, may get no program, or may continue doing what they have been doing all along ("usual care"). To guide the evaluation design, the evaluator hypothesizes that the children who make up the two groups are the *same* in terms of their symptoms before and after the program.

The evaluator administers standardized measures of depression symptoms to all the children in both groups before the experimental program begins and within 1 week of its conclusion. After analyzing the data using traditional statistical tests, the evaluator finds that in fact the children in the experimental group improve (have better scores on the depression symptom measure) whereas those in the control group do not. Using these statistical findings, the evaluator rejects the hypothesis that the two groups are the same after the program and concludes that because they differ statistically, the program is effective.

Some of the participant children's teachers, however, challenge the evaluator's conclusion by asking if the statistical difference is clinically meaningful. These teachers are not convinced that the improvement in scores in the experimental group means much. After all, the depression symptoms measure is not perfect, and the gains indicated may disappear over time. Through this experience, the evaluator learns that if you rely solely on statistical significance as a standard of effectiveness, you may be challenged to prove that the statistics mean something practical in clinical terms.

The difference between statistical and clinical significance is particularly important in program evaluations that focus on impact, outcomes, and costs. Suppose that students' scores on a standardized test of achievement increase from 150 to 160. Does this 10-point increase mean that students are actually more capable? How much money are policy makers willing to allocate for schools to improve scores by 10 points? On the other hand, consider a group of people in which each loses 10 pounds after being on a diet for 6 months. Depending on where each person started (e.g., some may need to lose no more than 10 pounds, some may need to lose at least 50), a loss of 10 pounds may be more or less clinically significant.

Another way to think of standards of clinical significance is through the concept of *effect size.* Consider this conversation between two evaluators:

Evaluator A: We have been asked to evaluate a Web-based program for high school students that aims to decrease their health-related risks through interactive education and the use of online support groups. We particularly want students to stop smoking. How will we know if the program is effective? Has anyone done a study like this?

Evaluator B: I don't know of anyone offhand, but we can e-mail some people I know who have worked with online programs to reduce health risks. Maybe they have some data we can use. Also, we can do a search of the literature.

Evaluator A: What would we look for?

Evaluator B: We want to know if a program like ours has ever been proven to result in significantly fewer smokers. If we find that any programs have had such results, we will then want to know if a sufficiently large number of students have quit smoking so that we have some truly meaningful results. We may need to work with the school district to find out how large the number of students who quit should be. Alternatively, we can use standard statistical methods to decide on the number.

Evaluator B is getting at the concept of effect size when she talks about having a sufficiently large number of students who quit smoking so that the results, if significant, are also meaningful.

How do you determine the effect size? As Evaluator B suggests, the best sources of information on how other programs have performed are consultations with colleagues and reviews of the literature. But you may not find performance data through such sources, especially if the program you are evaluating is especially innovative. Further, data are not always available because not everything is published. If you cannot find information on other programs similar to yours, you may have to conduct a small-scale or *pilot study* to get estimates of effect sizes for your program. You can also use statistical formulas to calculate effect sizes. Regardless of how you decide on the extent of the effect, you will probably want to ask experts to confirm its practical and clinical significance.

Setting Standards Using Experts

Experts can assist evaluators in setting standards and in confirming the practical or clinical significance of the findings. In this context, an *expert* is defined as any individual or representative of a professional, consumer, or community group who is likely to use the results of an evaluation.

Evaluators use a variety of techniques to consult with and promote agreement among experts. These usually include the selection of representative groups of experts who then take part in structured meetings. For example, for an evaluator who is concerned with setting standards for a program to improve the quality of instruction in health policy and health services research, an appropriate group of advisers would include experts in those fields, experts in education, and consumers of health services research and policy (such as representatives from the public).

The fields of health and medicine make extensive use of expert panels. For example, the National Institutes of Health has used consensus development conferences to help resolve issues related to knowledge about and use of particular medical technologies, such as intraocular lens implantation, as well as the care of patients with specific conditions, such as depression, sleep disorders, traveler's diarrhea, and breast cancer. The American College of Physicians, the American Heart Association, the Institute of Medicine, and the Agency for Health Care Research and Quality are some of the many organizations that consistently bring experts together to establish "guidelines" for practice concerning common problems such as pain, high blood pressure, and depression.

The main purpose of seeking consensus among experts is to define levels of agreement on controversial subjects and unresolved issues. These methods are therefore extremely germane to setting standards against which to judge the effectiveness of new programs when no comparison group data are available. True consensus methods, however, are often difficult to implement, because they typically require extensive reviews of the literature on the topic under discussion as well as highly structured methods.

The use of expert panels has proven to be an effective technique in program evaluation for setting standards of performance, as illustrated in Example 2.9.

Example 2.9 Using Experts to Set Standards

Sixteen U.S. teaching hospitals participated in a 4-year evaluation of a program to improve outpatient care in their group practices. Among the study's major goals were improvements in amount of faculty involvement in the practices, in staff productivity, and in access to care for patients. The evaluators and representatives from each of the hospitals used standards for care set by the Institute of Medicine as a basis for setting standards of program effectiveness before the start of the study. After 2 years, the evaluators presented interim data on performance and brought experts from the 16 hospitals together to come to consensus on standards for the final 2 years of the study. To guide the process, the evaluators prepared a special form, part of which appears in Figure 2.2.

Variable	Current Standard	Definitions	Interim Results	Question	Suggestion	Your Decision
Waiting Time	90% of patients should be seen within 30 minutes	Waiting time is time between scheduled appointment and when first seen by primary provider	70% of patients were seen within 30 minutes	Is 90% reasonable?	90%	__ %
	Compared to national data-bases, program patients should not have unduly long waiting times		Waiting times = 24.3 minutes. National data = 37.3 minutes for doctor's office or private clinic.	Should national data be used as standard?	Yes	__ Yes __ No

Figure 2.2. Selected Portions of a Form Used in Setting Standards of Effectiveness

It is interesting to note that a subsequent survey of the participants in the standard-setting process discussed in Example 2.9 found that they did not use the interim data to make their choices: No association was found between how well a medical center had previously performed with respect to each of 36 selected standards and the choice of a performance level for the remaining 2 years of the evaluation. Interviews with experts at the medical centers revealed that the standards they selected came from informed estimates of what performance might yet become and from the medical centers' ideals; the experts considered the interim data to be merely suggestive.

Program evaluators use a number of methods when they rely on panels of experts to promote understanding of issues, topics, and standards for evaluation, but the most productive of these depend on a few simple practices, as discussed in the following guidelines:

Guidelines for Expert Panels

1. *The evaluator must clearly specify the evaluation questions.* If the questions are not clearly specified, the experts may help in clarification and in specification. Here are examples:
   Not quite ready for standard setting: Was the program effective with high-risk women?
   More amenable to standard setting: Did the program improve the proportion of low-weight births among low-income women?
   Standard: Significantly fewer low-weight births are found in the experimental versus the control group.

2. *The evaluator should provide data to assist the experts.* These data can be about the participants in the experimental program, the intervention itself, and the costs and benefits of participation. The data can come from the published literature, from ongoing research, or from financial and statistical records. For example, in an evaluation of a program to improve birth weight among infants born to low-income women, experts might make use of information about the extent of the problem in the country. They might also want to know how prevalent low-weight births are among poor women and, if other interventions have been used effectively, what their costs were.

3. *The evaluator should select experts based on their knowledge, their influence, or how they will use the findings.* The number of experts an evaluator chooses is necessarily dependent on the evaluation's resources and the evaluator's skill in coordinating groups. (See Example 2.10 for two illustrations concerning the choice of experts.)

4. *The evaluator should ensure that the panel process is carefully structured and skillfully led.* A major purpose of the expert panel is to come to agreement on the criteria for appraising a program's performance. To facilitate agreement, and to distinguish the panel process from an open-ended committee meeting, the evaluator should prepare an agenda for the panel in advance, along with the other materials noted above (such as literature reviews and other presentations of data). When possible, the evaluator should try to focus the panel on particular tasks, such as reviewing a specific set of data and rating the extent to which those data apply to the current program. For example, the evaluator might give the experts data on past performance (e.g., 10 of 16 hospitals had continuous quality improvement systems for monitoring the quality of inpatient care) and ask them to rate the extent to which that standard should still apply (e.g., on a 5-point scale ranging from *strongly agree* to *strongly disagree*).

Example 2.10 Choosing Experts to Set Evaluation Standards

- The New Dental Clinic aimed to improve patient satisfaction. A meeting was held in which three patient representatives, a nurse, a physician, and a technician defined the "satisfied patient" and decided on how much time to allow the clinic to produce satisfied patients.
- The primary goals of the Adolescent Outreach Program are to teach teens about preventive health care and to make sure that all needed health care services (such as vision screening and immunizations) are provided. A group of teens participated in a teleconference to help the program developers and evaluators decide on the best ways to teach teens and to set standards of learning achievement. Also, physicians, nurses, teachers, and parents participated in a conference to determine the types of services that should be provided and how many teens should receive them.

Setting Standards Using Community Data Sets

Large data sets such as those maintained by the Centers for Disease Control and Prevention (CDC), the National Center for Health Statistics (which can be accessed through the CDC Web site at http://www.cdc.gov), and state and local governments come from scientific surveys of whole populations of various kinds and contain accurate information on individual and collective health status as well as on the composition, organization, and financing of the health system. Researchers also maintain data sets, and many make their data available to other investigators.

The information from large data sets is often presented in summary or report form. Such data sets provide benchmarks against which evaluators can measure the effectiveness of new programs. For instance, an evaluator of a hypothetical drivers' education program might say something like this: "I used the county's Surveillance Data Set to find out about use of seat belts. The results show that about 1 in 10 drivers between 18 and 21 years of age in this county do not use seat belts. An effective driver education program should be able reduce that number to 1 in 11 within 5 years."

Suppose you have been asked to evaluate a new program to prevent low-weight births in your state. If you know the current percentage of low-weight births in the state, then you can use that figure as a gauge for evaluating the effectiveness of a new program that aims to lower the rate. Example 2.11 shows some ways in which evaluators use existing data to set standards in program evaluation.

Example 2.11 Using Community Data to Set Standards in Program Evaluation

- The Obstetrical Access and Utilization Initiative serves high-risk women and aims to reduce the numbers of births of babies weighing less than 2,500 grams (5.5 pounds). One evaluation question asks, "Is the birth of low-weight babies prevented?" In the state, 6.1% of babies are low birth weight, but this percentage includes babies born to women who are considered to be at low or medium risk. The standard used as evidence that low-weight births are prevented is as follows: "No more than 6.1% of babies will be born weighing less than 5.5 pounds."
- The city's governing council has decided that the schools should become partners with the community's health care clinics in developing and evaluating a program to reduce motor vehicle crashes among children and young adults ages 10 to 24 years. According to the Centers for Disease Control's findings from the Youth Risk Behavior Surveillance System (accessed through the CDC Web site, http://www.cdc.gov), the leading cause of death (31% of all deaths) among youth of this age is motor vehicle accidents. Council members, community clinic representatives, teachers and administrators from the schools, and young people meet to discuss standards for program effectiveness. They agree that they would like to see a statistically and clinically meaningful reduction in deaths due to motor vehicle crashes over the program's 5-year trial period. They will use the 31% figure as the baseline against which to evaluate reduction.

When you use data from large sets of data as the standards against which you are evaluating a local program, you must make certain that they are truly applicable. The only data available to you may have been collected a long time ago or under circumstances that are very different from those surrounding the program you are evaluating, and so they may simply not apply. For example, data gleaned from an evaluation conducted with men may not apply to women, and data on older men may not apply to younger men. Data from an evaluation conducted with hospitalized patients may not apply to people in the community. Also, there may be geographic and cultural variations in how people perceive and deal with health; standards for the entire community may not always apply locally.

Setting Standards Using the Literature

The literature consists of all published and unpublished reports of evaluation studies. To identify standards for your program, you should use only the most scientifically rigorous evaluations of other programs. You must also be careful to base your standards on programs and participants reported in the literature that are sufficiently similar to the program and participants you are evaluating. Example 2.12 illustrates how evaluators might use the literature in setting standards in program evaluations.

Example 2.12 Using the Literature to Set Evaluation Standards

The Community Cancer Center has inaugurated a new program to help families deal with the depressive symptoms that often accompany a diagnosis of cancer in a loved one. A main program objective is to reduce symptoms of depression among participating family members.

The evaluators want to convene a group of potential program participants to assist in developing standards of program effectiveness. In specific, the evaluators want assistance in defining "reduction in symptoms." They discover, however, that it is very difficult to find a time when all of the potential participants are available to meet. Also, the center does not have the funds to sponsor a face-to-face meeting. Because of these constraints, the evaluators decide against convening a meeting and instead turn to the literature.

The evaluators go online to find articles that describe the effectiveness of programs to reduce depressive symptoms in cancer patients. Although they find five published articles, only one of the programs evaluated is exactly the same as the Community Cancer Center's program, although it takes place in an academic cancer center. Nevertheless, given the quality of the evaluation and the similarities between the two programs, the evaluators believe that they can apply this other program's standards to the present program. This is what the evaluators found in the article:

> At the 6-month assessment, family members in the first group had significantly lower self-reported symptoms of depression on the Depression Scale than did family members in the second group (8.9 versus 15.5). The mean difference between groups adjusted for baseline scores was –7.0 (95% confidence interval, –10.8 to –3.2), an effect size of 1.08 standard deviations. These results suggest that 86% of students who underwent the program reported lower scores of depressive symptoms at 6 months than would have been expected if they had not undergone the program.

The evaluators decide to use the same measure of depressive symptoms (the Depression Scale) as did the evaluator of the published study and to use the same statistical test to determine the significance of the results.

When adopting standards from the literature, you must compare the characteristics of the program you are evaluating and the program or programs whose evaluation standards you plan to adopt. You need to make certain that the participants, settings, interventions, and main outcome variables are similar, if not identical.

Then, when you do your evaluation, you must choose exactly the same measures or instruments and statistical methods to interpret the findings.

Evaluation Standards and Economic Evaluations

In a cost-effectiveness analysis, a program is considered to be effective if no other program is available at lower cost (that is, other programs may be available, but they cost more). Four generic standards apply in economic evaluations:

- *Cost-effectiveness evaluation:* Program A is effective and is the lowest-cost program around.
- *Cost-benefit analysis:* Program A has merit if its benefits are equal to or exceed its costs; the benefit-to-cost ratio of Program A is equal to or greater than 1.0 and exceeds the benefit-to-cost ratio of Program B.
- *Cost minimization analysis:* Programs A and B have identical benefits, but Program A has lower costs.
- *Cost utility analysis:* Program A produces *N* (the evaluation figures out exactly how many) quality adjusted life years at lower cost than Program B.

Example 2.13 illustrates the uses of economic standards in evaluations.

Example 2.13 Setting Standards for Economic Evaluations

RISK-FREE is a new preventive health education program. The evaluators have three study aims and associated hypotheses. Two of the study aims (Aims 2 and 3) pertain to an economic evaluation.

- *Aim 1:* To evaluate the comparative effectiveness of a patient and physician educational intervention to prevent risky health behaviors in adults relative to usual care
  Hypothesis 1: When baseline levels are controlled for, the experimental patients will have a significantly lower probability of risky health behaviors over a 12-month period than patients in the usual care arm.
  Hypothesis 2: When baseline levels are controlled for, the experimental patients will have significantly better health-related quality of life over a 12-month period than patients in the usual care arm.

As part of an impact evaluation, the evaluators will also examine proximal outcomes (mediating factors in the relationship between the randomized intervention and the effectiveness end points), testing two additional hypotheses:

> *Hypothesis 3:* When baseline levels are controlled for, the experimental patients will demonstrate significantly greater self-efficacy and knowledge over a 12-month period than patients in the usual care arm.

Hypothesis 4: When baseline levels are controlled for, the experimental providers will demonstrate significantly greater knowledge and more positive attitudes, and patients will report that their providers engage in more counseling, over a 12-month period than providers in the usual care arm.

- *Aim 2:* To evaluate the comparative costs of the patient and physician educational intervention relative to usual care

  Hypothesis 5: When baseline levels are controlled for, the experimental patients will have significantly lower utilization and net (intervention + nonintervention) costs over a 12-month period than patients in the usual care arm. (This hypothesis is based on the expectation that the intervention will increase nonintervention costs by more than the cost of the intervention itself, leading to net cost savings.)
- *Aim 3:* To evaluate the cost-effectiveness of the patient and physician educational intervention relative to usual care

  Hypothesis 6: The experimental intervention will be cost-effective relative to care as usual, based on generally accepted threshold values for incremental cost-effectiveness ratios (dollars per quality-adjusted life year).

If Aim 2 demonstrates that the intervention is cost saving with equal outcomes or cost neutral with better outcomes, then the intervention is cost-effective by definition and the Aim 3 analyses are unnecessary.

Evaluation Questions and Standards: Establishing a Healthy Relationship

An evaluation question may have just one standard, or several standards may be associated with it. For example:

Question: Did nurses learn to abstract medical records reliably?

Standard 1: 80% of all nurses learn to abstract medical records reliably.

Standard 2: A statistically significant difference in learning is observed between nurses at Medical Center A and those at Medical Center B. Nurses at Medical Center A have participated in a new program, and the difference is in their favor.

The reason the question in this example has two standards is that if 80% of nurses at Medical Center A are found to be able to abstract medical records reliably, we cannot really attribute this positive result to a program unless we have access to the abstractions of nurses who were not in a program. After all, nearly all nurses might know from the start how to abstract medical records. So why not just rely on the second standard? Because differences alone, no matter how great, may not be enough.

Suppose that the nurses' learning at Medical Center A was actually significantly higher than the learning that took place at Medical Center B. If the learning levels of both groups were low (say, average scores of 50% in the new program group and 20% in the comparison), then the difference, although statistically meaningful, might not be educationally or clinically meaningful, and thus it has little practical merit. We can conclude, for example, that, even though the program successfully elevated performance, the amount of improvement was insufficient, and so the program was simply not satisfactory.

When to Set Standards

The evaluator should have standards in place before continuing with the evaluation's design and analysis. Consider the following two examples.

Example 1

Program goal: To teach nurses to abstract medical records reliably

Evaluation question: Have nurses learned to abstract medical records reliably?

Standard: 90% of all nurses learn to abstract medical records reliably

Program effects on: Nurses

Effects measured by: Reliable abstraction

Design: A survey of nurses' abstractions

Data collection: A test of nurses' ability to abstract medical records

Statistical analysis: Computation of the percentage of nurses who abstract medical records reliably

Example 2

Program goal: To teach nurses to abstract medical records reliably

Evaluation question: Have nurses learned to abstract medical records reliably?

Standard: A statistically significant difference in learning is observed between nurses at Medical Center A and nurses at Medical Center B. Nurses at Medical Center A have participated in a new program, and the difference is in their favor.

Program effects on: Nurses at Medical Center A

Effects measured by: Reliable abstraction

Design: A comparison of two groups of nurses

Data collection: A test of nurses' ability to abstract medical records

Statistical analysis: A t test to compare average abstraction scores between nurses at Medical Center A and nurses at Medical Center B

The evaluation questions and standards contain the independent and dependent variables on which the evaluation's design, measurement, and analysis are subsequently based. Independent variables are sometimes called *explanatory* or *predictor* variables because, as these variables are present before the start of the program (that is, are independent of it), evaluators use them to "explain" or "predict" outcomes. In the example above, reliable abstraction of medical records (the outcome) is to be explained by nurses' participation in a new program (the independent variable). In evaluations, the independent variables often are the program (experimental and control), demographic features of the participants (such as gender, income, education, experience), and health characteristics of the participants (such as functional status and physical, mental, and social health).

Dependent variables, also termed *outcome* variables, are the factors the evaluator expects to measure. In program evaluations, these include health status, functional status, knowledge, skills, attitudes, behaviors, costs, and efficiency.

Thus the evaluation questions and standards necessarily contain the independent and dependent variables: those on whom the program is to have effects and measures of those effects, as illustrated in Example 2.14.

Example 2.14 Questions, Standards, and Independent and Dependent Variables

Program goal: To teach nurses to abstract medical records reliably

Evaluation question: Have nurses learned to abstract medical records reliably?

Standard: A statistically significant difference in learning is observed between nurses at Medical Center A and nurses at Medical Center B. Nurses at Medical Center A have participated in a new program, and the difference is in their favor.

Program effects explained by (independent variable): Participation versus no participation in a new program

Effects measured by this outcome (dependent variable): Reliable abstraction

---

The QSV Report: Questions, Standards, Variables

The relationships among evaluation questions, standards, and variables can be depicted in a reporting form such as the one shown in Figure 2.3. You will find that reporting questions, standards, and variables in this format is useful as you go about planning your evaluation and accounting for its methods. As the figure shows, the evaluation questions appear in the first column of the QSV (questions, standards, variables) report form, followed in subsequent columns by the standards associated with each question, the independent variables, and the dependent variables.

The QSV report in Figure 2.3 shows information on an evaluation of an 18-month program combining diet and exercise to improve health status and quality of life for persons 75 years of age or older who are living at home. Participants will be randomly assigned to the experimental or control groups according to the streets on which they live. Participants in the evaluation who need medical services can choose one of two clinics offering differing models of care delivery, one that is primarily staffed by physicians and one that is primarily staffed by nurses. The evaluators will be investigating whether any differences exist between male and female participants after program participation and the role of patient mix in those differences. (*Patient mix* refers to those characteristics of patients that might affect outcomes; these include sociodemographic characteristics, functional status scores, and presence of chronic disorders such as diabetes and hypertension.) The evaluators will also be analyzing the cost-effectiveness of the two models of health care delivery.

Evaluation Questions	Standards	Independent or Explanatory Variables	Dependent or Outcome Variables
To what extent has quality of life improved?	A statistically and practically significant improvement in quality of life over a 1-year period A statistically and practically significant improvement in quality of life between participants and nonparticipants	Gender, group participation (experimental and control participants), patient mix (sociodemographic characteristics, functional status scores, presence or absence of chronic disorders such as diabetes and hypertension)	Quality of life includes social contacts and support, financial support, perceptions of well-being
To what extent has health status improved?	A statistically and practically significant improvement in quality of life over a 1-year period A statistically and practically significant improvement in quality of life between participants and nonparticipants	Gender, group participation (experimental and control participants), patient mix (sociodemographic characteristics, functional status scores, presence or absence of chronic disorders such as diabetes and hypertension)	Health status includes functional status and perceptions of general health and physical functioning; measures of complications from illness (for diabetes would include cardiac, renal, ophthalmologic, or foot; for hypertension would include blood pressure control)
What is the relationship between cost and effectiveness of two clinic staffing models: primarily physicians and primarily nurses?	Effectiveness will be demonstrated by lower cost per visit and satisfactory health status and quality of life	Two models of care (primarily physician-based and primarily nurse-based)	Quality of life, health status, costs of personnel, hours delivering care, number of appointments made and kept

Figure 2.3. The QSV Reporting Form

As you can see, the QSV reporting form extracts the questions, standards, and variables from the description of the evaluation of the diet and exercise program for persons over 75 years of age. This evaluation has three questions: one about the program's influence on quality of life, one about the program's influence on health status, and one about the cost-effectiveness of two methods for staffing clinics. Each of the three questions has one or more standards associated with it. The independent variables for the questions about quality of life and health status are gender, group participation, and patient mix, and each of these terms is explained. The dependent variables are also explained in the QSV report. For example, the report notes that "quality of life" includes social contacts and support, financial support, and perceptions of well-being.

Summary and Transition to the Next Chapter on Evaluation Research Design

A program evaluation is conducted to determine whether a given program is meritorious. Is it worth the costs, or might a more efficient program accomplish even more? Evaluation questions focus the evaluation. They may be aimed at many different areas, such as the program's environment; the extent to which program goals and objectives have been met; the degree, duration, and distribution of benefits and effects; and the implementation and effectiveness of different program activities and management strategies.

Program evaluations are concerned with providing convincing evidence of programs' effectiveness. The standards are the specific criteria against which effectiveness is measured. The evaluator should set the questions and standards in advance of any evaluation activities because they prescribe the evaluation's design, data collection, and analysis. One question may have more than one standard associated with it. Evaluators set standards based on statistical comparisons, the opinions of experts, and reviews of the literature, past performance, and community data sets.

The next chapter will tell you how to design an evaluation so that you will be able to link any changes found in health, health practices, education, and attitudes to an experimental program and not to other competing events. For example, suppose you are evaluating a health education program that aims to encourage men and women over the age of 50 to get a colonoscopy—a rather uncomfortable procedure that has been shown to protect against colon cancer. You might erroneously conclude that your program is effective if you observe a significant increase in colonoscopies among program participants unless your evaluation's design is sufficiently sophisticated to distinguish between the effects of the health education program and those of other sources of education, such as television and newspapers. The next chapter discusses the most commonly used evaluation research designs.

Exercises

EXERCISE 1

Directions

Read the example below and, using only the information offered, list the evaluation questions.

> The University Medical Center is concerned with continuously auditing its transfusion practices to ensure the safety of the blood supply. Accordingly, the Committee on Blood Derivatives has been formed to establish guidelines for transfusing red blood cells, fresh-frozen plasma, platelets, and cryoprecipitated AHF. An education program is offered to all interested physicians and nurses to teach them about the guidelines, assist in ensuring appropriate transfusion practices, and, in general, improve the quality of care at the institution. A 2-year evaluation is conducted. Among the medical center's concerns is that all physicians use the guidelines.

EXERCISE 2

Directions

Read the example below and state the evaluation questions and associated standards as well as the independent and dependent variables.

> The director of the Infectious Disease Center wants all of the center's nonphysician staff members to acquire knowledge regarding some of the ethical issues pertaining to the care of patients with infectious diseases, including hepatitis and tuberculosis. These specifically include issues pertaining to patient privacy. The director is working with the center's Bioethics Committee and members of its Division of Medical Education to develop a program for nonphysicians. The plan is to institute the program and monitor its effects on staff each year for 5 years.

Suggested Readings

To learn more about questions and standards in economic evaluations, see the following evaluation reports, all of which are available in their entirety online through MEDLINE. (For instructions on how to find MEDLINE, see the "Suggested Readings" section in Chapter 1.)

Fleming, M. F., Mundt, M. P., French, M. T., Manwell, L. B., Stauffacher, E. A., & Barry, K. L. (2002). Brief physician advice for problem drinkers: Long-term efficacy and benefit-cost analysis. *Alcoholism: Clinical and Experimental Research, 26,* 36–43.

Objective: To describe the 48-month efficacy and benefit-cost analysis of Project TrEAT (Trial for Early Alcohol Treatment), a randomized controlled trial of brief physician advice for the treatment of problem drinking.

Jha, A. K., Perlin, J. B., Kizer, K. W., & Dudley, R. A. (2003). Effect of the transformation of the Veterans Affairs health care system on the quality of care. *New England Journal of Medicine, 348,* 2218–2227.

Objective: To determine the change in the quality of health care for veterans resulting from a mid-1990s systemwide reengineering of the VA health care system to improve quality of care and to compare the quality of care in the VA system with that of the Medicare fee-for-service program.

Jones, K., Colson, P. W., Holter, M. C., Lin, S., Valencia, E., Susser, E., & Wyatt, R. J. (2003). Cost-effectiveness of critical time intervention to reduce homelessness among persons with mental illness. *Psychiatric Services, 54,* 884–890.

Objective: To investigate the cost-effectiveness of the critical time intervention program, a time-limited adaptation of intensive case management, which has been shown to reduce recurrent homelessness significantly among men with severe mental illness.

Wheeler, J. R. (2003). Can a disease self-management program reduce health care costs? The case of older women with heart disease. *Medical Care, 41,* 706–715.

Objective: To assess the impact of a heart disease management program on use of hospital services, estimate associated hospital cost savings, and compare potential cost savings with the cost of delivering the program.

About Quality of Care

Donabedian, A. (1980). *Explorations in quality assessment and monitoring: Vol. 1. The criteria and standards of quality.* Ann Arbor, MI: Health Administration Press.

Donabedian, A. (1982). *Explorations in quality assessment and monitoring: Vol. 2. The definition of quality and approaches to its assessment.* Ann Arbor, MI: Health Administration Press.

Donabedian, A. (1983). *Explorations in quality assessment and monitoring: Vol. 3. Methods and findings of quality assessment and monitoring: An illustrated analysis.* Ann Arbor, MI: Health Administration Press.

Institute of Medicine. (2000). *Crossing the quality chasm.* Washington, DC: National Academy Press.

See Also

Drummond, M. F., Stoddard, G. L., & Torrance, G. W. (1997). *Methods for economic evaluation of health programs.* New York: Oxford University Press.

This book is an outstanding source of basic information on economic evaluation methods.

Fink, A., Kosecoff, J., & Brook, R. H. (1986). Setting standards of performance for program evaluations: The case of the teaching hospital general medicine group practice program. *Evaluation and Program Planning, 9,* 143–151.

This article describes the methods and usefulness of setting standards in a national study to improve the quality of care and education for health care practitioners. It is one of the few articles to date that discusses methods for standard setting, so even though it was published some time ago, it is still relevant.

Hulley, S. B., Cummings, S. R., Browner, W. S., Grady, D., Hearst, N., & Newman, T. B. (2001). *Designing clinical research* (2nd ed.). Philadelphia: Lippincott Williams & Wilkins.

For information on the origins of evaluation questions as well as other types of research questions, see Chapter 2 of this volume.

Purpose of This Chapter

An evaluation design is a structure that is created especially to produce an unbiased appraisal of a program's merits. The structure is built on the independent variables and the frequency and timing of measurement. This chapter discusses the relationships between evaluation designs and the evaluation questions and standards. It also explains the uses and limitations of experimental and descriptive evaluation designs. The chapter also discusses a chart known as the *evaluation design report,* which illustrates the logical connections between the purposes and methods of an evaluation.

3 Designing Program Evaluations

A Reader's Guide to Chapter 3

Evaluation Design: Creating the Structure

Selecting an Evaluation Design

What are the evaluation questions and standards? The independent variables? The inclusion and exclusion criteria? Will a control group be included? When will measures take place? How often will measures take place?

Designs for Program Evaluation

Experimental evaluation designs, descriptive (observational) evaluation designs, factorial and other combination evaluation designs

Internal and External Validity

The Evaluation Design Report: Questions, Standards, and Independent Variables

Evaluation Design: Creating the Structure

An evaluation design is a structure that the evaluator creates especially to appraise a program's effectiveness objectively and without bias. Consider Examples 3.1, 3.2, and 3.3.

Example 3.1 Evaluation Design: The Same Group Is Measured Over Time

Narrative

A new Spanish-language health education program for fifth graders is being evaluated in the district's 12 elementary schools. If effective, it will replace the traditional program. A key evaluation question is whether participating students' knowledge improves. To be eligible for participation, students must be able to read in Spanish at the fifth-grade level or better. Improvement is to be analyzed statistically. Students will be tested within 1 month of the beginning of the program and after 1 year to determine how much they have learned.

Abstract

Program: A new fifth-grade Spanish-language health education program

Evaluation question: Does students' knowledge improve?

Standard: Statistically significant improvement over time

Independent variable: Students in the new program

Eligibility for the evaluation: All 12 elementary schools are eligible

Eligibility for the program: Students must read at the fifth-grade level or better in Spanish

Measurement: A test of students' knowledge within 1 month of the beginning of the experimental program and a test of the same students' knowledge 1 year after completion of the program

---

Example 3.2 Evaluation Design With Random Selection and Measurement Over Time

Narrative

A new Spanish-language health education program for fifth graders is being evaluated in 6 of the district's 12 elementary schools. The 6 participating schools will be selected at random. If effective, the program will be introduced throughout all 12 of the district's elementary schools. A key evaluation question is whether students' knowledge improves. To be eligible to participate, students must be able to read in Spanish at the fifth-grade level or better. Improvement is to be analyzed statistically. Students will be tested within 1 month of the beginning of the program and after 1 year to determine how much they have learned.

Abstract

Program: A new fifth-grade Spanish-language health education program

Evaluation question: Does students' knowledge improve?

Independent variable: Students in 6 elementary schools participating in a new program

Standard: Statistically significant improvement over time

Eligibility for the evaluation: 6 of 12 elementary schools in the district

Selection for the evaluation: 6 schools will be selected at random

Eligibility for the program: Students who read at the fifth-grade level or better in Spanish

Measurement: A test of students' knowledge within 1 month of the beginning of the experimental program and a test of students' knowledge 1 year after completion of the program

---

Example 3.3 Evaluation Design With Random Selection and Randomly Assigned Groups Measured Over Time

Narrative

A new Spanish-language health education program for fifth graders is being evaluated in 6 of the district's 12 elementary schools. If effective, it will be introduced throughout all 12 of the district's elementary schools. The 6 participating schools will be chosen at random. Of these 6 schools, 3 will be randomly assigned to continue with their regular health education program, and the other 3 will participate in the new program. A key evaluation question is whether students' knowledge improves. Improvement is to be analyzed statistically. To be eligible to participate, students must be able to read in Spanish at the fifth-grade level or better. Students will be tested within 1 month of the beginning of the program and after 1 year to determine how much they have learned.

Abstract

Program: A new fifth-grade Spanish-language health education program

Evaluation question: Does students' knowledge improve?

Independent variable: Students in an experimental program and in a control program

Standard: Statistically significant improvement over time

Eligibility for the evaluation: 6 of 12 elementary schools in the district

Selection for the evaluation: 6 schools will be selected at random

Eligibility for the program: Students who read at the fifth-grade level or better in Spanish

Assignment to groups: 3 schools assigned at random to the experimental program; the other 3 assigned to continue with the traditional district-approved health education program

Measurement: A test of students' knowledge within 1 month of the beginning of the program and a test of students' knowledge 1 year after completion of the program

---

These three examples illustrate three basic program evaluation designs: experimental evaluation designs with nonrandom selection into the evaluation and reliance on one group to act as a control or comparison for itself (using a premeasure and a postmeasure), experimental evaluation designs with random selection into the evaluation and reliance on one group to act as a control or comparison for itself (using a premeasure and a postmeasure), and experimental evaluation designs with random selection into the evaluation and random assignment into experimental and control groups and a premeasure and postmeasure.

In Example 3.1, all 12 of the district's elementary schools will participate in the evaluation; eligible students will be measured before and after participation. In Example 3.2, 6 of the district's 12 schools will be selected at random to participate in the evaluation, and eligible students will be tested before and after participation. In Example 3.3, out of 6 of the district's 12 schools, 3 schools will be assigned at random into the new or experimental program; eligible students in the other 3 schools will receive the regular program. Students in the third example will also be measured twice: before and after the intervention.

Before designing an evaluation, the evaluator should answer at least the following six questions:

1. What are the evaluation questions and standards?
2. What are the independent variables?
3. What are the inclusion and exclusion criteria?
4. Will a control group be included? (If the answer to this question is yes, what are the characteristics of the control group?)
5. When will measures be taken?
6. How often will measures be taken?

The discussion of each of these questions below uses examples from the new Spanish-language health education program described above.

Selecting an Evaluation Design: Dealing With Six Questions

What Are the Evaluation Questions and Standards?

The first step in the selection of any evaluation design is to consider the evaluation questions and their associated standards. The standard is the guide to a *minimum* design. If your standard involves changes over time, for example, you know that you need a design in which two measurements are taken. This is the case for the three evaluation examples given above. In Example 3.3, however, the evaluation also combines the two measurements with two groups. The addition of a comparison group to a design always strengthens it. Suppose, for example, an evaluation found that fifth graders improved in their knowledge of preventive health care after their participation in an experimental program. Unless the evaluator can demonstrate that fifth graders in comparable programs did not also improve, claims that the new program is effective can be challenged. Fifth graders can improve in their knowledge for several reasons—among them, ordinary intellectual maturation.

What Are the Independent Variables?

Independent variables are also called *explanatory* or *predictor* variables because they are used to explain or predict the program's outcomes (the dependent variables). They are independent of the program and are part of the evaluation's structure or design.

In evaluations, the independent variables are often group participation (experimental group and control group) and the participants' social and health status. The evaluator uses these variables in hypothesizing or predicting the outcomes (dependent variables) of program participation. Consider the relationships among the following evaluation questions, standards, independent variables, and outcomes.

Relationships Among Evaluation Questions, Standards, Independent Variables, and Outcomes

Example A

Evaluation question: How do participants in the experimental and control groups compare in their social activity?

Standard: A statistically significant difference in social activity that favors the experimental group

Independent variable: Group participation (in the experimental group or in the control group)

Outcome (dependent variable): Social activity

Evaluator's prediction: Participation in the experimental program will be associated with increased and higher-quality social activity than will participation in the control program.

Example B

Evaluation question: How do low-income women in the new prenatal care program compare with low-income women in the traditional program in their attendance at childbirth and parenting classes?

Standard: A statistically significant difference between the new and traditional program in attendance that favors the new program

Independent variable: Group participation (in the new prenatal care program or in the traditional program)

Outcome (dependent variable): Attendance at childbirth and parenting classes

Evaluator's prediction: Participation in the new program will be associated with greater increases in attendance at childbirth and parenting classes than will participation in the traditional program.

Once the evaluator has established the questions, standards, independent variables, and outcomes, the design comes next.

Evaluation Questions, Standards, Independent Variables, Outcomes, and Design

Evaluation question: To what extent has quality of life improved for individuals who participated in the Healthy Adult Program?

Standard: A statistically and practically significant improvement in quality of life between male and female participants and nonparticipants whose problems vary in complexity

Independent variables: Group participation, gender, patient mix (a combination of economic characteristics and health and functional status)

Outcome (dependent variable): Quality of life

Design:

	Experimental	**Control**
Males		
Very complex problems		
Average complexity		
Not very complex problems		
Females		
Very complex problems		
Average complexity		
Not very complex problems		

The independent variables frame the evaluation design. In some cases, the frame is relatively easy to create because the categories are self-evident, as they are for gender (male and female) and group participation (experimental and control). But for other independent variables, such as patient mix, age, and health status, deciding on categories becomes more complicated. In this example, "patient mix," which refers to a combination of economic, health, and functional differences, was divided into three categories: very complex, average, and not very complex. But other categories might have been chosen to describe patient mix. For example, the three components of patient mix might have been treated separately, with patients assigned to groups depending on their scores on measures of health, functioning, and income. The evaluator's choice of categories depends on what the literature says (Are data available that suggest the most accurate way to define patient mix?) and the resources available (How many groups can the evaluator afford to include in the evaluation?).

What Are the Inclusion and Exclusion Criteria?

Inclusion and exclusion criteria (sometimes called *eligibility criteria*) separate those who are eligible for participation in the evaluation from those who are not. These criteria are the foundation for the evaluator's inference of conclusions about the groups who are most likely to benefit from participation. For example, assume that an evaluation of a program to improve preventive personal health practices includes only women less than 50 years of age with diabetes. Suppose also that the evaluation cannot afford to provide transportation to the program's location for women who do not have their own transportation, and so these women are excluded. If the program is effective, the nature of the exclusion criteria will necessarily limit the program's applicability to women under 50 years with diabetes who have access to transportation.

Criteria for inclusion in an evaluation sometimes come from primarily practical considerations, such as geographic and temporal proximity and demographic and health characteristics. Example 3.4 lists some typical kinds of inclusion criteria.

Example 3.4 Illustrative Inclusion Criteria

- Schools offering health education to fifth graders
- Women seen in the clinic during the past 2 years
- Health centers serving 50 or more new clients each week
- Health centers serving 50 or more new female clients each week

---

Evaluations sometimes also have exclusion criteria. These are special criteria aimed at excluding potential participants whose inclusion is likely to impair the actual functioning of the evaluation or skew its data. Consider the exclusion criteria listed in Example 3.5.

Example 3.5 Illustrative Exclusion Criteria

- Schools whose fifth-grade health education programs meet less than once a week
- Articles published before 1990
- People with major mental disorders (such as schizophrenia) who are unlikely to comply with program rules

---

In addition to practical considerations, eligibility criteria come from the evaluation questions, as illustrated in Example 3.6.

Example 3.6 Inclusion and Exclusion Criteria: The Evaluation Questions

Study 1

Evaluation question: Has access to prenatal care for high-risk pregnant women improved?

Ask: Which high-risk groups must be included for this program to receive a fair trial? To which high-risk groups are the findings to be applied? Where and when can I find appropriate women for participation?

Inclusion criteria:

- Residence within 10 miles of the clinic
- Teenage mothers with at least one other child living at home
- Women between 30 and 40 years of age who are eligible for Medicaid

Exclusion criteria:

- Women with private health insurance
- Women between 20 and 29 years of age

Study 2

Evaluation question: Have students improved their knowledge of health?

Ask: What are the characteristics of students that must be included for this program to receive a fair trial? To which groups of students should the findings be applicable? Where and when can I find appropriate students to participate?

Inclusion criteria:

- Enrollment in one of the district's elementary schools
- Students whose reading abilities in Spanish are at the fifth-grade level or better

Exclusion criteria:

- Students whose teachers have less than 1 year of experience in teaching health education
- Students with grade point averages of less than 3.0
- Students who were absent in the past year an average of 5 or more days each month

Will a Control Group Be Included?

The term *group* in this context refers to the institutions and individuals who participate in the evaluation, regardless of whether or not they receive the experimental intervention. A typical evaluation design consists of an experimental group, which receives the new program, and a control group, which receives some other program or no program at all. This fundamental design can be represented as in Figure 3.1.

Experimental Group	Control Group

Figure 3.1. A Basic Evaluation Design: The Experimental and Control Groups Compared

Some evaluation designs include more than one experimental group and also more than one control. For example, suppose the evaluator of a new school-based preventive health care program for fifth graders wants to compare two different styles of instruction: computer-assisted instruction (Program A) and small group discussion (Program B). Suppose also that the evaluator proposes two control groups: teacher-directed lecture and discussion (Control 1) and self-instructional learning modules (Control 2). The design for this evaluation is depicted in Figure 3.2. This design enables the evaluator to compare the achievement of learning objectives by students in the following situations:

- Experimental Program A versus Program B
- Control Programs 1 and 2
- Experimental Program A and Controls 1 and 2
- Experimental Program B and Controls 1 and 2

In an evaluation, what program should the control group receive? This very important question often is not given the attention it deserves. Frequently, the

	Experimental Program A: Computer-Assisted Instruction	Experimental Program B: Small Group Discussion
Control Program 1: Teacher-Directed Instruction		
Control Program 2: Self-Instructional Modules		

Figure 3.2. An Evaluation Design for a Program Comparing Instructional Methods: Two Experimental and Two Control Groups

control group's program consists of the usual services or no services at all. A control group must start out as demonstrably like the experimental group in its composition (health status, knowledge, attitudes, demographic characteristics) but definably and measurably unlike the experimental group in its program. Programs can differ in many different ways, such as in their philosophies, objectives, methods, settings, duration, management, and resources.

When Will Measures Take Place?

In evaluations, measures can be made before and after the program, during the program, or only after the program. Premeasures can serve many important evaluation purposes; for example, they can help the evaluator select groups to participate in the evaluation and program, check the need for the program, ensure comparability of groups, and provide a basis for calculating change or improvement. The merit of using premeasures can be compromised, however, if the premeasures are not demonstrably similar to the postmeasures, if they are administered very close in time to the postmeasures (because participants may simply repeat their responses from the premeasures), and if they influence participants to behave or perform in special ways (by focusing their attention on program content). Table 3.1 lists some examples of the uses of premeasures and postmeasures.

How Often Will Measures Take Place?

The frequency with which measures are made depends on how much time is needed for the program's effects to occur, the duration of the program and the evaluation, and the resources available for measurement. The amount of time that the evaluator needs to observe and be able to measure a program's hoped-for effects varies according to the characteristics of the expected outcomes, impact, and costs. For example, assessing students at the end of a year to determine the effects of a program to teach specific health education content to fifth graders is probably reasonable. Assessing changes in health habits and associated costs at the end of a year would be foolhardy, however, because it usually take longer than a year for such changes to become observable. An

Table 3.1 Examples of Uses of Premeasures and Postmeasures

Measure	*Uses*	*Comments*
Premeasure to select groups	Students were tested for their ability to read Spanish to identify those with reading levels at fifth grade or better. A financial analysis was conducted to identify women eligible for welfare assistance.	Data such as these (reading level and financial status) are often available from records. Using existing data can save time.
Premeasure to check the need for the program	A pretest of students' knowledge revealed that they already knew a substantial portion of the information to be imparted in the new curriculum. A financial analysis revealed that more women are eligible than the original estimates for the new program suggested.	This information can be used to revise the program or the evaluation questions and standards.
Premeasure to ensure comparability of groups	Schools A, B, and C, which volunteered for the program, were found to have more experienced health education teachers than Control Schools X, Y, and Z. No differences were found in the ages, marital status, health status, or income of women in the volunteer experimental and control groups.	Differences between or among groups before the start of the program can easily bias the results. Determining the nature and extent of potential "contaminants" is essential in program evaluation.
Premeasure to provide a basis for measuring change or improvement	Students in the experimental group gained significantly more knowledge than did students in a control group. Women in the experimental group did not enter care earlier than women in the control.	Premeasures provide a baseline against which to measure progress for single groups ("self controls") and for multiple groups.
Postmeasure to appraise benefit, outcome, impact, cost	Average scores on a test were compared between the experimental and control groups after participation in a health education program. The numbers of women entering prenatal care before the third trimester were compared after half participated in a program to improve access to care.	Postmeasures provide evidence of a program's merits. They include achievement tests, surveys (interviews, telephone, self-administered questionnaires), observations, and record reviews.

evaluator often needs to conduct a literature review or a survey of experts to identify the expected amount of time needed to uncover changes in health habits, practices, and costs. Remember as well that the longer the period needed for measurement and observation, the greater the likelihood that external effects (such as changes in the health care reimbursement system or changes due to children's physical and social maturation) will interact with and "confound" the results.

Yearly measurement to search for long-term changes may be indicated, but programs and their evaluations rarely last more than 3 to 5 years. To ensure the possibility of continuous evaluation, the evaluator can create a data collection system and continuously date the data.

Designs for Program Evaluation

Evaluations aim to be prospective investigations of the characteristics and effectiveness of particular programs. In a prospective investigation, data are collected for the specific purposes of the evaluation, commencing with the start of the evaluation. Example 3.7 illustrates this point.

Example 3.7 Evaluations Are Prospective

- *Prospective Evaluation A:* An evaluation asked if fifth graders' knowledge improved after their participation in a health education program. Students were tested 1 month before the program started and 1 year after their participation, and the test scores were used to compare their performance over time.
- *Retrospective Study B:* For the past 5 years, the school district has administered an achievement test to all fifth graders to find out about their knowledge of preventive health care. At the end of the fifth year, the evaluator reviewed these test records to identify high and low scorers. The two groups were compared to determine whether a relationship existed between participation in a new program and higher scores.
- *Prospective Evaluation C:* Does participation in the Obstetrical Access and Utilization Project improve birth outcomes for high-risk women? Data were collected on mothers from the time of their entry into the project and for 6 months after the birth of their babies. An evaluation was conducted that compared babies born to participating mothers and those born to nonparticipating mothers in terms of their mortality, morbidity, birth weight, and gestational age.
- *Retrospective Study D:* Does participation in the Obstetrical Access and Utilization Project improve birth outcomes for high-risk women? After 3 years of the project's installation, evaluators studied birth and death certificates. Among their findings was that significantly fewer babies of very low birth weight were born to women who took part in the project.

The best program evaluations are prospective because they are amenable to the most "control." Retrospective studies (sometimes called *summative evaluations*) are historical analyses. This kind of study leaves too much to chance to satisfy the demands of a diligent investigation of a program's characteristics and merits. For example, in Retrospective Study B, above, assume that all high scorers were found to have participated in the district's new program. Can the evaluator conclude that the program was effective? Perhaps the high scorers were more knowledgeable to begin with. In Prospective Evaluation C, the positive findings can be a reflection of the characteristics of women who participated in the project rather than a reflection of the effectiveness of the project (for instance, the participants may have been more educated about prenatal care than nonparticipants, or more willing to comply with medical and nursing advice). Advance control over the contents of the program, over selection and assignment to groups, and over data collection is essential to ensure the validity of an evaluation's findings.

The designs discussed in the following section have been selected because they are most appropriate for program evaluations. Descriptive designs are included because evaluators use them frequently, and such designs have a major role to play in evaluation. Because program evaluation borrows from a number of disciplines, you will find that evaluators sometimes use several different terms interchangeably (for example, *true experiment, randomized controlled trial,* and *control trial*). These terms are explained as they come up in the text.

A Classification of Program Evaluation Designs

I. Experiments
   A. Evaluations with concurrent controls in which participants are randomly assigned to groups (called *randomized controlled trials* or *true experiments*)
   B. Evaluations with concurrent controls in which participants are not randomly assigned to groups (called *nonrandomized controlled trials* or *quasi-experiments*)
   C. Evaluations with self-controls (require premeasures and postmeasures; called *before-and-after designs*)
   D. Evaluations with historical controls (make use of data collected on participants in other evaluations and research studies or in large community surveys such as the National Health Interview Survey)

II. Descriptive or observational designs
   A. Cross-sectional designs
   B. Cohort designs

III. Factorial designs (experimental or descriptive)

IV. Combination designs (both experimental and descriptive designs)

Experimental Evaluations

Evaluations With Concurrent Controls and Random Assignment

In evaluation designs utilizing concurrent controls and random assignment, potential program participants (e.g., persons over 75 years of age, children in need of polio vaccinations, high-risk men) are identified and then assigned at random to either the new program group or the control group. The program is introduced concurrently to both groups, and the two groups are compared on some outcome of interest (e.g., health status). This design is called a *randomized trial, a randomized controlled trial,* or a *true experiment.*

When both the participants and investigators in a randomized controlled trial (RCT) do not know which group is the experimental one and which is the control, this is known as a *double-blind experiment.* When participants do not know to which group they have been assigned but the investigators do, this is called a *blinded trial.*

In health program evaluation studies, it is often logistically or ethically difficult to "blind" participants, and this circumstance may introduce bias or error. Another potential source of bias is failure to deliver a program uniformly. For example, if two different professors are to teach the same program content, their teaching styles may be so different as to "bias" the results.

The RCT is the fundamental design against which all other designs are judged because causation can be inferred from the results of an RCT. To ensure the generalizability of the results, evaluators should probably conduct RCTs of the same intervention in many places, with a variety of participants, over a number of years.

From the evaluator's perspective, the experimental evaluation with randomly constituted concurrent controls is the ideal, but many factors militate against the use of this design:

- Evaluators typically lack the resources to conduct multicenter interventions.
- Evaluators have difficulty in getting enough participants to constitute groups.
- Evaluators are not granted the time and money they need to prepare and implement such designs.
- A disparity almost invariably exists between the urgency with which data are needed and the amount of time required to conduct the evaluation.
- Ethical and other problems arise when evaluators randomly assign and blind participants and investigators.
- In a very large evaluation, it can be a logistical nightmare to ensure that the program and assessment measures (such as tests and surveys) are being implemented across groups in a uniform way.

Evaluations With Concurrent Controls But No Randomization

Nonrandomized, concurrent controls (quasi-experimental designs) involve the creation of an experimental group and a control group without random assignment. This design is usually easier to implement than an RCT. For example, consider an evaluation of a gerontology fellowship program for physicians. Each year, three physicians in six medical schools will participate. The aim of the 3-year program is to enhance the physicians' ability to do health services research in the area of aging. By the end of the third year, 54 fellows in gerontology will have participated. In this example, because the numbers of students and medical schools are relatively small, random assignment really does not make sense.

The use of nonrandomly selected controls in evaluation raises the possibility of bias from additional sources, as illustrated in Example 3.8.

Example 3.8 Biases in Evaluations Using Concurrent Controls With No Randomization

- *Membership bias:* This bias is found in preexisting groups (e.g., students at one medical center versus students at another) because one or more of the same characteristics that cause people to belong to the groups (e.g., choice of medical centers with differing clinical emphases) are associated with the outcome being evaluated (e.g., attitude toward and knowledge of a particular clinical subject matter).
- *Nonresponse bias:* This bias occurs when participation in an evaluation study is voluntary. For example, suppose faculty are invited to participate in a new geriatrics and gerontology curriculum. Those who accept the invitation may be somewhat different from nonaccepters in their willingness to try new educational programs, in the amount of time they have to participate in a new activity, and so on.

Evaluations With Self-Controls

A design with self-controls uses a group of participants to serve as its own comparison. Suppose, for example, an educational evaluator tested nursing students three times: at the beginning of the year to find out how much they knew to begin with, immediately after their participation in a new course to find out how much they learned, and at the end of 2 years to ascertain how much learning they retained. This three-measurement strategy describes an evaluation design using the nursing students as their own control. In the example, the evaluator measures the nurses once before and twice after the intervention (a new course). Designs of this type are also called *before-and-after* or *pretest-posttest* designs.

Evaluations that use self-controls are prone to several biases. These come about when participants are excited about taking part in a new program and are thus especially motivated to do well; when participants mature physically, emotionally, and intellectually; and when historical events intervene. For example, an evaluator may find that nursing students in a new course have acquired important skills and retained them over time, but these results may be due to the new course or to the characteristics of the nursing students. The students may have been motivated from the start to learn because they were excited about being in an experimental program, or they may have matured intellectually, and this development rather than the program was responsible for the learning. Also, historical events may have occurred to cloud the effects of the new course. For instance, during the year in which the program took place, a visiting professor gave several inspiring lectures to the nursing students—the students' performance on subsequent tests may be due as much to the lectures as to the program.

The soundness of self-controlled designs depends on the appropriateness of the number and timing of measurements. If the evaluator of the nursing course wants to check retention of learning, for example, should he or she test students once? Twice? At what intervals? An evaluator might decide that a program is ineffective just because he or she collected final data before the hoped-for outcomes could occur.

Evaluations With Historical Controls

An evaluation with historical controls relies on data that are available from sources outside of the evaluation itself. Such data include established norms of height, weight, blood pressure, scores on standardized tests (such as the SAT and the MCAT), and laboratory values. They may also include data on participants in surveys of the community at large (community data sets such as the National Health Interview Survey), other programs, or the same program in another setting. Historical controls are convenient; their main source of bias is the potential lack of comparability between the groups on whom the data were originally collected and the group of concern in the evaluation.

Descriptive or Observational Evaluation Designs

The terms *descriptive* and *observational* are used interchangeably to describe study designs that lack interventions. For instance, an evaluator who wants to understand the feelings of hospitalized chronically ill children might interview a sample of such children. If the evaluator wants to track the children's feelings over time, he or she might interview them several times over a period of years. Studies of this kind are surveys, and some people refer to the designs of such studies as *survey designs.* Evaluators use surveys to obtain information that can guide them in developing programs and setting standards of program merit.

Cross-Sectional Designs

Evaluators use cross-sectional designs to collect baseline information on experimental and control groups, to guide program development, and as a source of data regarding programs and their environments. Cross-sectional designs enable evaluators to develop portraits of one or many groups at one period of time. Example 3.9 illustrates the use of cross-sectional designs in program evaluations.

Example 3.9 Cross-Sectional Designs and Program Evaluation

- *A test of student knowledge of program evaluation principles:* The Curriculum Committee wanted information on entering graduate students' knowledge of the methods and uses of program evaluation in improving the public's health. The committee asked the evaluator to prepare and administer a brief test to all students. The results revealed that 80% could not distinguish between cross-sectional and experimental evaluation designs, and only 20% could list more than one source for setting standards of program effectiveness. The Curriculum Committee used these findings to develop a course of instruction to provide entering graduate students with the skills they need to conduct and review evaluations.
- *A review of the care of hypertensive patients:* Evaluators conducted a review of the medical records of 2,500 patients in three medical centers to find out about the management of patients with hypertension. They are using the data to determine whether a program is needed to improve dissemination of practice guidelines for this common medical problem and to determine how that program should be evaluated.
- *A survey of satisfaction with transfusion practices.* Evaluators conducted a survey of all patients who received transfusions within the past 6 years at the medical center as well as the patients' family members. The findings revealed that nearly 60% of 1,000 patient respondents were females between 68 and 72 years of age. Nearly half of the patients reported that they were familiar with the concept of "autologous" donation. Just over 87% indicated that they were very satisfied with their treatment at the hospital and would not fear another transfusion if one became necessary. More than 50% of the 739 family members surveyed, however, indicated their concern over the entire process and the safety of transfusions. These findings suggested the need for an education program to reassure patients' family members.

Cohort Designs

A *cohort* is a group of people who have something in common and who remain part of that group over an extended period of time. In medical research, cohort studies are used to investigate the risk factors for a disease as well as the disease's cause, incidence, natural history, and prognosis. Cohort studies ask, What will happen? They are prospective designs, and the group is followed over time, or longitudinally.

In an evaluation, a cohort consists of participants in a program who are observed over time to determine the extent to which the program's effects have lasted and how and to what extent program participation influenced the future. For example, evaluators might monitor a cohort of students in an experimental program to train nurses to administer home health care programs over time to find out how many of the participants assume leadership positions and the extent to which the knowledge they acquired in the program was sustained and useful. Cohort studies are expensive to conduct because they are continued over long periods of time; they are also subject to biases from selection (that is, those who are chosen and willing to participate in the evaluation may be very different from those who do not participate) and attrition.

Either/Or: Factorial Designs

As noted above, factorial designs may be either descriptive or experimental.

Descriptive Factorial Designs

A descriptive factorial design lays out all combinations of several independent variables at one time. For example, suppose that the hospital you work in is interested in improving its supervisors' leadership skills. You decide to survey employees to find out who among the current supervisors are most effective and what makes them so effective. You plan to use the findings to guide the development and evaluation of a leadership-training program.

You have evidence that employees use different criteria to evaluate male supervisors and female supervisors. You also think that employees apply different criteria to supervisors who are 40 years of age and younger and those who are 41 years and older. Your experience at the hospital also suggests that, regardless of management style, older male supervisors will be perceived as more effective than younger males or females of any age, regardless of supervisory style. To find out if this is true, you decide to categorize supervisors as primarily participatory (i.e., they use an inclusive decision-making style) or autonomous (they make decisions with a minimum of collaboration). To measure supervisor style, you use a validated self-administered survey of supervisory styles.

You survey employees to find out how and whether the gender or age of the supervisor and supervisory style affects staff perceptions of effectiveness (as measured by a validated survey of effectiveness), as shown in Example 3.10.

Example 3.10 Descriptive Factorial Design: Effective Hospital Supervisors

Dependent variable: Employees' perceptions of supervisors' effectiveness

Independent variables (or factors):

Style (participatory or autonomous)
Gender (male or female)
Age (40 and younger or 41 and older)

Design: A graphic representation of this factorial design looks like this:

	Participatory		Autonomous	
	Male	Female	Male	Female
40 years and under				
41 years and older				

The design depicted in Example 3.10 is a 2 (participatory or autonomous) × 2 (male or female) × 2 (40 and younger or 41 and older) factorial design. With this design, you can study *main effects* and *interaction effects.* Main effects are the effects of each factor (e.g., participatory versus autonomous) on the dependent variable (perceptions of effectiveness). Interaction effects are the effects on the dependent variable that occur as a result of the interaction between two or more independent variables (e.g., gender and age).

Questions about main effects

With respect to employees' perceptions of effectiveness:

1. How do participatory supervisors compare with autonomous supervisors?
2. How do men compare with women?
3. How do supervisors who are 40 and under compare with supervisors who are 41 and older?

Questions about interaction effects

Do differences exist that are not due to supervisory style or gender or age alone but due to interactions between them? For example:

1. How do male (or female) participatory supervisors 40 years of age and under compare with male (or female) participatory supervisors 41 years of age or older?
2. How do male (or female) autonomous supervisors 40 years of age and under compare with male (or female) autonomous supervisors 41 years of age or older?
3. How do male participatory (or autonomous) supervisors 40 years of age and younger (or 41 years of age and older) compare with female participatory (or autonomous) supervisors 40 years of age and younger (or 41 years of age and older)?

Experimental Factorial Designs

Factorial designs may also be experimental. Suppose that you are interested in comparing the effectiveness of print materials versus interactive online materials for the purpose of teaching diabetic patients how to care for themselves. Three hospital-based pediatric endocrinology clinics agree to participate in your evaluation. The clinics also agree to assign patients at random to receive the print or online materials. All participants are interviewed before they receive the intervention and 6 months later. This design is illustrated in Example 3.11.

Example 3.11 Experimental Factorial Design: Educating Patients in Self-Management of Diabetes

Clinic 1		Clinic 2		Clinic 3	
Print	**Online**	**Print**	**Online**	**Print**	**Online**
1	2	4	1	2	1
6	3	5	2	5	3
7	4	8	3	6	4
8	5	9	6	7	8
9	12	11	7	10	8
11	10	12	10	11	12

The numbers in the cells of the figure in this example are the identification numbers of the participants, which are assigned at random to one of two types of education: print or online. If the teens had not been assigned at random, the design would still be factorial. In this case, the design is a 2 (clinic) × 2 (educational methods) factorial design.

Experimental designs with three or more factors or independent variables are possible. If you are testing to see if there are differences in outcomes, as in Example 3.10, you must be certain that you have enough people in each cell so that if a difference exists, you will have the statistical *power* to uncover it. If you need many people, then you must carefully plan how you will recruit and keep them in the program and its evaluation. Recruiting and maintaining a large number of participants can be difficult, time-consuming, and costly.

To complicate matters, you may prejudice the results if you make many comparisons. Suppose you have three independent variables or factors (e.g., gender), each with two levels (e.g., male and female). You then have the possibility of 8 comparisons (2 × 2 × 2). If one factor has two levels, another has three, and the third has four, you end up with 24 comparisons (2 × 3 × 4). Just by chance alone, the probability is quite high that you will find that one or more of the comparisons are statistically significant.

Combinations: The Solomon Four-Group Design

Evaluation designs can involve two groups who are observed both before and after an intervention. A very powerful design of this type is the Solomon four-group design, in which participants are randomly assigned to four groups. The design can be depicted as shown in Figure 3.3. In this example, Groups 1 and 3 participated in a new program, but Groups 2 and 4 did not. Suppose the new program aimed to improve employees' knowledge of health hazards at their place of work. Using the Solomon four-group design (and assuming an effective program), the evaluator can expect to find the following:

1. In Group 1, knowledge on the postmeasure should be greater than knowledge on the premeasure.
2. More knowledge should be observed in Group 1's postmeasure than in Group 2's.
3. Group 3's postmeasure should show more knowledge than Group 2's premeasure.
4. Group 3's postmeasure should show more knowledge than Group 4's postmeasure.

Group 1	Premeasure	Program	Postmeasure
Group 2			Postmeasure
Group 3	Premeasure	Program	Postmeasure
Group 4			Postmeasure

Figure 3.3. The Solomon Four-Group Design

This design is a randomized controlled trial, and it incorporates self-controls and concurrent controls.

Table 3.2 summarizes the benefits of the eight major evaluation designs discussed above as well as the concerns they raise.

Table 3.2 Summary of Evaluation Designs: Benefits and Concerns

Evaluation Design	*Benefits*	*Concerns*
Design with concurrent controls and random assignment (randomized controlled trial, true experiment)	If properly conducted, can establish the extent to which a program caused its outcomes	Difficult to implement logistically and methodologically
Design with concurrent controls without randomization (quasi-experiment)	Easier to implement than a randomized controlled trial	May result in a wide range of potential biases because, without equal chances of selection, participants in the program may be systematically different from those in the control group; two groups in the evaluation may be systematically different from other, nonparticipating groups
Design with self-controls	Relatively easy to implement logistically; provides data on change and improvement	Measurements must be appropriately timed; with no control group, impossible to tell whether seemingly experimental effects are also present in other groups
Design with historical controls	Easy to implement; unobtrusive	"Normative" comparison data must be applicable to participants in the evaluation
Descriptive (cross-sectional) design	Provides baseline information on the evaluation's participants and descriptive information on the program and its setting and resources	Offers a static picture of participants and program at one point in time
Cohort design	Provides longitudinal or follow-up information	Can be expensive because of long-term nature; participants who are available over time may differ in important ways from those who are not
Factorial design	Expands the possible number of evaluation questions; allows study of main effects and interaction effects	May need large numbers of people to fill "cells" if too many questions are asked; may obtain false results if many statistical tests are performed to help answer a long list of questions
Solomon four-group design	Enables evaluator to infer causation; guards against effects of the premeasure on subsequent performance	Needs enough participants to constitute four groups; expensive to implement

Internal and External Validity

The terms *internal validity* and *external validity* are sometimes used in connection with evaluation design. A design is internally valid if it enables the evaluator to be confident that a program is effective in a specific experimental instance. If a design has external validity, then the evaluator can also demonstrate that the program's results are applicable to participants in other places and at other times.

Internal validity is essential because without it the evaluator cannot tell if a finding is due to the program or to some other factors or biases. For example, over the course of a 5-year preventive health education program for high school students, the students may mature intellectually and emotionally, and this new maturity may be as important as the program in producing changes. This phenomenon is called *maturation.* Other common risks to internal validity include the following:

- *History:* Historical events may occur that can bias an evaluation's results. For example, suppose a national campaign has been created to encourage people to make use of preventive health care services. If a change in health insurance laws favoring reimbursement for preventive health care occurs at the same time as the campaign, the evaluator will have difficulty separating the effects of the campaign from the effects resulting from increased access to care created by more favorable reimbursement for health care providers.
- *Instrumentation:* Unless the measures used to collect data are dependable, the evaluator cannot be sure that the findings are accurate. For example, if the postmeasure in a before-and-after design is easier than the premeasure, the results will erroneously favor the program. Also, untrained but lenient observers or test administrators might rule in favor of a program, whereas untrained but harsh observers or test administrators might rule against it.
- *Attrition:* Sometimes the participants who remain in the evaluation sample are different from those who drop out.

Risks to an evaluation design's external validity are most often consequences of the ways in which participants are selected and assigned. For example, participants in an experimental evaluation may behave in atypical ways because they know they are in a special program; this is called the *Hawthorne effect.* Evaluators also risk external validity whenever they test, survey, or observe participants, because this may alert the participants to the kinds of behaviors that are expected or favored.

The Evaluation Design Report: Questions, Standards, and Independent Variables

The evaluation design report (EDR) form shown in Figure 3.4 is useful for planning and explaining an evaluation. Designs begin with evaluation questions, standards, and independent variables, and the EDR depicts the relationships among these elements and the design.

Evaluation Questions	Standards	Independent Variables	Evaluation Design
To what extent has quality of life improved?	A statistically and practically significant improvement in quality over a 1-year period A statistically and practically significant improvement in quality of life between male and female participants and nonparticipants with differing sociodemographic characteristics and health and functional status	Group participation, gender, patient mix	An experimental design with randomly assigned concurrent controls in which participating men and women of differing sociodemographic characteristics and health and functional status are compared over two periods of time
To what extent has health status improved?	A statistically and practically significant improvement in health over a 1-year period A statistically and practically significant improvement in health status between participants and nonparticipants with differing sociodemographic characteristics and health and functional status	Group, gender, patient mix	An experimental design with randomly assigned concurrent controls in which participating men and women of differing sociodemographic characteristics and health and functional status are compared over two periods of time

Figure 3.4. The Evaluation Design Report

The example EDR in Figure 3.4 reports on the design for an 18-month program combining diet and exercise to improve health status and quality of life for persons 75 years of age or older. An experimental group of elderly people who still live at home will receive the program, and another group will not. Participants will be randomly assigned to the experimental group or the control group according to the streets on which they live. That is, participants living on Street A will be randomly assigned, as will participants living on Streets B, C, and so on. Participants in the evaluation who need medical services can choose one of two clinics offering differing models of care: One clinic is primarily staffed by physicians and the other is primarily staffed by nurses. The evaluators will be investigating whether any differences exist after program participation for men and women and the role of patient mix in those differences.

The EDR shows that there are two evaluation questions, each of which has two standards associated with it. The evaluation questions ask whether the program has improved quality of life and health status, and their independent variables are the same: group, gender, and patient mix. The evaluation will use an experimental design with randomly assigned concurrent controls. Figure 3.5 is a pictorial representation of this design.

Patient Mix	Gender	Time 1		Time 2	
		Experimental Participants	Control Participants	Experimental Participants	Control Participants
Very complex patient mix	Men				
	Women				
Average patient mix	Men				
	Women				
Not very complex patient mix	Men				
	Women				

Figure 3.5. Experimental Evaluation Design and Randomly Assigned Concurrent Controls

Summary and Transition to the Next Chapter on Sampling

This chapter has focused on ways to structure an evaluation so that program effects can be observed objectively. The structure, or evaluation design, includes the independent variables (such as the number and characteristics of the experimental and control groups) and number and timing of measures. The benefits and concerns associated with experimental and descriptive designs have been discussed. Randomized controlled trials are recommended for evaluators who want to establish causation, but these designs are difficult to implement. Although not as rigorous, nonrandomized trials and descriptive designs are useful, and evaluators employ such designs. The next chapter discusses sampling—that is, what you need to do when you cannot obtain an entire given population for your evaluation. Among the issues that will be discussed are how to obtain a random sample and how to select a large enough sample so that, if program differences exist, you will find them.

Exercise

Directions

Read the narrative below and identify the evaluation questions, standards, independent variables, and design. Comment on the potential for bias or error in your choice of evaluation design.

> The Center for Refugee Health wants to find out if its 3-year program will result in improved quality of care. Among the center's planned strategies is to evaluate the appropriateness of pain management for children and persons in other special populations (e.g., the elderly) before and after the program. The evaluators will survey a sample of health care providers and patients to find out their perceptions of the quality of care given and received.

Suggested Readings

Brink, P. J., & Wood, M. J. (Eds.). (1998). *Advanced design in nursing research* (2nd ed.). Thousand Oaks, CA: Sage.

This book provides examples of the kinds of research designs used in nursing research.

Campbell, D. T., & Stanley, J. C. (1963). *Experimental and quasi-experimental designs for research.* Chicago: Rand McNally.

This is the classic book on differing research designs. The authors describe "threats" to internal and external validity in detail. They also address the important issues of generalizability and how to get at "truth."

de Vaus, D. (2001). *Research design in social research.* Thousand Oaks, CA: Sage.

This book defines research design and discusses experimental as well as cross-sectional and case study designs.

Kazdin, A. E. (1998). *Methodological issues and strategies in clinical research* (2nd ed.). Washington, DC: American Psychological Association.

This book provides a general review, with examples, of the principles of experimental design in clinical settings.

Purpose of This Chapter

This chapter discusses the reasons for sampling and explains the advantages and limitations of several commonly used sampling methods: random, systematic, stratified, cluster, and convenience sampling. The chapter also discusses the issues evaluators need to consider in deciding on appropriate sample size. A form for reporting on sampling strategy is also offered. This form is designed to show the logical relationships among the evaluation questions, standards, independent variables, sampling strata, inclusion and exclusion criteria, dependent variables, measures, sampling methods, and sample size.

4 Sampling

A Reader's Guide to Chapter 4

What Is a Sample?

A *sample* is a portion or subset of a larger group called a *population.* The evaluator's *target population* consists of the institutions, persons, problems, and systems to which or to whom the evaluation's findings are to be applied or "generalized." Consider the three target populations and samples in Example 4.1.

Example 4.1 Three Target Populations and Three Samples

Study 1

Target population: All homeless veterans throughout the United States

Program: Outreach, provision of single-room occupancy housing, medical and financial assistance, and job training: the REACH-OUT Program

Sample: 500 homeless veterans in four states who receive outpatient medical care between April 1 and June 30

Comment: The REACH-OUT Program is designed for all homeless veterans. The evaluator plans to select a sample of 500 homeless veterans in four states between April 1 and June 30. The findings are to be applied to all homeless veterans in all 50 states.

Study 2

Target population: All academic medical centers

Program: Continuous Quality Improvement, a program to monitor and change the system of care, including its efficiency, one index of which is scheduling practices

Sample: A 10% sample, gathered over a 1-year period, of the records of all scheduled office visit times for patients with diabetes, hypertension, and depression in each of 20 medical centers

Comment: The target for this evaluation is all academic medical centers. A sample of 20 medical centers will be selected for the Continuous Quality Improvement program. To appraise the program's efficiency, the evaluator will sample 10% of the records for patients with three medical conditions. The findings are to be applied to all medical centers.

Study 3

Target population: All newly diagnosed breast cancer patients

Program: Education in Options for Treatment

Sample: Five hospitals in three states; within each hospital, 15 physicians; for each physician, 20 patients seen between January 1 and July 31 who are newly diagnosed with breast cancer

Comment: Women newly diagnosed with breast cancer are the targets of an educational program. The evaluators will select five hospitals and, within them, 20 patients seen from January through July by each of 15 doctors. The findings are to be applied to all patients newly diagnosed with breast cancer.

Inclusion and Exclusion Criteria or Eligibility

A sample is a constituent part of a larger population to which the evaluation's findings will be applied. If an evaluation is intended to investigate the impact of an educational program on women's knowledge of their options for surgical treatment for cancer, for example, and not all women with cancer are to be included in the program, the evaluator has to decide on the types of women who will be the focus of the study. Will the evaluation concentrate on women of a specific age? Women with a particular kind of cancer? Example 4.2 presents hypothetical inclusion and exclusion criteria for an evaluation of such a program.

Example 4.2 Inclusion and Exclusion Criteria for a Sample of Women to Be Included in an Evaluation of a Program for Surgical Cancer Patients

Inclusion: Using the Medicare claims database, of all patients hospitalized during 1993, those with diagnosis or procedure codes related to breast cancer; for patients with multiple admissions, only the admission with the most invasive operation

Exclusion: Women under the age of 65 (because women under 65 who receive Medicare are generally disabled or have renal disease), men, women with only a diagnostic biopsy or no breast surgery, women undergoing bilateral mastectomy, women without a code for primary breast cancer at the time of the most invasive operation, women with a diagnosis of carcinoma in situ, and women with metastases to regions other than the axillary lymph nodes

The evaluator of this program has set criteria for the sample of women who will be included in the evaluation and for which its conclusions will be appropriate. The sample will include women over 65 years of age who have been operated on for breast cancer. The findings of the evaluation will not be applicable to women under age 65 with other types of cancer who have had only a diagnostic biopsy, have not had surgery, or have had bilateral mastectomy.

The independent variables are the evaluator's guide to determining where to set inclusion and exclusion criteria. For example, suppose that, in an evaluation of the effects on teens of a preventive health care program, one of the questions asks whether boys and girls benefit equally from participation. In this evaluation question, the independent variable is gender and the dependent variable is benefit. If the evaluator plans to sample boys and girls, he or she must set inclusion and exclusion criteria. Inclusion criteria for this evaluation might include boys and girls under 18 years old who are likely to attend all of the educational activities for the duration of the evaluation and who are able to read at levels appropriate for their ages or grades. Teens might be excluded if they already participate in another preventive health care program, if they do not speak English, or if their parents object to their participation. If these hypothetical inclusion and exclusion criteria are used to guide sampling eligibility, then the evaluation's findings can be generalized only to English-speaking boys and girls under age 18 who read at grade level and tend to be compliant with school attendance requirements. The evaluation is not designed to enable the findings to be applicable to teens who have difficulty reading or speaking English and who are unlikely to be able to complete all program activities.

Sampling Methods

Sampling methods are usually divided into two types: probability sampling and convenience sampling. Probability sampling is considered the best way to ensure the validity of any inferences made about a program's effectiveness and its generalizability. In probability sampling, every member of the target population has a known probability of being included in the sample.

In convenience sampling, participants are selected because they are available. Thus in this kind of sampling, some members of the target population have a chance of being chosen whereas others do not. As a result, the data that are collected from a convenience sample may not be applicable at all to the target group as a whole. For example, suppose an evaluator examining the quality of care provided by student health services decided to interview all students who came for care during the week of December 26. Suppose also that 100 students came and all agreed to be interviewed: a perfect response rate. The problem is that in some parts of the world the end of December is associated with increased rates of illness from respiratory viruses as well as with high numbers of skiing accidents; moreover, many universities are closed during that week, and most students are not around. Thus the data collected by the happy evaluator with the perfect response rate could very well be biased, because the evaluation excluded many students simply because they were not on campus (and so, if they were ill, received care elsewhere).

Simple Random Sampling

In simple random sampling, every subject or unit has an equal chance of being selected. Because of this equality of opportunity, random samples are considered relatively unbiased. Typical ways of selecting a simple random sample include applying a table of random numbers (available in almost any statistics textbook) or a computer-generated list of random numbers to lists of prospective participants.

Suppose an evaluation team wanted to use a table of random numbers and had the names of 20 physicians from which 10 were to be selected at random. First, the evaluators would assign a number, from 01 to 20, to each name (e.g., Adams = 01, Baker = 02, . . . Thomas = 20). This list of numbers is called the *sampling frame.* Then, using the table of random numbers, the evaluators would choose the first 10 digits between 01 and 20. Alternatively, the evaluators could use a computer program to generate a list of 10 numbers between 01 and 20. Figure 4.1 presents a portion of a table of random numbers to illustrate how the evaluators would use such a table to select a sample of 10 doctors from a list of 20.

18283 46453 19076 36743 22125	19704[2] 21547 23453 89563 19786	45387 39246 32760 **12**378 23498	23476 93198 27166 98223 76575	12323 98005 75032 23465 76435	34865 65988 99945 25408 63442
76009 09878 34534 83109 89063	77099 76549 44475 75899 43555	43788 88877 56632 34877 32700	36659 26587 34350 21357 76497 94656	74399 44633 **01**768 24300 36099 34689	**03**432 77659 29027 00869 97956
09887 23280 93856 21256 14575[1]	67770 34572 23090 50863 35490[3]	69975 99443 22257 56934 23645	54465 98765 67400 70993 22179	**13**896 34978 23580 34765 35788	**04**645 42880 24376 30996 37600
23276 87530 00791 99003 14367	7[4]0870 45738 32164 32567 64999	**20**087 **09**998 97665 **02**878 78453	66665 45397 27589 38602 40078	78876 47500 90087 **18**700 53727	58007 34875 **16**004 23455 28759

1 = Two rolls of a die yield 1 (column) and 5 (block).
2 = Two rolls of a die yield 2 (column) and 1 (row).
3 = Intersection of[1] and[2].
4 = Start here to get the sample.

Figure 4.1. A Portion of a Table of Random Numbers

NOTE: Numbers that are **bold** and underlined = sample of ten, consisting of numbers between 01 and 20.

One way to get a random sample: using a table of random numbers. The evaluation team needs a randomly drawn sample of 10 physicians from a list of 20. Using a table of random numbers, the evaluators first identify a row of numbers at random and then a column. Where the two intersect, they begin to identify their sample.

1. *How they randomly identify the row:* A member of the evaluation team tosses a die twice. On the first toss, the die's number is 3; the number on the second toss is 5. Starting with the first column in the table, these numbers correspond to the third block and the fifth row of that block, or the row containing numbers 1 4 5 7 5 in Figure 4.1.

2. *How they randomly identify the column:* A member of the team tosses the die twice and gets 2 and 1. These numbers identify the second block of columns and the first column beginning with 1. The starting point for this sample is where the row 1 4 5 7 5 and the column beginning with 1 intersect, at 3 5 4 9 0.

3. *How they select the sample:* The evaluators need 10 physicians from their list of 20—or two-digit numbers. Moving down from the second column, the 10 numbers between 01 and 20 that appear (starting with the numbers below 3 5 4 9 0, and beginning with the first number, 7) are 12, 20, 09, 01, 02, 13, 18, 03, 04, and 16. These are the physicians selected for the random sample.

Random Selection and Random Assignment

In any given evaluation, the process of random selection may be different from the process of random assignment, as is illustrated in Example 4.3.

Example 4.3 Random Selection and Random Assignment: Two Illustrations

Evaluation A

Evaluation A had 6 months to identify a sample of teens to participate in an evaluation of an innovative school-based preventive health care program. At the end of the 6 months, all eligible teens were assigned to the innovative program or the traditional (control) program. Assignment was based on how close to a participating school each teen lived. The evaluators used this method because participation meant that students would be required to attend several after-school activities, and no funding was available for transportation.

Evaluation B

Evaluation B had 6 months to identify a sample of teens to participate in an evaluation of an innovative school-based preventive health care program. At the end of the 6 months, a sample was randomly selected from the population of all teens who were eligible. Half the sample was randomly assigned to the innovative program and half to the traditional (control) program.

In Evaluation A in this example, the evaluators selected all eligible teens and then assigned them to the experimental and control groups according to how close each one lived to a participating school. In Evaluation B, the evaluators selected a random sample of all those who were eligible and then randomly assigned the participants either to the experimental group or the control group. Of these two methods, the latter is usually considered preferable to the former. *Random selection* means that every eligible person has an equal chance of becoming part of the sample; if all are included because they just happen to appear during the time allocated for sampling, biases may be introduced. Random assignment can also guard against bias.

Systematic Sampling

Suppose an evaluator has a list with the names of 3,000 nurse practitioners from which a sample of 500 is to be selected. In systematic sampling, the evaluator would divide 3,000 by 500 to yield 6, and then select every sixth name on the list. An alternative would be to select a number at random—say, by tossing a die. If the toss came up with the number 5, for example, the evaluator would select the fifth name on the list, then the tenth, the fifteenth, and so on, until he or she had the necessary 500 names.

Systematic sampling is not an appropriate method to use if repetition is a natural component of the sampling frame. For example, if the frame is a list of names, those beginning with certain letters of the alphabet might get excluded because, for certain ethnicities, they appear infrequently.

Stratified Sampling

A *stratified random sample* is one in which the population is divided into subgroups, or *strata,* and a random sample is then selected from each group. For example, in a program to teach women about options for the treatment of breast cancer, the evaluator might choose to sample women of differing general health status (as indicated by scores on a 32-item test), age, and income (high = +, medium = 0, and low = –). In this case, health status, age, and income are the strata. This sampling blueprint can be depicted as shown in Figure 4.2.

The evaluator chooses the strata, or subgroups, based on his or her knowledge or beliefs about their relationship to the dependent variable or outcome measure—in this case, the options chosen by women with breast cancer. That is, the evaluator in this example has reason to believe that general health status, age, and income influence women's choices of treatment. The evaluator must be able to justify his or her selection of the strata with evidence from the literature or other sources of information (such as historical data or expert opinion).

If the evaluator neglects to use stratification in the choice of a sample, the final results may be confounded. For example, if the evaluation neglects to distinguish among women with different characteristics, good and poor performance may be

Health Status Scores and Income	Age (years)				
	< 35	35–55	56–65	66–75	> 75
25–32 points High income					
Average					
Low					
17–24 points High income					
Average					
Low					
9–16 points High income					
Average					
Low					
1–8 points High income					
Average					
Low					

Figure 4.2. Sampling Blueprint for a Program to Educate Women in Options for Breast Cancer Treatment

averaged among them, and the program will seem to have no effect even if women in one or more groups benefited. In fact, the program actually might have been very successful with certain women, such as those over age 75 who have moderate incomes and General Health Status scores between 25 and 32.

When evaluators do not use stratification, they may apply statistical techniques (such as analysis of covariance and regression) retrospectively (after the data have already been collected) to correct for confounders or "covariates" on the dependent variables or outcomes. Evaluators generally agree, however, that it is better to anticipate confounding variables by sampling prospectively than to correct for them retrospectively, through analysis. This is because statistical corrections require very strict assumptions about the nature of the data, assumptions for which the sampling plan may not have been designed. With few exceptions, using statistical corrections afterward results in a loss of power, or the ability to detect true differences between groups (such as the experimental and control groups).

The strata in stratified sampling are subsets of the independent variables. If the independent variables are gender, health status, and education, the strata are how each of these is defined. For example, gender is defined as male and female. A variable such as health status can be defined in many ways, depending on the measures available to collect data and the needs of the evaluation. For example, health status may be defined as a score on some measure or may be rated as excellent, very good, good, fair, or poor.

Cluster Sampling

Cluster sampling is used in large evaluations—those that involve many settings, such as universities, hospitals, cities, states, and so on. In cluster sampling, the population is divided into batches that are then randomly selected and assigned, and their constituents can be randomly selected and assigned. For example, suppose that California's counties are trying out a new program to improve emergency care for critically ill and injured children, and the control program is the traditional emergency medical system. If you want to use random cluster sampling to evaluate this program, you can consider each county to be a cluster and select and assign counties at random to the new program or the traditional program. Alternatively, you can randomly select children's hospitals and other facilities treating critically ill children within counties and randomly assign them to the experimental system or the traditional system (assuming this were considered ethical). Example 4.4 gives an illustration of the use of cluster sampling in a survey of Italian parents' attitudes toward AIDS education in their children's schools.

Example 4.4 Cluster Sampling in a Study of Attitudes of Italian Parents Toward AIDS Education

Epidemiologists from 14 of Italy's 21 regions surveyed parents of 725 students from 30 schools chosen by a cluster sampling technique from among the 292 classical, scientific, and technical high schools in Rome. Staff visited each school and selected students using a list of random numbers based on the school's size. Each of the students selected for participation was given a letter to deliver to his or her parents explaining the goals of the study and when they would be contacted.

Nonprobability or Convenience Sampling

Convenience samples are samples for which the probability of selection is unknown. Evaluators use convenience samples simply because they are easy to obtain. This means that some people have no chance at all of being selected simply because they are not around to be chosen. Convenience samples are considered to be biased, or not representative of the target population, unless proven otherwise.

In some cases, evaluators can perform statistical analyses to demonstrate that convenience samples are actually representative. For example, suppose that during the months of July and August, an evaluator conducts a survey of the needs of county institutions concerned with critically ill and injured children. Because many county employees take their yearly vacations in July and August, the respondents may be different from those who would have answered the survey during other times of the year. For example, those present to respond in July and August may not be eligible for vacation because they have been on the job for a relatively short period of time, and they may be less experienced than other employees as well. If the evaluator wants to demonstrate that those employees who were around to respond and those who were not available in July and August are not different, he or she can compare the two groups on key variables, such as time on the job and experience with critically ill and injured children. If this comparison reveals no differences, the evaluator is in a relatively stronger position to assert that, even though the sample was chosen on the basis of convenience, the characteristics of the participants do not differ on certain key variables (such as length of time on the job) from those of the target population.

The Sampling Unit

A major concern in sampling is the *unit* to be sampled. Example 4.5 illustrates the concept of the sampling unit.

Example 4.5 What Is the Target? Who Is Sampled?

An evaluation of a new program is concerned with measuring the program's effectiveness in altering physicians' practices pertaining to acute pain management for children who have undergone operations. The target population is all physicians who care for children undergoing operations. The evaluation question is "Have physicians improved their pain management practices for children?" The standards are that physicians in the experimental group show significant improvement over a 1-year period and significantly greater improvement than physicians in a control group. Resources are available for 20 physicians to participate in the evaluation.

The evaluators will randomly assign 10 physicians to the experimental group and 10 physicians to the control. They plan to find out about pain management through a review of the medical records of 10 patients of each of the physicians in the experimental and control groups, for a total sample of 200 patients. (This is sometimes called a *nested design.*) A consultant to the evaluation team says that, in actuality, the evaluators are comparing the practices of 10 physicians against those of 10 physicians, and not the care of 100 patients against that of 100 patients. The reason is that characteristics of the care of the patients of any single physician will be very highly related. The consultant advises the evaluators to correct for this lack of "independence among patients of the same physician" by using one of the statistical methods available for correcting for "cluster" effects. Another consultant, in contrast, advises the evaluators to use a much larger number of patients per physician and suggests a statistical method for selecting the appropriate number. Because the evaluators do not have enough money to enlarge the sample, they decide to "correct" statistically for the dependence among patients.

In this example, the evaluators want to be able to apply the evaluation's findings to all physicians who care for children undergoing operations, but they have enough resources to include only 20 physicians in the evaluation. In an ideal world, the evaluators would have access to a very large number of physicians, but in the real world, they have only the resources to study 10 patients per physician and access to statistical methods to correct for possible biases. These statistical methods enable evaluators to provide remedies for the possible dependence among the patients of a single physician, among students at a single institution, among health care workers at a single hospital, and so on.

Sample Size

Power Analysis and Alpha and Beta Errors

An evaluation's ability to detect an effect is referred to as its *power.* A power analysis is a statistical method of identifying a sample size that will be large enough to allow the evaluator to detect an effect if one actually exists. A commonly used evaluation research design is one in which the evaluator compares two randomly assigned groups to find out whether differences exist between them. "Does Program A differ from Program B in its ability to improve quality of life?" is, accordingly, a typical evaluation question. To answer this question accurately, the evaluator must be sure that enough people are in each program group so that any difference that is actually present will be uncovered. Conversely, if there is no difference between the two groups, the evaluator does not want to conclude falsely that there is one. To begin the process of making sure that the sample size is adequate to detect any true differences, the evaluator's first step is to reframe the appropriate evaluation questions into null hypotheses. Null hypotheses state that no difference exists between groups, as illustrated in Example 4.6.

Example 4.6 The Null Hypothesis in a Program to Improve Quality of Life

Question: Does Experimental Program A improve quality of life?

Standard: A statistically significant difference is found in quality of life between Experimental Program A's participants and Control Program B's participants, and the difference is in Program A's favor.

Data source: The Quality of Life Assessment, a 30-minute self-administered questionnaire with 100 questions; scoring ranges from 1 to 100, with 100 meaning excellent quality of life.

Null hypothesis: No difference in quality of life exists between participants in Program A and participants in Program B (that is, the average scores obtained in Program A and in Program B are equal).

One accepted way of identifying a sample that is large enough to detect actual effects is to conduct a power analysis. As noted above, the power of an experimental evaluation is its ability to detect a true difference—in other words, to detect a difference of a given size (say, 10%) if the difference actually exists.

When an evaluator finds that differences exist among programs but in reality there are no differences, that is called an *alpha error* or *Type I error.* A Type I error is analogous to a false-positive test result—that is, a result indicating that a disease is present when in actuality it is not. When an evaluator finds that no differences exist among programs but in reality there are differences, that is termed a *beta error* or *Type II error.* A Type II error is analogous to a false-negative test result—that is, a result indicating that a disease is not present when in actuality it is. The relationship between what the evaluator finds and the true situation can be depicted as shown in Figure 4.3.

		Truth	
		Differences exist	**No differences exist**
Evaluator's conclusions from hypothesis test	Differences exist (reject null)	Correct	Type I or alpha error
	No differences exist (keep null)	Type II or beta error	Correct

Figure 4.3. Type I and Type II Errors: Searching for a True Difference

To select sample sizes that will maximize the power of their evaluations, evaluators must rely on formulas whose use requires an understanding of hypothesis testing and a basic knowledge of statistics. Evaluators using these formulas usually must perform the following steps:

- State the null hypothesis
- Set a level (alpha, or ∝) of statistical significance—usually .05 or .01—and deciding whether it is to be a one- or two-tailed test
- Decide on the smallest meaningful health-related difference (e.g., the difference in average scores between groups must be at least 15 points)

- Set the power $(1 - \beta)$ of the evaluation, or the chance of detecting a difference (usually 80% or 90%)
- Estimate the standard deviation (assuming that the distribution of the measure is normal) in the population

Some researchers have proposed alternative sample size calculations based on confidence intervals. A confidence interval is computed from sample data that have a given probability that the unknown parameter (such as the mean) is contained within the interval. Common confidence intervals are 90%, 95%, and 99%.

Calculating sample size is a technical activity that requires some knowledge of statistics. Several easy-to-use programs for calculating sample size are currently available for free on the Internet; to find one, enter the search term "sample size" into any search engine.

Why Sample?

Evaluators sample because it is efficient to do so and because it contributes to the precision of their research. Samples can be studied more quickly than entire target populations, and they are also less expensive to assemble. In some cases, it would be impossible to recruit a complete population for an evaluation, even if the necessary time and financial resources were available. For example, it would be futile for an evaluator to attempt to enroll all homeless veterans in an investigation of a program that targets them (see Example 4.1, above). Sampling is also efficient in that it allows the evaluator to invest resources in important evaluation activities, such as monitoring the quality of data collection and standardizing the implementation of the program, rather than in the collection of data on an unnecessarily large number of individuals or groups.

Sampling enables the evaluator to focus precisely on the characteristics of interest. For example, suppose an evaluator wants to compare older and younger patients with differing health and functional statuses. A stratified sampling strategy can give the evaluator just what he or she needs. A sample of the population with precise characteristics is more suitable for many evaluations than the entire population.

The Sampling Report

Evaluators can use the sampling report (SR) form illustrated in Figure 4.4 for both planning and explaining their evaluations. The SR contains the evaluation questions and standards, the independent variables and strata, the evaluation design, inclusion and exclusion criteria, the dependent variable, the measure, the criteria for level of acceptable statistical and clinical (or educational or practical) significance, the sampling methods, and the size of the sample.

The Evaluation	The Report
Evaluation questions	1. To what extent has quality of life improved? 2. Do men and women differ in quality of life after participation?
Standard	1. A statistical and clinically meaningful difference between experimental and control group, favoring the experimental group 2. Thus no standard is necessary. If differences between men and women are found, they will be examined to determine if they are clinically meaningful.
Evaluation design	An experimental design, with randomly assigned concurrent controls
Independent variables	Group participation; gender
Strata	Group participation: experimental and control Gender: male and female
Inclusion criteria	1. Must be living at home 2. Must be functionally independent (e.g., can feed, clothe, and shop for themselves)
Exclusion criteria	1. Unable to speak English or Spanish 2. Under 65 years of age
Dependent variable	Quality of life
Measure	Quality of Life Questionnaire: a 100-point survey. The Questionnaire's manual states that, when used with persons over 70 years of age, the standard deviation (a measure of how much the score "spread" from the mean or average score) is 10 points.
Criterion for clinical meaning	A difference of at least 5 points on the Quality of Life Questionnaire between experimental and control, favoring the experimental group. Statistical significance (alpha) = .01; power is 80% (beta = .20).
Sampling method	For group assignment: cluster sampling. All streets in the town are eligible. All eligible persons in a given street are randomly assigned to the experimental or control group. For gender: An equal number of men and women will be randomly selected from all who are eligible; men and women will be randomly assigned to an experimental or a control group. No two participants will live on the same street.
Sample size	To compare men and women, a total of 188 people are needed: 94 men and 94 women; 47 of each will be assigned to the experimental or control groups.

Figure 4.4. The Sampling Report Form

The form in Figure 4.4 shows the use of the SR for one evaluation question asked in an 18-month program combining diet and exercise to improve health status and quality of life for persons 65 years of age or older. An experimental group of elderly people who still live at home will receive the program and another group will not. To be eligible, participants must be able to live independently and feed, clothe, and shop for themselves. Persons who are under 65 years of age and those who do not speak English or Spanish are not eligible. Participants will be randomly assigned to the experimental or control groups according to the streets on which they live (that is, participants living on Street A will be randomly assigned, as will participants living on Streets B, C, and so on). The evaluators will be investigating whether the program effectively improves quality of life for men and women equally. A random sample of men and women will be selected from all who are eligible, but no two will live on the same street. Then men and women will be assigned at random to the experimental group or the control group.

Summary and Transition to the Next Chapter on Collecting Information

In this chapter and Chapter 3, the focus has been on independent or predictor variables. These often consist of groups (e.g., experimental and control), demographic characteristics, and settings (e.g., teaching and community-based hospitals). As this chapter has discussed, associated with research design are issues of sampling. Is sampling appropriate? Who should be sampled? How many people should be in each group? How will they be selected and assigned? Once these questions are answered, the evaluator's emphasis shifts to data collection, the topic of the next two chapters.

The next chapter discusses the issues involved in the collection of evaluation data and describes the sources of information available to evaluators, including the advantages and limitations of each kind of source. In health program evaluations, data are collected to describe participants as well as to measure the effects of the programs examined on health, education, and quality and efficiency of care.

Exercise

Directions

For each of the following situations, choose the best sampling method from among these choices:

A. Simple random sampling

B. Stratified sampling

C. Cluster sampling

D. Systematic sampling

E. Convenience sampling

Situation 1

The Rehabilitation Center has 40 separate family counseling groups, each with about 30 participants. The director of the center has noticed a decline in attendance rates and has decided to try out an experimental program to improve them. The program is very expensive, and the center can afford to finance only a 250-person program at first. If the evaluator randomly selects individuals from among all group members, this will create friction and disturb the integrity of some of the groups. As an alternative, the evaluator has suggested a plan in which five of the groups—150 people—will be randomly selected to take part in the experimental program and five groups will participate in the control.

Situation 2

The Medical Center has developed a new program to teach patients about cardiovascular fitness. An evaluation is being conducted to determine how effective the program is with males and females of different ages. The evaluation design is experimental, with concurrent controls. In this design, the new and traditional cardiovascular programs are compared. About 310 people signed up for the winter seminar. Of these, 140 are between 45 and 60 years old, and 62 of these 140 were men. The remaining 170 are between 61 and 75 years old, and 80 of these are men. The evaluators randomly selected 40 persons from each of the four subgroups and randomly assigned every other person to the new program and the remainder to the old program.

Situation 3

A total of 200 health education teachers signed up for a continuing education program. Only 50 teachers from this group, however, are to participate in an evaluation of the program's impact. The evaluator assigns each participant a number from 001 to 200 and, using a table, selects 50 names by moving down columns of three-digit random numbers and taking the first 50 numbers within the range 001 to 200.

Suggested Readings

Bailar, J. C., & Mosteller, F. (1988). Guidelines for statistical reporting in articles for medical journals. *Annals of Internal Medicine, 108,* 266–273.

This article explains the logic behind discussing the eligibility of experimental participants and the relationship between who is included and the population about which inferences are to be made. The authors also describe the characteristics of comprehensible reporting about randomization, blinding, and losses to observation.

Centers for Disease Control. (1992). Attitudes of parents of high school students about AIDS, drug, and sex education in schools—Rome, Italy, 1991. *Journal of the American Medical Association, 267,* 2160.

This article describes the cluster sampling method used in a survey of Italian parents' attitudes toward AIDS education in their children's schools.

Cohen J. (1988). *Statistical power analysis for the behavioral sciences* (2nd ed.). Hillsdale, NJ: Lawrence Erlbaum.

This book is a classic primer on power analysis.

Dawson, B., & Trapp, R. G. (2001). *Basic and clinical biostatistics* (3rd ed.). New York: Lange Medical/McGraw-Hill.

This book is a basic and essential guide to the use of statistics in medicine and medical care settings. The authors explain study designs and sampling, providing very clear explanations of the statistics involved in sampling along with numerous examples.

Hulley, S. B., Cummings, S. R., Browner, W. S., Grady, D., Hearst, N., & Newman, T. B. (2001). *Designing clinical research* (2nd ed.). Philadelphia: Lippincott Williams & Wilkins.

Although tailored to clinical research, the discussion of sampling in Chapters 5 and 6 of this volume is easy to understand and pertinent for evaluation researchers who are doing studies in medical settings.

Lachin, J. M. (1981). Introduction to sample size determination and power analysis for clinical trials. *Controlled Clinical Trials, 2,* 93–113.

This article explains the logic behind sample size determination.

Purpose of This Chapter

This chapter covers the criteria evaluators use for choosing among differing sources of information: self-administered printed and online questionnaires and achievement tests, medical record reviews, observations, interviews (whether conducted in person, over the telephone, or through computer-assisted methods), large data sets (containing administrative, clinical, and research data), performance tests, clinical scenarios, physical examinations, and the literature. The advantages and limitations of each kind of source are discussed as well. Special emphasis is given to the evaluator's review of the published literature for information because of the importance of the literature as a source of data in competent evaluations.

5 Collecting Information: The Right Data Sources

A Reader's Guide to Chapter 5

Information Sources: What's the Problem?

Choosing the Best Sources of Data

Sources of Data in Program Evaluation and Their Advantages and Limitations

Self-administered surveys, tests of achievement, medical record reviews, observations, interviews, physical examinations, large data sets, performance tests, clinical scenarios, and the literature

Guidelines for Reviewing the Literature

Information Sources: What's the Problem?

An evaluator is asked to study the effectiveness of the At-Home Program, an intervention whose main objectives include providing high quality of health care and improving the health status and quality of life for elderly persons over 75 years of age who are still living at home. The experimental intervention consists of a comprehensive assessment of each elderly participant by an interdisciplinary team of health care providers and a home visit every 3 months by a nurse practitioner to monitor progress and reevaluate health and function. The control group consists of elderly people in the same communities who are not visited by the nurse practitioner and continue with their usual sources of care. What information should the evaluator collect to find out whether the intervention's objectives have been achieved? Where should the information come from? The first place the evaluator should go for answers is to the evaluation questions and standards and their associated independent and dependent variables. Consider the illustrations from the evaluation of the At-Home Program in Example 5.1.

Example 5.1 Evaluation Questions, Standards, Variables, and Data Sources

Evaluation Question 1

Question: Has quality of care improved for diabetic patients?

Standard: A statistically and clinically meaningful improvement in quality of care is observed in experimental diabetic patients compared with control diabetic patients.

Independent variable: Group participation (experimental diabetics and control diabetics)

Potential data sources: Physical examination, medical record review, surveys of health care practitioners and patients

Dependent variable: Quality of care

Potential data sources: Medical record review, surveys of health care practitioners and patients

Evaluation Question 2

Question: Is quality of life improved for patients?

Standard: One aspect of good quality of life is the availability of a social network of family and friends. For the program, evidence of availability of a social network of family and friends is defined as a statistically significant difference in the adequacy of social networks that favors the experimental group.

Independent variable: Group participation (experimental and control)

Potential data source: Names or ID codes of participants in the experimental and control groups

Dependent variable: Sociability

Potential data sources: Surveys of patients and their family members and friends, surveys of health care practitioners, reviews of diaries kept by patients, observations

---

To answer the first question in Example 5.1, the evaluator has at least two implicit tasks: identifying persons with diabetes and assigning them to the experimental and control groups. Patients with diabetes can be identified through physical examination, medical record review, or surveys of health care practitioners and patients. Quality of care for diabetes can be measured through medical record review or through a survey of health care practitioners.

To identify persons in the experimental and control groups for the second question in Example 5.1, the evaluator would examine the study's database. To measure the adequacy of each patient's social network, the evaluator could survey all patients and ask them to keep records or diaries of outings with their friends and lists of their daily activities. The evaluator might also survey the patients' friends and family members.

Given the range of choices for each evaluation question, on what basis should the evaluator choose, say, to interview patients' families rather than administer a questionnaire to the study's participants? How should the evaluator decide between medical record reviews and physical exams as data sources? Answering these questions is at the heart of a program evaluation's data collection.

Choosing the Best Sources of Data

Evaluators have access to an arsenal of ways to collect information. Among these are self-administered questionnaires, tests of performance and achievement, face-to-face and telephone interviews, observations, large data sets, vital statistics (such as infant mortality rates), the literature, and personal, medical, financial, and other statistical records. There are advantages and limitations to using each of these kinds of sources. To choose appropriate data sources for your program evaluation, you need to ask the following questions:

Guidelines: Questions to Ask in Choosing Data Sources

- What variables need to be measured? Are they defined and specific enough to measure?
- Can you borrow or adapt a currently available measure, or must you create a new one?

- If an available measure seems to be appropriate, has it been tried out in circumstances that are similar to those in which your evaluation is being conducted?
- Do you have the technical skills, financial resources, and time to create a valid measure?
- If no measure is available or appropriate, can you develop one in the time allocated for the evaluation?
- Do you have the technical skills, financial resources, and time to collect information with the chosen measure?
- Are participants likely to be able to fill out forms, answer questions, and provide information called for by the measure?
- In a study that involves direct services to patients and use of information from medical and other confidential records, can you obtain permission to collect data in an ethical way?
- To what extent will users of the evaluation's results (e.g., practitioners, students, patients, program developers, and sponsors) have confidence in the sources of information on which they are based?

Example 5.2 shows what can happen when evaluators neglect to answer these questions.

Example 5.2 (Not) Collecting Evaluation Information: A Case Study

The evaluators of an innovative third-year core surgery clerkship prepared a written examination to find out whether students learned to test donor-recipient compatibility before transfusion of red blood cells. The examination (to be given before and after the clerkship) included questions about the mechanisms involved in and consequences of transfusing incompatible red cells, the causes of incompatible transfusions, what to do about Rh-negative females who may bear children, how to identify unusual red cell antibodies, and what to do when no compatible blood is available.

The evaluators also planned to prepare a measure of students' understanding of ethical issues in blood transfusion that would consist of 10 hypothetical scenarios with ethical components. They intended to compare students' responses to standards of ethics set by the University Blood Bank.

Finally, the evaluators anticipated distributing a self-administered survey to students before and after their participation in the clerkship to find out if their attitudes toward transfusion medicine changed. The results of the evaluators' activities were to be presented at a special meeting of the School of Medicine's Curriculum Committee 1 year after the start of the innovative program.

The evaluators' report turned out to be very brief. Although they were able to locate a number of achievement tests with questions about donor-recipient compatibility, and thus did not have to prepare these measures "from scratch," they could not find an appropriate time to give all students a premeasure and postmeasure. This meant that the evaluators had incomplete information on the performance of many students, with only pretests for some and only posttests for others. In addition, the evaluators found that developing the measure involving scenarios took about 9 months because it was more difficult to create the scenarios than they had anticipated. A sample of students found the original scenarios hard to understand and ambiguous, so the evaluators had to rewrite and retest them. In the end, the scenario measure was not even ready for use at reporting time.

Finally, many students refused to complete the attitude questionnaire. Anecdotal information suggested that students felt they were overloaded with tests and questionnaires and that they did not believe this additional one was important. Because of the poor quality of the data, the evaluators were unable to provide any meaningful information about the third-year surgery clerkship's progress.

In the case study presented above, the evaluators encountered difficulties for three major reasons:

- They did not have enough time to collect data on students' achievement before and after.
- They did not have enough time and possibly lacked the skills to prepare the scenarios for a planned measure.
- They chose a method of information collection that was not appropriate for the participants because they were unwilling to complete it.

Sources of Data in Program Evaluation and Their Advantages and Limitations

This section provides descriptions of the characteristics, advantages, and limitations of the most commonly used sources of data in program evaluations.

Self-Administered Surveys

In self-administered surveys (or questionnaires), respondents answer questions or respond to items, whether on paper or online. Typical self-administered questionnaire items might look like those shown in Figure 5.1, whereas a typical item in an online self-administered questionnaire might look like the one in Figure 5.2.

During the past 4 weeks, have you had any of the following problems with your work or other regular daily activities as a result of any emotional problems (such as feeling depressed or anxious)? Please answer YES or NO for each question by circling 1 or 2 on each line.

	Yes	No
Cut down the amount of time you spent on work or other activities?	1	2
Accomplished less than you would like?	1	2
Didn't do work or other activities as usual?	1	2

Figure 5.1. Examples of Items in a Self-Administered Survey Item

Which of the following best describes your type of practice? Please select the ONE choice that best applies.

- ○ University hospital
- ○ Community practice WITH academic affiliation in a rural setting
- ○ Community practice WITH academic affiliation in an urban setting
- ○ Community practice WITHOUT academic affiliation in a rural setting
- ○ Community practice WITHOUT academic affiliation in an urban setting
- ○ Other (please specify) [ ]

Figure 5.2. Example of an Item in an Online Self-Administered Survey

Self-administered surveys in hard-copy form (whether distributed through the mail, through a doctor's office, or in some other way) differ from online surveys in that the answers respondents write on paper questionnaires must later be scanned into a database or entered into it by hand, whereas online survey responses can be automatically entered into a database, which means that the responses can be analyzed instantly. From the evaluator's perspective, online surveys are efficient because they save paper, save the time needed for data entry (and the errors that may go with it), and do away with the need to find storage space for completed forms. However, to maximize the efficiency of online surveys, evaluators must be sure they have the technical expertise necessary to prepare online questionnaires properly and also to ensure respondent privacy. Because of the strict rules regarding participant privacy in many evaluation studies, evaluators using online surveys may need to acquire dedicated computers or set up firewalls, each of which consumes resources.

Advantages

- Many people are accustomed to completing questionnaires, regardless of where or how they are administered.
- Many questions and rating scales are available for adaptation.
- Mailed and online questionnaires can reach large groups of people at relatively low cost.
- Online surveys can easily produce findings immediately for both the evaluator and the evaluation consumer.

Disadvantages

- Survey respondents may not always tell the truth.
- The self-administered survey format is not suitable for obtaining explanations of behavior or sensitive information.
- Without supervision, some respondents may fail to answer some or even all questions on a survey, leaving the evaluator with incomplete information.

Tests of Achievement

The most commonly used method of collecting information on educational accomplishment is the written achievement test. Written tests tend to measure individuals' knowledge, understanding, and application of theories, principles, and facts. To assess higher levels of learning, such as the evaluation of evidence or the synthesis of information from varying sources, other methods, such as observation of performance or analysis of written papers and scientific studies, are more appropriate.

Most evaluations of educational programs rely to some extent on written tests of achievement. Many of these employ multiple-choice questions, as in the example shown in Figure 5.3.

What is the best medical therapy for a patient experiencing a mild urticarial reaction from blood transfusion? **Please circle one choice only.**

Steroids	1
Antihistamines	2
Lasix	3
Epinephrine	4
Aspirin	5

Figure 5.3. Example of a Multiple-Choice Question on an Achievement Test

Medical Record Reviews

Medical record reviews are used in audits of medical practices and in research that aims to study the quality of medical care. Figure 5.4 displays a component of a medical record review form that an evaluator might use to find out about adverse outcomes for Medicare patients admitted to the hospital with a heart attack.

VII. Physician Care

Answers should be based on physicians' notes including history and physical, consult reports, progress notes, and ER [emergency room] notes.

Adverse Outcomes

Did a physician document the occurrence of the following adverse outcomes <u>during</u> the marker admission for hospitalized Medicare patients with myocardial infarction [heart attack]? If so, give the date when each was <u>first</u> noted.

	Occur During Admission?		If YES, Give Date (nd = 9999)
Adverse Outcome	**Yes**	**No/nd**	**Mo/Day**
i. Chest pain on day 3 or later, and present for at least two consecutive days.	1	9	______
ii. Shock beginning on day 2, or later (physician notes patient developed shock or had a systolic BP < 90).	1	9	______
iii. Arrest (cardiac, respiratory or unspecified, sudden death, CPR or resuscitation); exclude arrests in ER.	1	9	______
iv. Death.	1	9	______
v. Insertion of temporary or permanent pacemaker.	1	9	______

Check here if none of the above adverse outcomes occurred: [______________]

Figure 5.4. Portion of a Medical Record Review Form: Adverse Outcomes for Medicare Patients Admitted to the Hospital With a Heart Attack

Advantages

- Collecting data from medical records can be relatively unobtrusive in that the evaluator need not disturb medical office and hospital procedures.
- Medical records are excellent sources of data on actual practice (e.g., performance of procedures, medications prescribed).
- Medical records may be good sources for accurate data on some patient demographic characteristics (e.g., age, sex, insurance status, medical history).

Disadvantages

- Finding the information of interest within medical records can be time-consuming, especially if the records are not available completely in electronic form. Even if they are in electronic form, the evaluator may have to learn how to use the system and go through an elaborate process to gain access to them.
- Evaluation personnel who review medical records may need extensive practice and training to ensure that the review process is reliable and accurate.
- Certain types of information are not always part of patients' medical records (e.g., functional or mental status).
- Medical records do not provide data on the appropriateness of practice or on the relationship between what the practitioner did (the process of care) and patient results (the outcomes of care).
- The evaluator cannot assume that medical records are readily available for review; he or she must find out about the rules for extracting information from private records within each institution.

Observations

Observations are appropriate for describing the environment (e.g., the size of an examination room or the number, types, and dates of magazines in the office waiting room) and for obtaining global portraits of the dynamics of a situation (e.g., a typical problem-solving session among medical students or a "day in the life" of a clinic). A commonly used observational technique is the time-and-motion study, in which measures are taken of the amount of time spent by patients and physicians as they go through the health care system. Usually, time-and-motion studies are used to measure the efficiency of care. Figure 5.5 displays a portion of a typical observation form.

Advantages

- Observation provides the evaluator with an opportunity to collect firsthand information.
- Observation may provide the evaluator with information that cannot be anticipated.

	Circle One
Is the waiting room carpeted?	
Yes, all areas	1
Yes, some areas	2
No, no areas	3
Do the windows have drapes or blinds?	
Yes	1
No	2
Not applicable because no windows	3

Figure 5.5. Portion of an Observation Form

Disadvantages

- Evaluation personnel must receive extensive training and follow a very structured format in order to collect dependable observations.
- The process of observation is both labor-intensive and time-consuming.
- Observers can influence the environment they are studying, and observed individuals may behave differently than they might otherwise because they are being "watched."

Interviews

Interviews can be conducted in person (with or without the assistance of a computer) or over the telephone. Figure 5.6 presents an excerpt from a typical patient face-to-face interview questionnaire.

Advantages

- Interviews allow the evaluator to ask respondents about the meanings of their answers.
- Interviews can be useful for collecting information from people who may have difficulty reading or seeing.

Disadvantages

- The process of conducting interviews is both time-consuming and labor-intensive.
- Interviewers must receive extensive training before they begin interviewing, and their work must be monitored on an ongoing basis.
- Interviewers may need special skills to interpret responses that are "off the record."

9. **ASK:** Have you ever been told by a doctor, nurse, or other health care professional that you had a heart attack, myocardial infarction (MI), or coronary?

   [ ] No: **GO TO QUESTION 10**

   [ ] Yes: **CONTINUE**

9a. **ASK:** How long ago did you have your heart attack, myocardial infarction (MI) or coronary? (**Read list to patient. SAY:** Before you answer, I will read you a list.)

   [ ] Less than one month

   [ ] 1–2 months

   [ ] 2–3 months

   [ ] 3–6 months

   [ ] 6–9 months

   [ ] 9–12 months

   [ ] More than 12 months

9b. **ASK:** Since your most recent heart attack was diagnosed, have you had any further episodes of angina (chest pain)? **SAY:** Before you answer, I will read you a list.

   [ ] Yes, more than 1 a day

   [ ] Yes, about 1 a day

   [ ] Yes, about 1 a week

   [ ] Yes, about 1 a month

   [ ] No

Figure 5.6. Portion of an Interview Form

Computer-Assisted Interviews

Computer-assisted telephone interviewing (CATI) is an efficient method for conducting interviews. With CATI, the interviewer reads instructions and questions to the respondent directly from a computer monitor and enters the responses directly into the computer. The computer, not the interviewer, controls the progression of the interview questions. Because no paper copies of the interview are produced, CATI eliminates the evaluator's need to find secure storage space for completed questionnaires.

CATI software programs enable the researcher to enter all telephone numbers and call schedules into the computer. When an interviewer logs on, he or she is prompted with a list of phone numbers to call, including new scheduled interviews and callbacks. For example, suppose the interviewer calls someone at 8:00 a.m. but receives no answer. The CATI program can automatically reschedule the call for some other time. CATI programs are also available that enable specially trained interviewers to contact respondents with unique needs. For instance, suppose your study sample consists of people who speak different languages. CATI allows multilingual interviewers to log on with certain keywords; the computer then directs them to their unique set of respondents.

The major advantage of CATI is that once the data are collected they are immediately available for analysis. However, having easy access to data may not always be a blessing. Such availability may tempt some evaluators to analyze the data before they have completed data collection, and the preliminary results may be misleading. The main value of easy access to data, especially in the early stages of data collection, is that it gives the evaluator the means to check on the characteristics of the respondents and to monitor the quality of the CATI interviewers in obtaining complete data.

Intensive interviewer training is crucial when CATI is used in field studies. Interviewers must first learn how to use the CATI software and handle computer problems should they arise during the course of an interview. For instance, what should the interviewer do if the computer "freezes"? Further, interviewers need to practice answering the questions that respondents invariably pose regarding the study's objectives, methods, human subject protections, and incentives. In fact, given the complexity of CATI, interviewer training may take up to a week. Evaluators should probably consider using CATI primarily when their investigations are well funded, because it is a relatively expensive and specialized form of data collection.

CATI takes two forms. In one, the interviews are conducted from a lab, a facility furnished with banks of telephone calling stations equipped with computers linked to a central server. The costs of building such a lab, which must have soundproof cubicles and either a master computer that stores the data from the individual computers or linkage to a server, are extremely high. Additional resources are needed to cover the cost of leasing CATI software and hiring a programmer to install it. Training for this type of CATI is expensive, because the interviewers require a great deal of practice. Numerous incidental costs are also associated with establishing a CATI lab, including those for headsets, seats and desks, instructional manuals, and service contracts for the hardware.

The second type of CATI system uses software programs that are run on laptops. With this type of CATI, the evaluator needs only a laptop and access to a telephone line to enable connection to the Internet. In time, we can expect that the need for a telephone line will be superseded by wireless access to the Internet, making this type of interviewing a desirable method for collecting data in the field and sending them to a central server. Moreover, this type of CATI is appropriate for studies with a variety of funding levels because it is portable and relatively inexpensive. The portability of laptops, however, raises concerns about patient privacy in health program evaluation. Laptops are sometimes shared or stolen, either of which can endanger the confidentiality of respondent data. In anticipation of these concerns, evaluators who use laptops for CATI should dedicate those computers to a single study, enforce strict privacy safeguards, and give interviewers special training to ensure proper CATI implementation and respondent protection. Patient privacy rules have become increasingly strict (e.g., through the Health Insurance Portability and Accountability Act, discussed in Chapter 1) and the penalties for violating those rules are costly.

Physical Examinations

Physical examinations are invaluable sources of data for evaluators because they produce primary data on health status. Physical examinations for evaluation purposes may intrude on the time and privacy of the physician and the patient, however, and, because they are labor-intensive, they are an expensive data source.

Because of the possibility that a physical examination will be conducted or received differently if the physician and patient are aware that they are part of an experiment, "blinding" is recommended for evaluations. With blinding, participants consent to be in an experimental study, but they do not know whether they are in the experimental group or a comparison group. In a double-blind evaluation, neither physicians nor patients know which groups they are in; in a single-blind evaluation, only one type of participant knows.

Large Data Sets

Governments and researchers compile data sets to keep track of individual and community health as well as to describe and monitor large health care systems. Among the most familiar data sets of this kind in the United States are those compiled by the Medicare system and by the National Health Interview Study. Many other countries around the world as well as the United Nations also maintain large health-related databases. In addition, evaluators and other researchers often store their own sets of data so that once their main study questions are answered, they can investigate other topics of interest without having to collect new data.

Evaluators typically use large data sets (or reports of their contents) to help program planners understand the extent of the need for particular programs and to set evaluation standards. Evaluators who want to use recently collected data from such data sets, rather than summaries or statistical reports on those data, must be prepared to analyze the data themselves, because the summaries and reports that are available to the public may lag behind the data collection by a few years.

Many useful summaries of large data sets are available on the Internet. For instance, suppose an evaluation team is asked to find out whether an alcohol prevention program is needed for older adults and, if it is, to provide advice on evaluating the program's effectiveness. The evaluators decide to go to the Centers for Disease Control and Prevention's Web site (http://www.cdc.gov) to gather data on the frequency of drinking in people who are 65 years of age and older. They want to know what the percentage of drinkers is and whether or not it is changing (that is, getting "worse.") Once at the CDC site, the evaluators explore, clicking on "Surveillance," "Behavioral Risk Factor Surveillance System," and "Trends Data." On the "Trends Data" page, they use the pull-down menu to get to "Alcohol Use: Chronic Drinking." They are next directed to a summary of U.S. national statistics on chronic alcohol use. They then click on "Grouped by Age" to find a table of statistics and a graph of the results. They learn that the median percentage of persons 65 plus who are chronic drinkers increased to 2.7% in 2001 (the latest year for which figures were available in 2004), up from 1.5% in 1997. This increase is rather hefty when one considers the number of people it represents. Further, the evaluators reason, the number of older adults is going to increase over the next few decades, so the problem is going to remain an important one.

Using the data from the CDC's survey, the evaluation team tells the program planners that chronic use of alcohol is a growing problem in older adults and that they should reasonably consider developing and evaluating preventive programs. The evaluators suggest that, as a standard of effectiveness, any new program should aim to reverse the current trend toward increasing chronic alcohol use. The program planners decide to investigate the characteristics of a program that is likely to achieve this aim.

Other large data sets and statistical summaries that evaluators may find useful include those compiled by the National Center for Health Statistics (NCHS), the National Library of Medicine (through its National Information Center of Health Services Research and Health Care Technology), and the U.S. Bureau of the Census. The NCHS, for example, has data sets that include vital registration systems (e.g., reporting systems that include deaths, fetal deaths, birth registrations, marriage registrations, divorce registrations, and abortions). The NCHS publishes these data in *Vital Statistics of the United States.*

The NCHS also makes available data from surveys based on the registration systems, which include the National Maternal and Infant Health Survey (with data collected by the U.S. Census Bureau) and the national Mortality Followback Surveys. Data from provider-based surveys (such as the National Health Care Survey), population-based surveys (such as the National Health Interview Survey), and longitudinal population surveys (such as the Longitudinal Study of Aging) are also available through the NCHS. Health data are usually published in *Vital and Health Statistics.* (For more information on the many printed data reports and tables published by U.S. agencies, you can contact the U.S. Government Printing Office directly.)

Statistical data are also available to evaluators from state and local (city, county) health departments. The best way to get information about the content and availability of public use data sets is to contact the agency involved (this may take some creative Web searching) and ask about the technical requirements (e.g., system requirements) and costs.

Performance Tests: The Standardized Patient

Performance tests aim to measure participants' abilities to perform specific tasks, such as preparing a slide for a microscope, delivering cardiopulmonary resuscitation, or conducting an interview over the telephone. One performance testing technique that is unique to the health care field is the use of "standardized patients" in the observation and measurement of the skills and behaviors required of physicians. Standardized patients may be real (that is, they may have the disorder or problem to be studied) or they may be actors. These individuals undergo extensive training and monitoring to ensure their consistent adherence to scripts that are prepared for them by clinical experts and educators.

Many medical educators consider the standardized patient to be an invaluable tool for educating physicians and for evaluating medical education. They argue that the costs of preparing the scripts, training the patients, monitoring patient performance over time, maintaining sufficiently large cadres of patients, and updating clinical concepts are more than offset by the value of the method for teaching clinical skills and aiding in their assessment.

Clinical Scenarios

Clinical scenarios are particularly useful in the collection of data on "what if" situations. Example 5.3 illustrates; this clinical scenario is taken from a study of physicians' attitudes toward using deception to resolve difficult ethical problems.

Example 5.3 A Sample Clinical Scenario

You are seeing Mrs. Lewis, a 52-year-old patient of yours, for her annual physical, which reveals no abnormalities. You tell her that everything looks normal and that you are going to order routine blood tests and her annual screening mammography, saying that the last time you ordered it she had to pay for it herself. You know she is of modest means and cannot easily afford it. You are surprised that her health insurance does not cover it. Upon asking your secretary, you learn that insurance covers the cost of mammography only if there is a breast mass or objective clinical evidence of the possibility of cancer. The secretary tells you that the way to get around this is to put down "rule out cancer" instead of "screening mammography" on the form.

1. How would you fill out the form?
   a. Rule out cancer
   b. Screening mammography
2. If you choose (a) to question 1, was it because (choose one, or rank your choices):
   a. You think the insurance company's distinctions are unreasonable.
   b. You feel a stronger obligation to your patient than to the insurance company.
   c. You feel that everyone else does it.
   d. You feel the financial hardship on Mrs. Lewis would be greater than on the insurance company.
   e. Other (please explain).
3. Again, if you chose (a) to question 1, do you feel you deceived the insurance company? (Y/N)

4. If you chose (b) to question 1, was it because (choose one, or rank your choices):
   a. You think the insurance company's distinctions are reasonable.
   b. It is wrong to deceive a third party for a patient's benefit.
   c. You are worried about the legal/professional liability involved.
   d. You feel such practices are responsible for increased health care costs.
   e. Other (please explain).

SOURCE: The text of this example is from D. H. Novack, B. J. Detering, R. Arnold, L. Forrow, M. Ladinsky, and J. C. Pezzullo. (1989). Physicians' attitudes toward using deception to resolve difficult ethical problems. *Journal of the American Medical Association, 261*, 2980–2985.

The preparation of clinical scenarios requires great skill in writing and test construction, and the evaluator cannot be certain of the accuracy of the responses.

The Literature

Evaluators turn to the literature for reasons that range from gathering ideas for research designs and data collection and analysis methods to comparing data and conclusions across research. The broad term *the literature* refers to all published and unpublished reports of studies or statistical findings. Published reports are often easier to locate than those that remain unpublished, given that they have appeared in books and journals that are accessible in libraries and online. In addition, because published reports have the advantage of public scrutiny, their authors' methods (and the conclusions they have drawn) may be more dependable. Reports on evaluation studies may be published in peer-reviewed journals, in books, or as stand-alone reports or monographs produced by local, state, or national agencies.

Program evaluators generally use the literature for the following reasons.

Reasons for Evaluators' Use of the Literature

1. *To set standards:* The literature can provide information on the past performance of programs and populations. Evaluators may use this information in planning an evaluation and as a yardstick against which to compare the findings of one that has already been completed.

2. *To define variables:* The literature is a primary source of information about the ways others have defined and measured commonly used key health care variables, such as child abuse and neglect; high-risk behaviors; comorbid conditions; social, physical, and emotional functioning; quality of care; and quality of life.

3. *To determine sample size:* Power calculations, which evaluators use to arrive at sample sizes that are large enough to reveal true differences (if they exist),

require estimation of the variance—a measure of dispersion—in the sample or population. Sometimes, however, evaluators have no readily available data on the variance in the sample of interest. They can conduct a pilot study to obtain the data, but appropriate data may be available in the literature, enabling the evaluators to build on and expand the work of others.

4. *To obtain examples of designs, measures, and ways of analyzing and presenting data:* Evaluators can use the literature as a source of sound information on research methods and data collection, analysis, and reporting techniques.

5. *To determine the significance of the evaluation and its findings:* Evaluators often use the literature to justify the need for particular programs and for their evaluation questions. They also use the literature to show whether their evaluation findings confirm or contradict the results of other studies and to identify areas in which little or no knowledge is currently available.

6. *To conduct meta-analyses:* Meta-analysis is a technique in which the results of two or more randomized controlled trials are pooled and reanalyzed. The idea is that by combining the results of relatively small, local studies, one can increase the power of the findings. Evaluators have conducted meta-analyses to evaluate the results of tests of treatments for heart attack and breast cancer. The use of meta-analysis is predicated on data from experimental studies. Given that not all experiments are of equal quality, understanding how to review and interpret the literature is an important first step in conducting a meta-analysis. Very few program evaluations to date have been randomized controlled trials, and so this technique has not been used often. Evaluations are becoming more sophisticated, however, so perhaps meta-analyses will be more appropriate and common in the near future.

The following section presents a six-step guide to the evaluator's review of the literature.

Guidelines for Reviewing the Literature

As an evaluator, you should take the following six steps in conducting a literature review:

1. Assemble the literature.
2. Identify inclusion and exclusion criteria.
3. Select the relevant literature.
4. Identify the "best" literature.
5. Abstract the information.
6. Consider the unpublished literature.

Each of these steps is discussed in turn below.

Assemble the Literature

Hundreds of online bibliographic databases are available to health program evaluators. A commonly used one is the National Library of Medicine's database, MEDLINE, which you can access for free online at http://www.nlm.nih.gov. Some useful databases are proprietary—that is, you have to pay to use them. One such database is the American Psychological Association's PsycINFO, which includes citations from the literature of psychology and the social sciences. Other, more specialized electronic databases available through the National Library of Medicine include AIDSLINE, HEALTHLINE, TOXLINE, AVLINE, and ENVIROLINE.

The key to an efficient literature search is specificity. If you search for all articles published by Jones from 1980 through 2004 in English about evaluations of the quality of care in U.S. teaching hospitals, you are much more likely to get what you want than if you search for all published evaluations of quality of care in U.S. teaching hospitals. If Jones has published articles about evaluations in U.S. teaching hospitals that have appeared in the education, public policy, or social science literature rather than the health care literature, then certain articles may not turn up if you rely solely on a computerized search of a health care–related database. To conduct a more comprehensive search, you should investigate all potentially relevant databases, scrutinize the references in key articles, and ask experts in the field to recommend references and bibliographic databases.

To search any database efficiently, you must carefully specify the variables and populations in which you are interested. A first step is to decide on specific criteria for including a study in or excluding it from the literature review. Once you have established these criteria, you can employ terms that describe them to guide the search. These are called *search terms* or *keywords.*

Identify Inclusion and Exclusion Criteria

The inclusion and exclusion criteria define whether a study is appropriate or inappropriate for review. These criteria usually include attention to the variables and populations of concern, where and when the study was published, and its methodological quality, as can be seen in Example 5.4, which illustrates the use of inclusion and exclusion criteria for a review of the effectiveness of prenatal care programs.

Example 5.4 Inclusion and Exclusion Criteria for a Review of Evaluated Prenatal Care Programs

The evaluators decide to include in their review of the literature on prenatal care programs any evaluations of programs aiming to integrate medical and social services to improve the health outcomes of mothers and newborns. They select only published evaluations because the editorial review process screens out the poorest studies. They choose 1980 as a starting point so that they will have a decade's data reflecting the increased accessibility to prenatal care begun by the federal government in the 1960s and 1970s. The evaluators exclude research that was primarily medical (e.g., aggressive treatment of preterm births) or psychosocial (e.g., improving mothers' self-esteem) and in which the focus was on the organization of the medical care system (e.g., centralizing a region's prenatal care).

With these inclusion and exclusion criteria as guides, the evaluators in Example 5.4 can focus on a search for studies published from 1980 forward and in all languages. Their search terms will probably include "program evaluation," "prenatal care," and "health outcomes."

Example 5.5 shows some of the search terms used in reviews of the literature in two studies. The first search compared the literature (randomized controlled trials only) to experts' recommendations for treating myocardial infarction (heart attack), and the second reviewed the efficacy of treatments for posttraumatic stress disorder in victims of rape, combat veterans, torture victims, and the tragically bereaved.

Example 5.5 Keywords Used in Two Studies to Search Electronic Bibliographic Databases

1. To search *the literature on treatments for myocardial infarction:* "myocardial infarction," "clinical trials," "multicenter studies," "double-blind method," "meta-analysis," "random"
2. *To search the literature on posttraumatic stress disorder:* "traumatic stress," "treatment," "psychotherapy," "flooding," "PTSD," "behavior therapy," "pharmacotherapy," "drugs," "cognitive therapy"

Select the Relevant Literature

After you have conducted your searches and assembled the articles you have found, you will usually need to screen the articles for irrelevant material. Because few searches (or searchers) are perfect, they invariably turn up studies that do not address the topic of interest or that are methodologically unsound.

Screening often consists of applying methodological criteria. For example, you may screen out reports of studies that did not use control groups, those that include data from unreliable sources, those that present insufficient data on some important variable, or those in which the findings are preliminary.

Identify the "Best" Literature

Regardless of the scope of your literature review, you must employ a method that distinguishes among articles with differing levels of quality. Selecting the best literature means finding the most methodologically rigorous studies.

At least two individuals are needed to make an adequate appraisal of a study's quality. These individuals should be given a definition of the parameters of quality and should be trained to apply that definition. Before they begin the formal review, they should test out their understanding of the system by collaborating on the appraisal of the quality of one to ten articles. A third knowledgeable person can act as adjudicator in cases of disagreement.

Figure 5.7 presents as an example the set of methodological features and definitions that the evaluators from Example 5.4, above, used to appraise the quality of the published literature on prenatal care program evaluations.

The evaluator must decide how a study is to be categorized as "best"—for example, does it have to meet all the criteria or some fraction (say, a score of more than 5 of 8), or does it have to achieve certain minimum criteria (such as random

Criteria for Selecting the Best Literature
Description of the experimental program is clear (data are given on program's duration, funding level, services, providers, patients, standardization across sites, and so on).
Participants are randomly selected into the evaluation (all patients are selected or a random sampling).
Participants are randomly assigned to groups.
The data are collected prospectively.
Data that are collected for the evaluation are demonstrated to be valid for all main variables.
Evaluation focuses on outcomes (e.g., birth weight, gestational age, drug status of mother and baby).
Evaluation collects more than one measurement after participants complete the program.
Statistical information is sufficient to determine clinical and practical significance of the findings (e.g., confidence intervals, exact *p* values).

Figure 5.7. Rating Methodological Features of the Literature: Identifying the Best Published Prenatal Care Program Evaluations

assignment and valid data collection)? Needless to say, these choices are somewhat arbitrary, and the evaluator must be able to defend their merits on a case-by-case basis.

An important component of the process of deciding on a study's quality is agreement among reviewers. To identify the extent of agreement, one can examine each item in the review independently or compare reviewers' scores on the entire set of items.

When two or more persons measure the same item and their measurements are compared, an index of interrater reliability is obtained. One statistic that is often used in deciding on the degree of agreement among two reviewers on a dichotomous variable (valid data were collected: yes or no) is kappa (κ). The statistic used to examine the relationship between two numerical characteristics (Reviewer A's score of 5 points versus Reviewer B's score of 7 points) is correlation.

Not all literature reviews are done by two or more persons. When only one person conducts a review, *intra*rater reliability can be calculated using kappa or correlation. In this procedure, a single reviewer rates or scores a selection of articles at least twice and the results are compared.

Abstract the Information

The most efficient way to get data from the literature is to standardize the abstraction process. A uniform abstraction system guards against the possibility that some important information will be missed, ignored, or misinterpreted. To obtain information on a study's data collection, a form such as that shown in Figure 5.8 is useful.

If you want to abstract information on the characteristics of the programs that were being evaluated, you might collect information using a form such as the one depicted in Figure 5.9.

Consider the Unpublished Literature

Various analyses of the published literature have suggested the existence of a bias in favor of positive results. This means that if a review is based solely on published articles, negative findings may be underrepresented. It is not easy, however, to locate and gain access to unpublished evaluation reports. Published studies have been reviewed by experts as well as the researchers' peers and colleagues, and probably the most unreliable have been screened out. Nevertheless, when you are interpreting the findings from the published literature, you should consider the potential biases that may exist because unpublished reports are excluded.

SECTION IV: Methods (continued)

Data Sources:

A. Methods:
(check all that apply)

[ ] Direct observation
[ ] Medical record review
[ ] Telephone survey
[ ] Face-to-face interview
[ ] Literature review
[ ] Vital statistics
[ ] Self-administered questionnaire
[ ] Billing records
[ ] Administrative records
[ ] Other, specify: ______________

B. Variables measured:
(check all that apply)

[ ] Age
[ ] Race/ethnicity
[ ] Number of red cells ordered
[ ] Perioperative hemoglobin (g/dl)
Type of surgery
[ ] Orthopedic
[ ] Cardiac
[ ] General
[ ] Obstetric-gynecologic
[ ] Urological
[ ] Vascular
[ ] Thoracic
[ ] Plastic
[ ] Oral
[ ] Other ____________

C. Reliability/Validity:

1. Is any information regarding the reliability of selected forms, surveys, or other data collection methods discussed?

   [ ] YES ——> If YES, specify (e.g., Cronbach's alpha, Kuder-Richardson):

   ____

   [ ] NO/CANNOT TELL

2. Is any information regarding the validity of study design, data collection or findings discussed?

   [ ] YES ——> If YES, specify (e.g., used previously validated forms, reported validation studies):

   ____

   [ ] NO/CANNOT TELL

3. Are data collection procedures **standardized?** *(check all that apply)*

   [ ] YES
   [ ] NO/CANNOT TELL

D. Duration of Data Collection Period: ____ months *(convert all periods to months and sum if > 1 period)*

Years of Data Collection Period: 19 ______ to 19 ______

Figure 5.8. Excerpts From a Form for Obtaining Information on a Study's Data Collection

Programs / Interventions

Program/Site combinations *(check one):*

[ ] One program, one site (Go to A)
[ ] One program, several sites (Go to B)
[ ] Multifaceted program, one site (Go to C)
[ ] Multifaceted program, several sites (Go to D)

A. ONE PROGRAM / ONE SITE:

1. Program adequately described?

   [ ] YES ——> If YES, provide brief synopsis of program description:

   ____

   ____

   ____

   [ ] NO

2. Duration of program: __________ months
   (enter "99" if unknown or not reported)
   (e.g., convert 3 years to 36 months)

3. Funding level:
   (check one)

   [ ] Not stated
   [ ] $50,000
   [ ] $50,000 to < $100,000
   [ ] $100,000 to < $250,000
   [ ] $250,000 to < $500,000
   [ ] $500,000 to < $1 million
   [ ] $1 million to < $2 million
   [ ] $2 million to < $5 million
   [ ] > $5 million

B. ONE PROGRAM / SEVERAL SITES:

1. Program adequately described?

   [ ] YES ——> If YES, provide brief synopsis of program description:

   ____

   ____

   ____

   [ ] NO

2. Duration of program: ________ months
   (enter "99" if unknown or not reported)
   (e.g., convert 3 years to 36 months)

3. Funding level:
   (check one)

   [ ] Not stated
   [ ] $50,000
   [ ] $50,000 to < $100,000
   [ ] $100,000 to < $250,000
   [ ] $250,000 to < $500,000
   [ ] $500,000 to < $1 million
   [ ] $1 million to < $2 million
   [ ] $2 million to < $5 million
   [ ] > $5 million

4. Number of sites: ________ [ ] CHECK HERE IF THERE ARE 100 OR MORE SITES

5. Is the program standardized across sites?
   [ ] YES [ ] NO [ ] DON'T KNOW

Figure 5.9. A Form for Abstracting Program Information

Summary and Transition to the Next Chapter on Evaluation Measures

This chapter has explained the factors that the evaluator should take into account when deciding on measures or sources of data. First, the evaluator must carefully review the evaluation question so that all variables are known and clarified. Then the evaluator should consider the possible measures that are likely to provide information on each variable. Among the possibilities are self-administered questionnaires, tests of achievement and performance (e.g., clinical scenarios and standardized patients), medical record reviews, observations and interviews, physical examinations, databases, and statistical records. Each type of data source has advantages and limitations. For example, interviews enable the evaluator to question program participants in a relatively in-depth manner, but conducting them can be time-consuming and financially costly. Self-administered questionnaires may be less time-consuming and costly, but they lack the intimacy of interviews, and the evaluator must always worry about the rate of responses. In selecting a source of data for your evaluation, you must look first at the evaluation question and decide whether you have the technical and financial resources and the time to develop your own measure; if not, you must consider adopting or adapting an already existing measure. You must also consider the credibility to participants and consumers of whatever data source you choose. Remember to consult the literature whenever possible to identify what is available and where the current evaluation fits into the larger scheme of things.

The next chapter addresses the concepts of *reliability* (the consistency of the information from each source) and *validity* (the accuracy of the information). The chapter also discusses the steps you will need to take in developing and validating your own measure and outlines the activities involved in selecting a measure that has been developed by other evaluators. Among the other topics addressed in the next chapter are "coding" (that is, making sure that your measure is properly formatted or described from the point of view of the person who will enter the data into the computer) and making sure that the components of the evaluation are logically linked. A measurement chart is presented that is helpful for portraying the logical connections among the evaluation's variables and measures.

Exercises

EXERCISE 1

Directions

Match each of the following descriptions with the appropriate measure.

Description	Measure
1. Requires excellent writing skills	A. Self-administered questionnaires
2. May alter the experimental environment	B. Medical record reviews
3. Inexpensive, but may not get responses to all questions	C. Clinical scenarios
4. May measure what you know but does not measure what you can do	D. Literature
5. Not intrusive but may not contain much psychosocial information	E. Vital statistics
6. Particularly useful in the standard- setting process	F. Achievement tests
7. Requires that you take care to ensure that the data apply to your program	G. Observations

EXERCISE 2

Directions

You are the evaluator of a prenatal care program. One of the evaluation questions asks about characteristics of the babies born to participating mothers. The project routinely collects data on mothers and babies, but you need data on birth weight, gestational age, whether the baby was stillborn, whether a drug toxicology screen was performed at birth on the mother and the baby (and, if so, the results), the number of prenatal care visits, and the birth date. Create a form that will aid you in obtaining this information.

Suggested Readings

Bernard, H. R. (1999). *Social research methods: Qualitative and quantitative approaches.* Thousand Oaks, CA: Sage.

Part 3 of this book provides more information on many of the data collection techniques discussed in the present volume.

Fink, A. (Ed.). (2002). *The survey kit* (10 vols., 2nd ed.). Thousand Oaks, CA: Sage.

See especially three volumes in this set: *How to Ask Survey Questions* (Volume 2), *How to Conduct Self-Administered and Mail Surveys* (Volume 3), and *How to Conduct In-Person Interviews for Surveys* (Volume 5).

Patton, M. Q. (2001). *Qualitative research and evaluation methods* (3rd ed.). Thousand Oaks, CA: Sage.

This book examines alternative interviewing strategies such as focus groups, group interviews, and cross-cultural interviews.

Examples of Literature Reviews

Boustani, M., Peterson, B., Hanson, L., Harris, R., & Lohr, K. N. (2003). Screening for dementia in primary care: A summary of the evidence for the U.S. Preventive Services Task Force. *Annals of Internal Medicine, 138,* 927–937.

Cherkin, D. C., Sherman, K. J., Deyo, R. A., & Shekell, P. G. (2003). A review of the evidence of the effectiveness, safety and costs of acupuncture, massage therapy and spinal manipulation for back pain. *Annals of Internal Medicine, 138,* 898–906.

Fink, A., & McCloskey, L. (1990). Moving child abuse and neglect prevention programs forward: Improving program evaluations. *Child Abuse & Neglect, 14,* 187–206.

MacDonald, H. P., Garg, A. X., & Haynes, R. B. (2002). Interventions to enhance patient adherence to medication prescriptions. *Journal of the American Medical Association, 288,* 2868–2879.

Solomon, S. D., Gerrity, E. T., & Muff, A. M. (1992). Efficacy of treatments for posttraumatic disorder: An empirical review. *Journal of the American Medical Association, 268,* 633–638.

Wathen, C. N., & MacMillan, H. L. (2003). Intervention for violence against women: Scientific review. *Journal of the American Medical Association, 289,* 589–600.

Wilk, A. I., Jensen, N. M., & Havighurst, T. C. (1997). Meta-analysis of randomized control trials addressing brief interventions in heavy alcohol drinkers. *Journal of General Internal Medicine, 12,* 274–283.

Purpose of This Chapter

This chapter begins with a discussion of the concepts of reliability and validity. *Reliability* refers to the consistency of a measure, and *validity* refers to its accuracy. Reliable and valid measures are the key to a sound evaluation because they are indicators of the quality of the data on which the findings and conclusions are based. This chapter also discusses how to develop new measures, how to select among already existing measures, and how to use a measurement chart to establish logical connections among the evaluation's questions, design, and measures.

6 Evaluation Measures

A Reader's Guide to Chapter 6

Reliability
Test-retest, equivalence, homogeneity, and inter- and intrarater reliability

Validity
Content and face, criterion (predictive and concurrent), and construct validity

Checklist for Creating a New Measure
Subject matter, item choices, rating scales, format, testing, and revision

Checklist for Selecting an Already Existing Measure
Costs, content, reliability, validity, and format

The Measurement Chart
Dependent variables, measures, sampling, timing and duration of measurement, content, reliability, and validity

Reliability and Validity

Evaluators sometimes create their own measures and sometimes adapt or adopt parts or all of already existing ones. Because the conclusions of an evaluation are based on data from the measures used, the quality of the measures must be demonstrably high for the evaluation's results to be sound. (Otherwise, we have the well-known phenomenon of "garbage in–garbage out.") To determine the quality of their data collection measures, evaluators must understand the concepts of reliability and validity.

Reliability

A *reliable* measure is one that is relatively free of "measurement error," which causes individuals' obtained scores to be different from their true scores (which can be obtained only through perfect measures). What causes measurement error? In some cases, it results from the measure itself, as when the measure is difficult to understand or poorly administered. For example, a self-administered questionnaire regarding the value of preventive health care might produce unreliable results if it requires a level of reading ability that is beyond that of the teen mothers who are to use it. If the respondents' reading level is not a problem but the directions are unclear, the measure will also be unreliable. Of course, the evaluator could simplify the measure's language and clarify the directions and still find measurement error, because such error can also come directly from the people being questioned. For example, if the teen mothers who are asked to complete the questionnaire are especially anxious or fatigued at the time, their obtained scores could differ from their true scores.

In program evaluation, four kinds of reliability are often discussed: test-retest, equivalence, homogeneity, and inter- and intrarater reliability. A measure has *test-retest reliability* if the correlation between scores on the measure from one time to another is high. Suppose a survey of patient satisfaction is administered in April and again in October to the same group of patients at Hospital A. If the survey is reliable, and no special program or intervention has been introduced between April and October, on average, we would expect satisfaction to remain the same. The major conceptual difficulty in establishing test-retest reliability is in determining how much time is permissible between the first and second administrations. If too much time elapses, external events might influence responses on the second administration; if too little time passes, the respondents may remember and simply repeat their answers from the first administration.

Equivalence, or *alternate-form reliability,* refers to the extent to which two assessments measure the same concepts at the same level of difficulty. Suppose that students were given an achievement test before participating in a course and then again 2 months after completing it. Unless the evaluator is certain that the two tests were of equal difficulty, better performance on the second test could be a result of that test's being easier than the first rather than improved learning. And, as with test-retest reliability, because this approach requires two administrations, the evaluator must worry about the appropriate interval between them.

As an alternative to establishing equivalence between two forms of the same instrument, evaluators sometimes compute a *split-half reliability.* This requires dividing an instrument into two equal halves (or alternate forms) and obtaining the correlation between the two halves. Problems arise if the two halves vary in difficulty; however, because only one administration is required, at least the concern over the duration of intervals between testing is eliminated.

Homogeneity refers to the extent to which all the items or questions in a measure assess the same skill, characteristic, or quality. Sometimes this type of reliability is referred to as *internal consistency.* The extent of homogeneity is often determined through the calculation of a Cronbach's coefficient alpha, which is basically the average of all the correlations between each item and the total score. For example, suppose that an evaluator has created a questionnaire to find out about patients' satisfaction with Hospital A. An analysis of homogeneity will tell the extent to which all items on the questionnaire focus on satisfaction.

Some variables do not have a single dimension. Patient satisfaction, for example, may consist of satisfaction with many elements of the hospital experience: nurses, doctors, financial arrangements, quality of care, quality of surroundings, and so on. If you are unsure of the number of dimensions included in your instrument, you can perform a factor analysis. This statistical procedure identifies relationships among the items or questions in a measure.

Interrater reliability refers to the extent to which two or more individuals agree on a given measurement. Suppose that two individuals are sent to a prenatal care clinic to observe patient waiting times, the appearance of the waiting and examination rooms, and the general atmosphere. If these observers agree perfectly in their ratings of all these items, then interrater reliability is perfect. Evaluators can enhance interrater reliability by training data collectors thoroughly, providing them with guidelines for recording their observations, monitoring the quality of the data collection over time to ensure that data collectors are not "burning out," and offering data collectors opportunities to discuss any difficult issues or problems they encounter in their work.

Intrarater reliability refers to a single individual's consistency of measurement. Evaluators can also enhance this form of reliability through training, monitoring, and continuous education.

Validity

Validity refers to the degree to which a measure assesses what it purports to measure. For example, a test that asks students to recall information would be considered an invalid measure of their ability to apply information. Similarly, a survey of patient satisfaction cannot be considered valid unless the evaluator can prove that the people who are identified as satisfied on the basis of their responses to the survey think or behave differently than people who are identified as dissatisfied.

Content validity refers to the extent to which a measure thoroughly and appropriately assesses the skills or characteristics it is intended to measure. For example, an evaluator who is interested in developing a measure of quality of life for cancer patients has to define *quality of life* and then make sure that items in the measure adequately include all aspects of the definition. Because of the complexity of this task, evaluators will often consult the literature for models or conceptual frameworks from which to derive the definitions they need. A conceptual model of "quality of life," for instance, consists of the variables included when the concept is discussed in differing kinds of patients, such as those with cancer, those who are depressed, and those who are very old or very young. It is not uncommon for evaluators to make a statement such as the following in establishing content validity: "We used XYZ cognitive theory to select items on knowledge, and we adapted the ABC Role Model Paradigm for questions about social relations."

Face validity refers to how a measure appears on the surface: Does it seem to ask all the needed questions? Does it use language that is both appropriate and geared to the respondents' reading level to do so? Face validity, unlike content validity, does not rely on established theory for support.

Criterion validity is made up of two subcategories: predictive validity and concurrent validity. *Predictive validity* is the extent to which a measure forecasts future performance. A medical school entry examination that successfully predicts who will do well in medical school has predictive validity. *Concurrent validity* is demonstrated when two assessments agree or a new measure compares favorably with one that is already considered valid. For example, to establish the concurrent validity of a new aptitude test, the evaluator can administer the new measure as well as a validated measure to the same group of examinees and compare the scores. Alternatively, the evaluator can administer the new test to the examinees and compare the scores with experts' judgment of students' aptitude. A high correlation between the new test and the criterion measure indicates concurrent validity. Establishing concurrent validity is useful when the evaluator has created a new measure that he or she believes is better (e.g., shorter, cheaper, fairer) than any previously validated measure.

Construct validity, which is established experimentally, demonstrates that a measure distinguishes between people who have certain characteristics and those who do not. For example, an evaluator who claims construct validity for a measure of compassionate nursing care will have to prove in a scientific manner that nurses who do well on the measure are more compassionate nurses than nurses who do poorly. Construct validity is commonly established in at least two ways:

1. The evaluator hypothesizes that the new measure correlates with one or more measures of a similar characteristic (convergent validity) and does not correlate with measures of dissimilar characteristics (discriminant validity). For example, an evaluator who is validating a new quality-of-life measure might posit that it is highly correlated with another quality-of-life instrument, a measure of functioning, and a measure of health status. At the same time, the evaluator might hypothesize that the new measure does not correlate with selected measures of social desirability (individuals' tendency to answer questions so as to present themselves in a positive light) or measures of hostility.

2. The evaluator hypothesizes that the measure can distinguish one group from the other on some important variable. For example, a measure of compassion should be able to demonstrate that people who are high scorers are compassionate and that people who are low scorers are unfeeling. This

requires that the evaluator translate a theory of compassionate behavior into measurable terms, identify people who are compassionate and people who are unfeeling (according to the theory), and prove that the measure consistently and correctly distinguishes between the two groups.

A Note on Language: Data Collection Terms

The language used to discuss reliability and validity (terms such as *examinees, scores, scales, tests,* and *measures*) comes from test theory, or psychometrics. Program evaluators often use the terms *data source, measure, scale, test,* and *instrument* interchangeably. This is sometimes confusing, to say the least, especially because evaluators also talk about *outcome measures* and *outcome indicators* when referring to evaluation study outcomes. The following brief lexicon can be helpful for sorting out data collection terms.

A Guide to Data Collection Terms

- *Data source:* Any source of information for the evaluation. This may include data from questionnaires or tests, literature reviews, existing databases (such as Medicare's), and vital statistics (such as the number of live births in a given year).
- *Index:* A way of rank ordering things. Scores on an index of function give an indication of where people stand in relation to one another. This term is sometimes used interchangeably with *scale.*
- *Instrument:* A device or strategy used to collect data; instruments include laboratory tests, self-administered questionnaires, and interviews. This term is often used interchangeably with *measure.*
- *Measure:* Very much like a data source. This term is often used interchangeably with *instrument, test,* and *assessment.*
- *Outcome:* The consequences of participating in a program. Outcomes may be changes in areas such as health status and emotional well-being.
- *Outcome measure or outcome indicator:* Often used as a synonym for *outcome.*
- *Rating scale:* A graded set of choices. Scales may be nominal (or categorical) (e.g., race, gender), ordered (or ordinal) (e.g., with response categories such as *often, sometimes,* and *never;* Stages I, II, and III of a disease), or numerical, including continuous (age, height) and discrete (number of pregnancies, number of arrests for driving drunk). The most commonly used type of rating scale is the Likert scale, with response categories such as *strongly agree, agree, neither agree nor disagree, disagree,* and *strongly disagree.*
- *Scale:* A combination of items or questions that measure the same concept, such as a 10-item scale that measures emotional well-being or a 36-item scale that measures health status.
- *Test:* Achievement test, laboratory test.

Checklist for Creating a New Measure

Knowing the types of measures that are available and how to demonstrate their reliability and validity enables the evaluator to get down to the serious business of developing a measure that is tailored to the needs of the investigation or selecting and adapting one that is already in use. Before you attempt to create a new measure for your evaluation study, you must make sure that you have identified the domain of content (through observation or with the help of experts, research, and theory) and have the expertise, time, and money to complete the task. The following is a checklist of the basic steps you need to take in creating a new measure.

_____ **1. Set boundaries.**

- _____ *Decide on the type of measure* (e.g., questionnaire, observation).
- _____ *Determine the amount of needed and available time for administration and scoring* (e.g., a 15-minute interview and 10 minutes for summarizing responses).
- _____ *Select the kinds of reliability and validity information to be collected* (e.g., to establish alternate-form reliability, you must develop two forms; to establish concurrent validity, you will need an already existing instrument).

_____ **2. Define the subject matter or topics that will be covered.** For definitions, consult the literature, experts, or health care consumers. Example 6.1 illustrates how the definitions for an evaluation of prenatal care programs were found in the literature and corroborated by nurses, physicians, and evaluators.

Example 6.1 Defining Terms: The Case of Prenatal Care Programs

Prenatal health care refers to pregnancy-related services provided to a woman between the time of conception and delivery and consists of monitoring the health status of the woman; providing patient information to foster optimal health, good dietary habits, and proper hygiene; and providing appropriate psychological and social support. *Programs* have preset, specific purposes and activities for defined populations and groups. *Outcomes of prenatal care programs* include the newborn's gestational age and birth weight and the mother's medical condition and health habits.

These definitions tell the evaluator something like the following: If you want to evaluate prenatal care programs, your measures should include attention to patient education, dietary habits and hygiene, and psychosocial support. If you are interested in outcomes, you will need measures of gestational age and mother's medical condition and health habits. You will also need to decide which medical conditions (e.g., diabetes, hypertension) and health habits (e.g., drinking, smoking) will be the focus of your evaluation.

_____ **3. Outline the content.**

Suppose that an evaluator is concerned with the outcomes of a particular prenatal care program: the Prenatal Care Access and Utilization Initiative. Assume also that the evaluator's review of the literature and consultation with experts reveal the importance of collecting data on the following variables: still or live birth, birth weight, gestational age, number of prenatal visits, and drug toxicology status of mother and baby. An outline of the contents might look like this:

I. Baby's birth date

II. Birth weight

III. Gender

IV. Gestational age

V. Whether a drug toxicology screen was performed on baby and results

VI. Whether a drug toxicology screen was performed on mother and results

VII. Number of visits

_____ **4. Select item choices.**

An *item* on a measure is a question asked of the respondent or a statement to which the respondent is asked to react. Example 6.2 presents a sample item and its answer choices.

Example 6.2 Item Choices

Item: *What are the test results?*	***Choose one***
Choices:	
Normal or negative	☐
Not significant but abnormal	☐
Positive	☐
Equivocal/No Data	☐

Selecting choices for items requires skill and practice. Whenever possible, you should use item choices that others have used effectively. The possibilities of finding appropriate choices are greater when you are collecting demographic information (e.g., age, gender, ethnicity, income, education, where a person lives), for example, than when you are collecting data on the knowledge, attitudes, or behaviors that result from a specific program designed for a particular group of people. You can find effective item choices in the literature and can obtain many from measures prepared by U.S. Bureau of the Census; the health departments of cities, counties, and states; and other public and private agencies.

_____ **5. Choose rating scales.**

You should adapt rating scales from scales that have already been proven in earlier research whenever possible. Like the choices for items, rating scales are available from measures designed by public and private agencies and those described in the literature. Example 6.3 displays an item that uses a simple true-and-false scale.

Example 6.3 Item With a True-False Rating Scale

Please circle the number that best describes whether each of the following statements is true or false for you.

	Definitely True	Mostly True	Not Sure	Mostly False	Definitely False
I am somewhat ill.	1	2	3	4	5
I am as healthy as anybody I know.	1	2	3	4	5
My health is excellent.	1	2	3	4	5
I have been feeling bad lately.	1	2	3	4	5

_____ **6. Review the measure with experts and potential users.**

It is wise to ask other evaluators, subject-matter experts, and potential users to review your measure. The following are some important questions to ask them.

Questions to Ask of Those Reviewing Your Measure

- **Ask experts**
  1. Is all relevant content covered?
  2. Is the content covered in adequate depth?

3. Are all item choices appropriate?
4. Are all rating scales appropriate?
5. Is the measure too long?

- **Ask users**
  1. Is all relevant content covered?
  2. Is the content covered in adequate depth?
  3. Do you understand without ambiguity all item choices and scales?
  4. Did you have enough time to complete the measure?
  5. Did you have enough time to administer the measure?
  6. Is the measure too long?

_____ **7. Revise the measure based on comments from the reviewers.**

_____ **8. Put the measure in an appropriate format.** For example:

_____ Add an ID code, because without such coding you cannot collect data on the same person over time.

_____ Add directions for administration and completion.

_____ Add a statement regarding confidentially (informing the respondent that participants are identifiable by code) or anonymity (informing the respondent that you have no means of identifying participants).

_____ Add a statement thanking the respondent.

_____ Give instructions for submitting the completed measure. If it is to be mailed, is an addressed and stamped envelope provided? By what date should the measure be completed?

_____ **9. Review and test the measure before administration.**

The importance of pilot-testing a new measure cannot be overemphasized. To conduct a meaningful pilot test, you must use the measure under realistic conditions. This means administering the measure to as many participants as your resources will allow. After they have completed the measure, you need to interview the participants to find out about any problems they might have had in completing the measure. When your study involves interviews, you must test the methods for interviewing as well the measure itself.

Checklist for Selecting an Already Existing Measure

Many instruments and measures are available for use by health program evaluators. Good sources for these are the published evaluation reports found in journals. In some cases, whole instruments are published as part of these articles. Even when the instruments themselves do not appear, the evaluators usually describe all of their main data sources and measures in the "methods" sections of their reports, and you can contact them for any additional information you need.

Using an already tested measure has many advantages, among which is that it saves you the time and other resources needed to develop and validate a completely new instrument. Choosing a measure that has been used elsewhere is not without pitfalls, however. For example, you may have to pay to use an established measure, you may be required to share your data, and you may have to modify the measure so substantially that its reliability and validity are jeopardized, requiring you to establish them all over again.

The following is a checklist for choosing an already existing measure.

_____ 1. **Find out the costs:** Do you have to pay? Share data? Share authorship?

_____ 2. **Check the content:** In essence, you must do your own fact and content validity study. Make sure that the questions are the ones you would ask if you were developing the instrument. Check the item choices and rating scales. Will they get you the information you need?

_____ 3. **Check the reliability and validity:** Make sure that the types of reliability and validity that have been confirmed are appropriate for your needs. For example, if you are interested in interrater reliability but only internal consistency statistics are provided, the measure may not be the right one for you. If you are interested in a measure's ability to predict but only content validity data are available, think again before adopting the instrument.

You will need to check carefully the context in which the measure has been validated. Are the settings and groups similar to those in your evaluation? If not, the instrument may not be valid for your purposes. For example, a measure of compliance with counselors' advice in a program to prevent child abuse and neglect that has been tested on teen mothers in Montana may not be applicable to nonteen mothers in Helena, Montana, or to teen mothers in San Francisco, California.

You must also decide whether the measure is sufficiently reliable and valid for use. Reliability and validity are often described as correlations (say, between experts or measures or among items). How high should the correlations be? The fast answer is that the higher, the better, and .90 is best. But the statistic by itself should not be the only or even the most important criterion. A lower correlation may be acceptable if the measure has other properties that are potentially more important. For example, the content may be especially appropriate or the measure might have been tested on participants who are very much like those in your evaluation.

_____ 4. **Check the measure's format:**

- Will the data collectors be able to score the measure?
- Does it make sense to use it, given your available technology? For example, if it requires certain software or expertise, do you have it? Can you afford to get it?
- Will the participants in the evaluation be willing to complete the measure? Participants sometimes object to spending more than 10 or 15 minutes on an interview, for example. Also, personal questions and complicated instructions can result in incomplete data.

The Measurement Chart: Logical Connections

A measurement chart assists the evaluator in the logistics of the evaluation by helping him or her to be sure that all variables will have the appropriate coverage. Such a chart is also useful when the evaluator is writing proposals, because it portrays the logical connections among what is being measured, how, for how long, and with whom. When the evaluator is writing reports, the chart provides a summary of some of the important features of the evaluation's data sources. As the sample measurement chart in Figure 6.1 illustrates, the information in the chart's columns enables the evaluator to make logical connections among the various segments of data collection. Each column in the chart is explained briefly below.

Variables. To ensure that all independent and dependent variables are covered, the evaluator uses the chart to check the evaluation questions and sampling strategies, including all strata and inclusion and exclusion criteria. For example, suppose that an evaluation asks about the effectiveness of a yearlong combined diet and exercise program in improving the health status and quality of life for people over 75 years of age. Suppose also that it excludes all persons with certain diseases, such as metastatic cancer and heart disease. Assume that the evaluators plan to compare men and women to determine whether any differences exist between them after program participation. The variables needing measurement in such an evaluation would include quality of life, health status (to identify persons with metastatic cancer and heart disease and to assess changes), and demographic characteristics (to determine who is male and who is female).

How measured. For each variable, the measure should be indicated. The measurement chart in Figure 6.1 shows that quality of life will be assessed through interviews with patients and observations of how they live, health status will be measured through physical examination, demographic characteristics will be measured through self-administered questionnaires or interviews, and costs will be measured through a review of financial records.

Sample. This column in the measurement chart contains information on the number and characteristics of individuals who will constitute the sample for each measure. For example, the measurement chart in Figure 6.1 shows that to measure quality of life the evaluator will interview all 100 patients (50 men and 50 women) in the experimental group and all 100 patients (50 men and 50 women) in the control group as well as observe a sample of the lifestyles of 50 patients (25 men and 25 women) in each group. Assessment of health status will be based on physical examination of all persons in the experimental and control groups, and demographic information will be collected on all experimental and control program participants. Data on costs will be collected only for those individuals who use one of the two staffing models.

Dependent Variables	How Measured	Sample	Timing of Measures	Duration of Measures	Content	Reliability and Validity	General Concerns
Quality of life	Interviews with patients	All 100 patients in experimental group and all 100 in control. In each group of 100, 50 men and 50 women	1 month before program participation, 1 month after, and 1 year after	1-hour interviews; 30 minutes to summarize	Social, emotional, and physical functioning; health beliefs; perceived joy and satisfaction: 35 questions	The Brandyse Functional Assessment (long form) and the University Quality of Living Scale will be adopted. The Brandyse has been validated on 4,000 community-dwelling elderly. Test-retest reliability is .85 and homogeneity for subscales is .90.	No costs will be incurred; data will be shared with the Brandyse group. The University Quality of Living Scale is available free to all researchers. All patients will complete informed consent forms. No special institutional review board–type procedure need be followed. No special software or hardware is necessary.
	Observations	50 patients in the experimental and 50 in the control groups; 25 men and 25 women in each	1 month before program participation and 6 months after	Half-hour observations; 15 minutes to summarize	Appearance and repair of household; number of visitors; fire and accident safety: 10 questions	Interrater reliability will be estimated between at least two observers.	

Figure 6.1. Measurement Chart for an Evaluation of a Health Care Program's Effects on Patient Quality of Life and Health Status (Continued)

Dependent Variables	How Measured	Sample	Timing of Measures	Duration of Measures	Content	Reliability and Validity	General Concerns
Health status	Physical examination	All persons in experimental and control groups	1 month before the program, within 1 month of completion, and 1 year later	30 minutes	Emphasis on presence or absence of serious chronic disorders (e.g., metastatic cancer, heart disease): 50 questions	A team of four physicians and nurse practitioners will be trained to administer the physical examinations in a uniform way.	
Demographic characteristics	Self-administered questionnaires or interviews	All persons in experimental and control groups	1 month before the start of the program	Less than 5 minutes	Gender, ethnicity, age, education, household income, region of country in which highest level of education was achieved: 10 questions	Standard items will be used to collect these data.	
Costs	Financial records	All persons receiving care in two clinics, one staffed primarily by physicians and one by nurses	Within 1 month of completion of the program	About 30 minutes to obtain data and make calculations	Number of staff; hourly wages; number of appointments to each clinic made and kept; number of minutes spent on care	A form will be created and data collectors will be trained to use it. Periodic quality checks will be made.	

Timing of measures. The information in this column refers to when each measure is to be administered. For example, the measurement chart in Figure 6.1 shows that interviews regarding quality of life and physical examination will be conducted 1 month before the program, immediately after the program (within 1 months), and 1 year after. Observations will be made 1 month before and 6 months after. Demographic information will be obtained just once: 1 month before the start of the program.

Duration of measures. This column of the chart contains information on the amount of time it will take to administer and summarize or score each measure. The measurement chart in Figure 6.1 shows that the quality-of-life interviews will take 1 hour to conduct and a half hour to summarize. The observations will take a half hour to conduct and 15 minutes to summarize. The physical examinations are expected to take 30 minutes, and collecting data on demographic characteristics will take less than 5 minutes.

Content. The evaluator should provide a brief description of the content in the measurement chart. For example, if measurement of quality of life is to be based on a particular theory, the evaluator should note the theory's name. If the interview has several sections (e.g., social, emotional, and physical function), the evaluator might mention them. It is important to remember that the chart's purpose is really to serve as a guide to the measurement features of an evaluation. Each one of its sections may require elaboration. For example, for some measures, the evaluator may want to include the number of items in each subscale.

Reliability and validity. If the measures being used are adapted from some other study, the evaluator might describe the relevant types of reliability and validity statistics in this part of the chart. For example, if the quality-of-life measure has been used on elderly people in another evaluation that showed that higher scorers had higher quality than low scorers, this information might be included. If additional reliability information is to be collected in the current evaluation, that, too, may be reported. A review of medical records to gather information on the number, types, and appropriateness of admissions to the hospital over a 1-year period, for example, could require estimations of data collectors' interrater reliability; such information belongs in this section of the chart.

General concerns. In this portion of the chart, the evaluator notes any special features of the entire data collection and measurement endeavor. These include information on costs, training, number of items, special software or hardware requirements, and issues pertaining to informed consent.

Summary and Transition to the Next Chapter on Managing Evaluation Data

Reliability refers to the consistency of a measure, and *validity* refers to its accuracy. Having reliable and valid measures is essential in a diligent evaluation. Sometimes the evaluator is required or chooses to create a new measure; at other times, a measure is available that appears to be suitable. Whether creating, adapting, or adopting, the evaluator must critically review the measure to ensure its appropriateness and accuracy for the current study.

A measurement chart is a useful way of showing the relationships among dependent variables, how and when the dependent variables are measured, and the content, reliability, and validity of the measures. Measurement charts are useful tools for evaluators as they plan and report on evaluations.

The next chapter discusses the activities in which the evaluator engages to ensure the proper management of evaluation data to preserve them for analysis. These activities include drafting an analysis plan, creating a codebook, establishing coder reliability, reviewing data collection instruments for incomplete or missing data, entering data into a database, cleaning the data, creating the final data set, and archiving the data set.

Exercises

EXERCISE 1: RELIABILITY AND VALIDITY

Directions

Read the following excerpts and determine which concepts of reliability and validity are covered in each.

Excerpt A

The self-administered questionnaire was adapted with minor revisions from the Student Health Risk Questionnaire, which is designed to investigate knowledge, attitudes, behaviors, and various other cognitive variables regarding HIV and AIDS among high school students. Four behavior scales measured sexual activity (4 questions in each scale) and needle use (5 questions); 23 items determined a scale of factual knowledge regarding AIDS. Cognitive variables derived from the health belief model and social learning theory were employed to examine personal beliefs and social norms (12 questions).

Excerpt B

All charts were reviewed by a single reviewer with expertise in this area; a subset of 35 charts was reviewed by a second blinded expert to assess the validity of the review. Rates of agreement for single items ranged from 81% ($\kappa = .77$; $p < .001$) to 100% ($\kappa = 1$; $p < .001$).

Excerpt C

Group A and Group B nurses were given a 22-question quiz testing evaluation principles derived from the UCLA guidelines. The quizzes were not scored in a blinded manner, but each test was scored twice.

EXERCISE 2: REVIEWING A DATA COLLECTION PLAN

Directions

Read the following information collection scenario and, acting as an independent reviewer, provide the evaluator with a description of your problems and concerns.

The School of Nursing is in the process of revising its elective course in research methods. As part of the process, a survey was sent to all faculty who currently teach the methods courses to find out whether and to what extent epidemiology topics were included. Among the expectations was that methods courses would aim to improve students' knowledge of epidemiology and their attitudes toward its usefulness in a number of nursing subjects, ranging from public health nursing to home health care administration. The results of the survey revealed little coverage of some important objectives. Many faculty indicated that they would like to include more epidemiology, but they were lacking educational materials and did not have the resources to prepare their own. To rectify this, a course with materials was developed and disseminated. The Center for Nursing, Education, and Evaluation was asked to appraise the effectiveness of the educational materials. Evaluators from the center prepared a series of knowledge and skill tests and planned to administer them each year over a 5-year period. The evaluators are experts in test construction, and so they decided to omit pilot testing and save the time and expense. Their purpose in testing was to measure changes (if any) in nurses' abilities. They also planned to interview a sample of cooperating students to get an in-depth portrait of their knowledge of clinical epidemiology.

Suggested Readings

Ganz, P., Schag, C. A. C., Lee, J. J., & Sim, M. (1992). The CARES: A generic measure of health-related quality of life for patients with cancer. *Quality of Life Research, 1,* 19–29.

This article describes the validation of the Cancer Rehabilitation Evaluation System (CARES). It provides an excellent example of the way in which a new measure is tested.

Litwin, M. (2002). *How to assess and interpret survey psychometrics.* Thousand Oaks, CA: Sage.

This book is an excellent source of information on the different types of reliability and validity.

McDowell, I., & Newell, C. (1987). *Measuring health: A guide to rating scales and questionnaires.* New York: Oxford University Press.

This book provides numerous examples of health measurement techniques and scales and also discusses the validity and reliability of important health measures.

Stewart, A. L., Hays, R. D., & Ware, J. E. (1988). The MOS short-form health survey: Reliability and validity in a patient population. *Medical Care, 26,* 724–735.

This article describes the statistics used to establish the reliability and validity of a widely used measure of health.

Tulsky, D. S. (1990). An introduction to test theory. *Oncology, 4,* 43–48.

This article provides definitions and examples of the concepts of reliability and validity.

Note: More information on reliability and validity is available on the Internet. Use your favorite search engine and the search phrase "reliability and validity."

Purpose of This Chapter

This chapter provides information on how to organize and manage the data collected during an evaluation so that it can be analyzed. The topics addressed include the kinds of software available to assist evaluators in data entry and storage, how to monitor data entry to avoid errors, and how to create a "clean" data set. Because evaluators often collect a great deal of data, even in relatively small evaluations, it is very important that they manage their data efficiently.

7 Managing Evaluation Data

A Reader's Guide to Chapter 7

Data Management: The Road to Data Analysis

Drafting an Analysis Plan

Creating a Codebook
  Establishing reliable coding, measuring agreement

Searching for Missing Data

Entering the Data

Cleaning the Data
  Information collection measures not completed and only partially completed, outliers, data in need of recoding

Creating the Final Data Set for Analysis

Storing and Archiving the Data Set

Data Management: The Road to Data Analysis

The term *data management* refers to all of the actions evaluators take to convert the data they collect from all sources about a program into an analytic database or data set for analysis. The terms *database* and *data set* are often used interchangeably, but *data set* might also refer to a subset of a larger database. Evaluators sometimes collect more information than they analyze; in such a case, the data used in the analysis is the data set. The data management activities in which evaluators engage are as follows:

- Drafting an analysis plan that defines the variables to be analyzed
- Creating a codebook
- Establishing the reliability of the coders
- Reviewing data collection instruments for incomplete data and missing data
- Entering data into a database and validating the accuracy of the entry
- Cleaning the data to check for missing data and outliers
- Creating the final data set for analysis
- Storing and archiving the data set

Suppose that you are the evaluator of a 3-year program to encourage primary care patients to use preventive health care services on a regular basis. Your plan is to survey patients four times over the 3 years. There are 400 patients in the evaluation, and you decide to survey them at baseline (just before the program begins) and at intervals 12, 24, and 36 months after. Each survey contains 25 questions. In addition, you also plan to survey 25 physicians at baseline and at the conclusion of the program, 36 months later. The physicians' survey has 50 questions. If everyone in your original sample stays in the evaluation and answers all of the questions on all of the surveys, you will have to find a way to manage data from 400 patients who answer 25 questions each four times (40,000 answers) plus the data from 25 physicians who answer 50 questions twice (2,500 answers). To complicate matters, you may need to combine answers from patients and physicians in order to answer some of the evaluation questions. For example, say that one of the evaluation questions is, How do the male and female patients of female internists compare with those of male internists in their use of preventive health services? To answer this question, you will need to be able to access the data so as to identify female and male internists as well as the services used by male patients versus female patients. To do so, you will need a database that is clean and accessible.

Even before data collection begins, the evaluator needs to think about the hardware and software that will be used for data management. The complexity and importance of data management are sometimes overlooked, even though some evaluators estimate that data management activities take up between 20% and 50% of the time typically allocated for the analytic process. As you plan your own evaluation, it is important that you be realistic about the amount of time you will need for data management and that you make sure you have sufficient resources (staff, time, money) to do the job. The principles that underlie good data management apply to qualitative data as well as to statistical information.

Drafting an Analysis Plan

The evaluator describes the statistical and other analytic methods he or she intends to use for each evaluation objective, hypothesis, and research question in the *analysis plan.* The objectives, hypotheses, and questions contain the independent and dependent variables of interest in the evaluation. Suppose that you are the evaluator of a health education program designed to reduce risks for harmful drinking. The program consists of three main components: (a) the Alcohol-Related Problems Screen (ARPS), a measure to determine drinking classification (harmful or not harmful); (b) a report to the participant describing the reasons for the classification (such as "A person who drinks four or more drinks at one sitting two or three times a week or more is a harmful drinker"); and (c) educational materials (a booklet and a list of related Web sites) to help the participant cut his or her drinking down to a healthier level. Example 7.1 shows portions of a simple plan for analyzing the data to answer two of this study's evaluation questions.

Example 7.1 Portion of an Analysis Plan for an Evaluation of a Program to Reduce Harmful Drinking in Adults

Evaluation Question 1

Question: How do men and women compare in terms of numbers of harmful drinkers?

Hypothesis: More men than women will be harmful drinkers.

Independent variable: gender (male and female)

Dependent variable: drinking status (a harmful drinker: yes or no)

Planned analysis: chi-square to test for differences between numbers of men and women who are or are not harmful drinkers

Evaluation Question 2

Question: How do men and women compare in their risks for harmful drinking as defined by scores on the Alcohol-Related Problems Screen? (The higher the score, the greater the risks are likely to be. Scores are numerical and continuous and range from 1 to 50.)

Independent variable: gender (male and female)

Dependent variable: risks for harmful drinking as measured by scores on the ARPS

Planned analysis: *t* test to test for differences in average scores obtained by men and by women

Regardless of how well you plan your analysis, the realities of sampling and data collection may force you to modify your plan. Suppose, for example, that you review preliminary data from the Alcohol-Related Problems Screen (Evaluation Question 2 in Example 7.1). Based on the results of your review, you decide that in addition to testing for differences in average scores, you also want to compare the number of men and women who attain scores of 25 or higher on the ARPS with the number who obtain scores of 24 or lower. You would then have to modify your original analysis plan to include a chi-square test (to compare proportions or numbers) as well as the planned *t* test (to compare averages). In general, evaluators can count on having to make modifications to their original analysis plans, especially in large studies that collect a great deal of data.

Creating a Codebook

In this context, *codes* are units that the evaluator uses to "speak" to a computer. Suppose that in your evaluation of a program to reduce harmful drinking, 1,000 men and women complete the health survey called the Alcohol-Related Problems Screen. One question of concern to you is how many men report drinking four drinks at one sitting two or three times a week or more. To find out this information from the participants' survey responses, you have to tell the computer which variables to look for (e.g., gender and quantity and frequency of alcohol use). Computer programs read about variables through codes. Example 7.2 displays two items from the ARPS.

Example 7.2 Excerpts From a Screening Measure to Detect Harmful Drinking

1. Are you male or female? [SEX]

   Male ❐$_0$

   Female ❐$_1$

   .

   .

   .

8. How often in the past 12 months have you had 4 or more drinks of alcohol at one sitting? [QFDRINK]

	Choose one answer
Daily or almost daily	❐$_1$
Four or five times a week	❐$_2$
Two or three times a week	❐$_3$
Two to four times a month	❐$_4$
One time a month or less	❐$_5$
Never	❐$_0$

In Example 7.2, the codes are the numbers to the right of the response boxes. You would use a statistical program to tell you how many people who answered "1" to question 1 also answered "4" to question 8. To do this, you must tell the computer the names of the variables (Question 1 = SEX and Question 8 = QFDRINK) and their values (0 = male and 1 = female; 1 = daily or almost daily to 0 = never). (Many statistical programs also require that you tell the computer where in the data line to find the variables; see the section "Entering the Data," later in this chapter.) The "words" in brackets in Example 7.2 (SEX and QFDRINK) correspond to the variables represented by each question.

The evaluator must create a *codebook* that contains descriptions of all of the questions, codes, and variables associated with a survey. Example 7.3 displays portions of a typical codebook.

Example 7.3 Portions of a Codebook

Variable Name	Variable Label	Values: Labels and Codes
PROJID	Project code	7-digit ID
AGE	Age	Date of birth: Mo/day/year
GENDER	Gender	Gender of respondent: 0 = male; 1 = female. Leave blank if missing.
CNTRY	Country born in	Country person is born in: 01 = Argentina; 02 = Bolivia; 03 = Chile; 04 = Colombia; 05 = Cuba; 06 = Ecuador; 07 = El Salvador; 08 = Guatemala; 09 = Honduras; 10 = Mexico; 11 = Nicaragua; 12 = Peru; 13 = Puerto Rico. Leave blank if no data.
GUILT	Feels guilty or sorry	1 = daily or almost daily; 2 = at least once a week, but less than daily; 3 = at least once a month, but less than weekly; 4 = less than once a month; 0 = never. Leave blank if no data.
DRIVE	Drinks and drives	1 = 20 or more days; 2 = 10–19 days; 3 = 6–9 days; 4 = 3–5 days; 5 = 1–2 days; 0 = never. Leave blank if no data.

As this example illustrates, each variable is broken down into discrete units, called *values*, that correspond to the codes for that variable. For instance, a participant's feeling guilty or sorry for something he or she did because of alcohol use has five values: 1 = daily or almost daily; 2 = at least once a week but less than daily; 3 = at least once a month but less than weekly; 4 = less than once a month; 0 = never. The codes are thus 0, 1, 2, 3, and 4. The codebook also notes that if no information is available, nothing is filled in.

The evaluator should assign missing data a code or value that is not numeric, because many statistical programs will treat all codes as data that need to be analyzed. Suppose that you are conducting a survey of teens, and one participant neglects to include his or her age on a questionnaire; if you code that missing information as 99, the statistical program will likely assume that the respondent is 99 years old.

There are several ways to code missing data, including using a period (.) or inserting a blank space. Some software programs allow users to select several codes for missing data, such as ".a" for missing, ".b" for "don't know," and ".c" for "not applicable." It is a good idea to distinguish among these three concepts. If a person in an evaluation of harmful drinking does not drink, for instance, then all variables pertaining to the quantity and frequency of that person's drinking should be coded as "not applicable," given that the data are not actually "missing." When you have selected the software you will use in your evaluation, check the manual to see which coding system is appropriate and to determine what will work best for your analysis.

Although statistical software programs vary in the terminology they use, many (but by no means all) require that variable labels appear in all capital letters (PQOL or EDUC) and do not permit the use of special characters (such as commas and semicolons) in these labels. Some programs limit the number of characters for variable labels to about eight. Variable labels should be based on the actual names of the variables (e.g., the variable name "perceived quality of life" is given the variable label PQOL). To understand the data, the computer needs to know the name of each variable, the variable's label, and the variable's values and their labels. For the variable named "community," for example, the computer needs to know that its label is COMM and that its values are 1 = urban and 2 = rural. (Note that although the statistical program you use may employ slightly different terms for all these concepts, the ideas will be exactly the same.)

Establishing Reliable Coding

To assure reliable data in a small evaluation—say, with just one person doing the coding—the evaluator should recode all or a sample of the data to check for consistency. The second coding should take place about a week after the first coding. This is enough time for the coder to forget the first set of codes so that he or she does not just automatically reproduce them. After the data are coded a second time, the evaluator should compare the two sets of codes for agreement. If there are disagreements, the evaluator may resolve them by calling in a second person to arbitrate.

In a large evaluation, a second person should independently code a sample of the data. To assure reliability between coders, the evaluator must provide the coders with formal training and make sure they have access to the definitions of all terms.

Despite the evaluator's best efforts at setting up a high-quality codebook and data management system, the coders may not always agree with one another. Agreement among coders is especially important in qualitative evaluations, as the discussion below suggests. To find out the extent of agreement between coders—intercoder or interrater reliability—the evaluator can calculate a statistic called *kappa,* which measures how much better than chance the agreement between a given pair of coders is. The following subsection explains the principle behind the kappa statistic.

Measuring Agreement: The Kappa

Suppose that two evaluators are asked to review independently 100 interviews with single working mothers of two or more children. These mothers have just completed a monthlong program, and the interviews are about their health-related quality of life. The reviewers are to study the transcripts of the interviews to find how many of the participants mention doing regular exercise during the discussion. The reviewers are asked to code 0, for "no," if a participant does not mention regular exercise at least once

	Reviewer 1		
Reviewer 2	*No*	*Yes*	
No	20[C]	15	35[B]
Yes	10	55[D]	65
	30[A]	70	

and 1, for "yes," if she does mention regular exercise. Here are the reviewers' codes:

Reviewer 1 says that 30 ([A]) of the 100 interviews do not contain reference to regular exercise, whereas Reviewer 2 says that 35 ([B]) do not. The two reviewers agree that 20 ([C]) interviews do not include mention of exercise.

What is the best way to describe the extent of agreement between these reviewers? The figure of 20 out of 100, or 20% ([C]), is probably too low, because the reviewers also agree that 55% ([D]) of the interviews include mention of exercise. The total agreement 55% + 20% is an overestimate, because with only two categories (yes and no), some agreement may occur by chance. This is shown in the following formula, in which *O* is the observed agreement and *C* is the chance agreement.

Measuring Agreement Between Two Coders: The Kappa (κ) Statistic

$$\kappa = \frac{O - C}{1 - C},$$

where $O - C$ = agreement beyond chance and $1 - C$ = agreement possible beyond chance. Here is how this formula works with the above example.

1. Calculate how many interviews the reviewers may agree by chance *do not* include mention of exercise. One does this by multiplying the number of no's and dividing by 100, because there are 100 interviews: (30 × 35)/100 = 10.5.
2. Calculate how many interviews the reviewers may agree by chance *do* include mention of exercise by multiplying the number of interviews that each reviewer found to include mention. One does this by multiplying the number of yeses and dividing by 100: (70 × 65)/100 = 45.5.
3. Add the two numbers obtained in steps 1 and 2 and divide by 100 to get a proportion for *chance agreement:* (10.5 + 45.5)/100 = 0.56.

The *observed agreement* is 20% + 55% = 75%, or 0.75. Therefore the agreement beyond chance is 0.75 – 0.56 = 0.19: the numerator.

The *agreement possible beyond chance* is 100% minus the chance agreement of 56%, or 1 – 0.56 = 0.44: the denominator.

$$\kappa = \frac{0.19}{0.44};$$

$$\kappa = 0.43.$$

What is a "high" kappa? Some experts have attached the following qualitative terms to kappas: 0.0–0.2 = slight, 0.2–0.4 = fair, 0.4–0.6 = moderate, 0.6–0.8 = substantial, and 0.8–0.10 = almost perfect.

How can an evaluator achieve substantial or almost perfect agreement—reliability—among reviewers? By making certain that all reviewers collect and record data on exactly the same topics and that they agree in advance on what each important variable means. The "fair" kappa of 0.43 obtained by the reviewers in the example above may be due to differences between the reviewers' and the evaluator's definitions, the evaluator's poor training of the reviewers in the use of the definitions, and/or mistakes in coding.

Searching for Missing Data

The evaluator should review the first completed data collection instruments as soon as they are available, before any data are entered. In any study using self-administered written surveys, especially mailed questionnaires, the evaluator can expect to find some survey items unanswered. Respondents may not answer questions for many reasons. For example, they may not want to answer particular questions, they may simply miss items because they do not see them, or they may not understand what they are being asked to do. Some respondents may not understand the directions for completing the survey or the questions because the questionnaire requires them to read too much or is written at a level beyond their reading capabilities. Respondents may be unsure about what methods they should use in responding (e.g., whether they should fill in boxes completely or mark them with checks, whether they should circle the correct answers). They may find that questions are presented in a format that is difficult to use, such as the one in Example 7.4.

Example 7.4 A Question That May Be Confusing

Please mark an X through the choice that best describes you. Please answer each question.

	0 	1 	2 	3 
32. How often over the past year have *you* told others that you would hurt them?	Never	Sometimes	Lots of times	Almost every day
33. How often over the past year have *you* slapped, punched, or hit someone *before* they hit you?	Never	Sometimes	Lots of times	Almost every day
34. How often over the past year have *you* slapped, hit, or punched someone *after* they hit you?	Never	Sometimes	Lots of times	Almost every day
35 How often over the past year have *you* beaten up someone?	Never	Sometimes	Lots of times	Almost every day
36. How often over the past year have *you* attacked or stabbed someone with a knife?	Never	Sometimes	Lots of times	Almost every day

STOP DID YOU MARK ONE ANSWER TO EACH QUESTION EVEN IF YOUR ANSWER IS NEVER?

In this example, the respondent has answered just one question even though he or she was asked (and reminded) to answer all of the questions. What do the unanswered items mean? Has the respondent declined to answer the questions because he or she never does the actions described in them? If so, why didn't the respondent mark "never"? In fact, it is not uncommon for respondents on self-administered surveys to answer only those questions that they believe are relevant to them.

The evaluator who designed the question in Example 7.4 probably used this tabular format in an attempt to save space and to avoid repeating the response choices over and over. Respondents may find such a format confusing, however, because they are used to questionnaires in which items are formatted more like the one shown in Example 7.5.

Example 7.5 A Question Format That Is Relatively Easy to Understand

Has a doctor, other medical person, relative, friend, or anyone else ever been concerned about your drinking or suggested that you cut down?

No	☐
Yes, but not during the past 12 months	☐
Yes, during the past 12 months	☐

Confusing question formats lead to missing data because respondents do not know how to answer the questions. The evaluator may overcome some of the problems that cause respondents to misunderstand survey questions by conducting extensive cognitive pretests and pilot tests. *Cognitive pretests* are interviews with potential respondents in which they are asked to interpret each question and response choice on a survey. *Pilot tests* are tests of the survey questions in the actual evaluation setting. These two activities will tell the evaluator if a particular question format is unusable or some questions do not make sense, so that the problems can be addressed before the start of data collection.

No matter what the evaluator does, however, it is inevitable that some data will be missing during the evaluation. One of the major issues the evaluator faces is deciding on the best way to handle the problem of missing data. Say that you mail 100 questionnaires and get 95 back. You proudly announce that you have a 95% response rate for your questionnaire. Then, on closer examination, you discover that half the respondents did not answer question 5, and that each of the remaining 24 survey questions also has missing data. With all that missing information, you cannot really claim to have a 95% response rate for all questions.

What should an evaluator do about missing responses? In some program evaluations, it may be possible to go back to the respondents and ask them to answer the questions they left unanswered. In small studies where the respondents are known (such as within one clinic), the evaluator may be able to recontact the respondents easily. But in most surveys, collecting information a second time is usually impractical, if not impossible. Some evaluations use one or more anonymous data collection methods, and so the evaluators do not even know who the respondents are. In an institutional setting, the evaluator may have to go back to the institutional review board to get permission to contact the respondents a second time—a process that takes time and may delay completion of the evaluation.

In online data collection, surveys can be programmed so that the respondent must answer one question before proceeding to the next. This approach can help to minimize the amount of missing data. Some evaluation participants may find this restriction frustrating, however, and may refuse to complete the survey if they are unable to skip questions. Some evaluators believe that forcing respondents to answer every question is coercive and unethical. In their view, a program that forces a respondent to answer a question even if he or she prefers not to may be construed as violating the ethical principle of autonomy, or respect for individuals. Moreover, using this approach may result in unreliable information, as some people may enter meaningless answers to some questions just to be able to move on in the survey.

Entering the Data

Data entry is the process of getting the survey's responses into the computer. It usually takes one of three forms. In the first kind of data entry, someone enters data from a coded survey into a database management or spreadsheet program. The data are then saved as text or ASCII files, so that they can be exported into a statistical program such as SPSS, SAS, or Stata.

In the second type of data entry, data are entered directly into a statistical program such as SPSS, SAS, or Stata. Most evaluation studies still rely on simple spreadsheet programs (such as Excel) or on relational databases (such as Oracle and Microsoft SQL server). Some database programs (e.g., Microsoft Access and Visual Basic) provide interface builders for data entry, which allow the evaluator to format the screen to look like the data collection form.

In the third form of data entry used in evaluation studies, the respondent or interviewer enters responses directly into the computer. Data entry of this type is associated with computer-assisted interviewing, online surveys, and scanned surveys. The responses are automatically entered into database management systems or statistical programs (usually through special translation software). Programs are also available that will automatically convert one file format into another (say, from SAS to Stata).

Each data entry, database management, and statistical program has its own conventions and terminology. Some programs refer to entering data as setting up a "record" for each respondent. The record consists of the person's unique ID (identification code) and the person's "observations" (response choices, scores, comments, and so on). Other programs consider the unit of analysis (such as the person) as the observation, and the data collected on each observation are referred to as "variables" or "fields."

Example 7.6 shows a simple data set for 6 people.

Example 7.6 Data on Six People

RESPID	GENDER	MARRIED	CHILDREN	GUILTY	REPORT
1	1	3	2	1	1
2	2	4	1	3	2
3	2	3	2	3	2
4	1	3	2	1	2
5	1	1	1	1	2
6	1	3	1	3	1

In this example, the table is organized so that, except for the first column, the respondents' identification (RESPID) numbers constitute the rows and the data on the respondents are the columns. That is, person 2's data are 2, 4, 1, 3, and 2. Many statistical programs require the user to tell the computer where on the data line a variable is located. For instance, in Example 7.6 the person's gender is called GENDER, and data on gender can be found in column 2. Feeling guilty because of drinking is called GUILT, and the data for this variable can be found in column 5.

Database management programs, statistical programs, and computer-assisted surveys with automatic data entry can facilitate the accuracy of data entry when they are programmed to allow the entry of only legal codes. For instance, if the codes should be entered as 001, 002, and so on, up to 010, the user can write rules so that an entry of 01 or 10 is not permitted—that is, if anyone tries to enter 01 or 10, the program will respond with an error message. With minimal programming, such software can also check each entry to ensure that it is consistent with previously entered data and that skip patterns in the questionnaire are respected. That is, the program can make sure that the fields for questions that are to be skipped by some respondents are coded as skips and not as missing data. Designing a computer-assisted data entry protocol requires skill and time. The evaluator should never regard any such protocol as error-free until it has been tested and retested in the field.

Cleaning the Data

Once the data are entered, they need to be cleaned. When a data set is clean, anyone who uses it will get the same results when running analyses. Data become "dirty" for a number of reasons, including miscoding, incorrect data entry, and missing responses. To avoid dirty data, the evaluator must make sure that coders and data entry personnel are experienced, well trained, and properly supervised. One way of checking the data is to compare variable values against preset maximum and minimum levels; if, for example, someone enters 50 when the maximum is 5, an error has clearly occurred. The evaluator can also minimize errors by making sure that the coding scheme distinguishes truly missing data (no response or no data) from responses of "don't know" or "not applicable."

The evaluator should run frequencies (i.e., tabulations of the responses to each survey question) on the data as soon as about 10% of the responses are in, and then run them again and again until it is clear that the survey is running smoothly. If the data set is relatively small, the evaluator can visually scan the frequencies for errors. For large databases with many records, variables, skip patterns, and open-ended text responses, a systematic computerized check may be required. All leading statistical programs provide for cleaning specifications that can be used during data entry and later as a separate data cleaning process.

Several other problems may require the evaluator to clean up the data. These include information collection measures that have not been completed at all, others that have been only partially completed, and still others that contain data that are very different from those of the average evaluation participant.

Information Collection Measures Not Completed

Invariably, some information collection activities will not be completed. For instance, some mailed surveys will not be returned regardless of how persuasive the evaluator's follow-up methods are. If the proportion of nonrespondents in your study is large, then you must compare the subjects from whom you have no data against the respondents from whom you have data. You can do this by comparing respondents and nonrespondents in terms of their demographic characteristics (age, gender, ethnicity, zip code, and so on) as in Example 7.7.

Example 7.7 One Way to Deal With Nonresponse

An e-mail survey is conducted to find out if patients at the Community Clinic who enrolled in an online health education program changed their health habits for the better. The evaluators send surveys to 100 patients, and 70 respond. The evaluators are concerned that responding patients and nonresponding patients differ in age. To account for the 30% nonresponse rate, they do the following:

1. They calculate the proportion of responders who are 25 years of age or younger and the proportion who are 26 years of age or older. They find that 28 of the 70 responders, or 40%, are 25 or under, and 42, or 60%, are 26 or older.
2. They hypothesize that all 30 nonresponders are 26 years of age or older, for a total in this age group of 30 + 42, or 72. This means that 72% of the sample may be 26 years or older, rather than the 60% the evaluators originally calculated.
3. They reason that it is unlikely that all nonresponders are 26 years and older. Some must be 25 years or younger, but how many? To solve the mystery, they telephone a random sample of 10 nonresponders, and they find that 7 are 25 or younger. They then use the following formula, which calculates the 95% confidence limits of a point (in this case, the percentage) estimate:

   P (the true proportion of students 25 years or younger) $= 1.96, \sqrt{PQ/n}$

or

$$1.96\sqrt{(.7)(.8)/10} = .28.$$

The probable answer for the 10 nonresponders is .70 – .28. Somewhere between 41% and 98% of the 30 nonresponders are 26 years and older. The evaluators can now guess that 42 (the responders who are 26 years of age and older) plus 17 to 30 patients are 26 years or older. This means that between 59% (17 + 42) and 72% (42 + 72) are in the older age group.

As you can see, the spread of possibilities is large. In fact, low response can ruin the value of a particular data collection activity.

It is important that evaluators plan to collect data on nonrespondents. If a survey has a low response rate but the evaluator can show that responders and nonresponders are similar, this strengthens the justification for accepting the survey's findings as legitimate. Sometimes evaluators need to be ingenious when comparing responders and nonresponders. If you are conducting an anonymous mailed survey, for example, you might compare responders and nonresponders by zip code. For an online survey, you might compare the number of returns from ".com" or ".net" addresses with the number from ".org" or ".edu" addresses.

To minimize low response rates, the evaluator must make sure that all data collection is meaningful to the intended participants. Is the topic important enough so that they feel compelled to answer the questions? The evaluator must also be sure to respect the rules of confidentiality. In addition, the level of reading ability that the instrument requires as well as its format and the aptness of the language it uses should be checked through pretesting and scientific translation. If the reading level is too high, or the format is cluttered, or the translation is poor (any one will do), potential respondents will ignore the survey. For interview surveys, the evaluator must spend the time and money necessary to train interviewers well and to monitor their work on an ongoing basis. Respondents will not complete surveys if they do not understand or like the interviewers. Response rates can sometimes be improved by offers of financial or other incentives (such as gifts or gift certificates) to encourage respondents to complete surveys. Follow-up activities such as contacting respondents with reminders through e-mail, conventional mail, or telephone can also be helpful.

Evaluators often use a statistical method called *weighting* to make up for nonresponse. Suppose that you expect 50% of men and 50% of women in a sample to complete a survey, but only 40% of men do. In such a case, you can weight the men's returns so that they are equivalent to 50%. There are several strategies for weighting, among them logistic regression analysis. In this method, the existence or nonexistence of a response is considered a dichotomous dependent variable and other variables are used to predict it. Dichotomous variables are divided into two components. For instance, if the variable age is dichotomous, then it is divided into two parts, such as 65 and older and 64 and younger. Scores can be dichotomized: 50 and under and 51 and older. Practically any variable can be dichotomized.

Suppose that you have information on age and gender, *and* you can predict whether or not a person responded using these two variables—that is, your respondents and nonrespondents differ on these characteristics. Logistic regression provides you with an estimate of the probability that a given respondent's data will be missing. The probabilities are assigned as weights for all cases. Cases that have missing data are given higher weights. All statistical software programs include mechanisms for weighting responses.

Information Collection Measures Only Partially Completed

Statisticians often *impute,* or estimate based on known information, how respondents would have answered particular questions if they had chosen to. Suppose you are conducting an evaluation of a program to teach people to be wise consumers of Internet-based health information. You ask all participants how much time they spend online searching for health information, but about 15 people do not answer the question. One method you might use to estimate what those 15 people would have reported is to identify others in the sample with similar health conditions or other variables of interest (such as age or education), compute the average of the time reported by those individuals, and assign that average to each of the 15 nonresponders.

Many researchers have mixed feelings about imputation. Little consensus is available about the validity of imputed data. If you choose to impute, you should consider analyzing your data both with and without the missing values replaced, and then compare the results to make certain that the method of replacement did not lead to very different interpretations.

Outliers

Outliers are pieces of data or observations that appear inconsistent with the rest of the data set. They may be detected by a statistical program's built-in checks, or the evaluator may discover them by running frequencies and other descriptive statistics and checking the results against acceptable values. For instance, suppose that you survey 50 people to find out if they like a particular movie. You review the returns and find that 48 respondents assigned ratings of 2, 3, and 4 on a scale of 1 (*hated it*) to 5 (*loved it*). One respondent is consistently negative and assigns ratings of 1 to all 75 questions about the movie. Another respondent assigns ratings of 5 to all 75 questions. These two people may be outliers—the question is what to do about them.

Many researchers simply discard outliers from their data analyses. Each evaluator must decide on a case-by-case basis what to do with data that clearly deviate from the norm. Such decisions should be made with caution: When you discard seemingly deviant data, you may also be tossing out important information. Methods of detecting outliers include regression analysis and formal tests that assume that variables are normally distributed. (See Chapter 8 for a discussion of the normal distribution.)

Data in Need of Recoding

Data management may continue until the last analysis is performed. For example, as time goes on, you may want to add additional people to your survey sample, or you may want to add additional variables. These activities will require coding, data entry, and data cleaning. You may need to recode the data you have collected, as illustrated in Example 7.8.

Example 7.8 Recoding Data

Example 1: A program is initiated to encourage 15 communities to participate in collaborative health services research. After the 2-day program is completed, the evaluators interview the participants to find out whether their attitudes have changed. The evaluators hypothesize that the older participants are more interested than the younger ones in collaboration. They have data on each person's birth date, and preliminary analysis reveals that the participants' ages range from 26 to 71. The median age of the sample is 42. The evaluators decide to compare the attitudes of older and younger people. They recode the data to make two age categories: 42 and younger and 43 and older.

Example 2: The evaluators of an intervention to improve family function adopt a standardized measure of family stability. The measure has 10 items, each rated on a scale of 1 to 5. The evaluators discover that 7 of the items are worded so that a score of 1 is high and a score of 5 is low. On the other 3 items, a score of 5 is high and a score of 1 is low. Because the evaluators want a total score of family stability, they have to recode the three reverse-worded questions so that a 1 is scored as if it were a 5, a 2 as if it were a 4, and so on. If they do not recode the data, the items will not have a common direction, and the evaluators will be unable to sum them to get a score.

Creating the Final Data Set for Analysis

Once the data are entered, evaluators typically transfer the database to a statistical or qualitative software program. (Although some statistical software programs have data management capabilities, special database management programs tend to allow users to edit more easily.) Once the analysis begins, the evaluator may alter the characteristics of some of the variables so that continuous variables are dichotomized and new categories and derived variables are created. Example 7.9 shows how this works.

Example 7.9 On the Way to an Analytic Data Set

Continuous Variables Are Dichotomized

1. Scores on the DRINK measure range from 1 to 100. For the analysis, the evaluators compare persons with scores of 25 and less with those who achieved 26 or more.
2. The Alcohol-Related Problems Screen (ARPS) asks participants to complete this question:

During the past 12 months, how often did you have six or more drinks of alcohol at one sitting?

	Please check one
Daily or almost daily.	❐
Four or five times a week.	❐
Two or three times a week.	❐
Two to four times a month.	❐
One time a month or less.	❐
Never.	❐

Because the evaluators are concerned with comparing people who drink in great excess of recommended limits with those who do not, they dichotomize the answers to this question by comparing the proportion of respondents who answer "never" to those who give any other response.

New Categories Are Created

The ARPS lists a number of medications and asks respondents to check off the ones they are taking. The evaluators decide to group the specific medications into categories, such as antidepressants, antihypertensives, and so on.

Derived Variables Are Produced

The evaluators create a variable called "drink years" by multiplying years of drinking times number of drinks per day.

Storing and Archiving the Data Set

The evaluator must be sure to create backup copies of the database and the analytic data set (before conversion to the statistical program). In addition, the evaluator must document in the codebook all changes made to the database or data set. Once the evaluator is confident that the data are clean and that all changes to the database are final, then the analysis can begin. The evaluator must then create a backup of the final, analytic database and store it in a safe place.

Summary and Transition to the Next Chapter on Data Analysis

This chapter has discussed the activities that evaluators engage in to ensure the proper management of evaluation data so that those data can be analyzed. These activities include drafting an analysis plan, creating a codebook, establishing coder reliability, reviewing data collection instruments for incomplete or missing data, entering data into a database, cleaning the data, creating the final data set, and archiving the data set.

The next chapter focuses on the types of analysis that are particularly useful in program evaluations. It describes how the evaluator should go about determining the characteristics of the data that describe or measure each main variable and that help determine the analytic strategy. The next chapter also discusses practical as well as statistical meaning through the use of confidence intervals. Special statistical tests involving odds and risks are discussed because of their importance in evaluation studies. In addition, the chapter discusses the analysis of qualitative data and meta-analysis.

Exercises

EXERCISE 1

Directions

Interpret the codes for this question asked on a telephone interview:

> [T_9] How much of the time during the PAST 4 WEEKS have you felt calm and peaceful? Would you say all of the time, most of the time, some of the time, a little of the time, or none of the time?

All of the time	☐	(100)
Most of the time	☐	(75)
Some of the time	☐	(50)
A little of the time	☐	(25)
None of the time	☐	(0)
DON'T KNOW	☐	(8)
REFUSED	☐	(9)

EXERCISE 2

Directions

Assign codes to this set of questions asked during the same telephone interview as in Exercise 1.

> My illness has strengthened my faith. Would you say this statement is very much, quite a bit, somewhat, a little bit, or not at all true?

Very much	☐
Quite a bit	☐
Somewhat	☐
A little bit	☐
Not at all	☐
DON'T KNOW	☐
REFUSED	☐

> How much of the time during the LAST 4 WEEKS have you wished that you could change your mind about the kind of treatment you chose for prostate cancer? Would you say all of the time, most of the time, a good bit of the time, some of the time, a little of the time, or none of the time?

All of the time	☐
Most of the time	☐
A good bit of the time	☐
Some of the time	☐
A little of the time	☐
None of the time	☐
DON'T KNOW	☐
REFUSED	☐

Suggested Readings

Hulley, S. B., Cummings, S. R., Browner, W. S., Grady, D., Hearst, N., & Newman, T. B. (2001). *Designing clinical research* (2nd ed.). Philadelphia: Lippincott Williams & Wilkins.

Chapter 16 of this volume provides an excellent overview of the tasks needed for data entry, data editing, and analysis. The chapter also reviews the programs needed in database design and management.

Shi, L. (1997). *Health services research methods.* Albany, NY: Delmar.

In Chapter 13 of this book, the author covers coding, the codebook itself, and data entry.

Trochim, W. M. K. (2000) *The research methods knowledge base* (2nd ed.). Cincinnati, OH: Atomic Dog.

This comprehensive textbook (available online at http://trochim.human.cornell.edu/kb) addresses all of the topics in a typical introductory undergraduate or graduate course in social research methods. It covers the entire research process, including data management (in a brief discussion) and data analysis.

Purpose of This Chapter

Program evaluators use statistical methods to analyze and summarize data and to come to conclusions about program improvement and effectiveness that can be applied to planning and policy. The statistical methods they use are derived from the fields of biostatistics and epidemiology. *Biostatistics* refers to the application of statistics to biological and health sciences. *Epidemiology* is the study of the origins, distribution, and control of disease in human populations (not individuals). Choosing a method to analyze program evaluation data is an intellectual process in which statistical technology and the outcomes of health interventions converge. This chapter discusses key components of that intellectual process.

Specifically, this chapter addresses the associations among the evaluation questions, design, sample, and data sources and shows how the choice of analysis is as much a function of the characteristics of the evaluation questions and the quality of the data available to the evaluator as it is dependent on the evaluator's ability to identify the appropriate statistical technique. The chapter does not focus on how evaluators program data for analysis or perform statistical operations (these topics are covered better in statistics texts and computer manuals), but it does discuss the pertinent uses of the procedures that health program evaluators most commonly employ. Because hypothesis testing, confidence intervals, the concepts of odds and risk, and meta-analyses are particularly important topics in evaluation, they receive special attention here. Because evaluators sometimes use qualitative methods along with statistical methods, the chapter includes discussion of a typical qualitative method: content analysis.

8 Analyzing Evaluation Data

A Reader's Guide to Chapter 8

A Suitable Analysis: Starting With the Evaluation Questions

To select the most suitable analysis for evaluation, the evaluator must answer these questions:

1. What independent and dependent variables are contained within each evaluation question (and its associated standard)?
2. In what form or from what kind of scale will data be provided? Data can come from nominal scales (e.g., male, female), ordinal scales (e.g., high, medium, low), or numerical scales (e.g., a score of 30 out of 100 possible points).
3. What statistical methods may be used to answer the evaluation question, given its independent and dependent variables?
4. Do the evaluation's data meet all of the assumptions of the statistical tests? (For example, is the sample size sufficient? Are the data "normally distributed"?)

Measurement Scales and Their Data

A first step in selecting a statistical method is to identify the type of data resulting from each measure used to collect data on the independent and dependent variables. A variable is a characteristic that is measurable. For example, a patient's weight is a variable, and all persons weighing 55 kilograms have the same numerical weight. A patient's satisfaction is also a variable. In this case, however, a numerical scale for measuring satisfaction has to be devised and rules must be created for its interpretation. For example, in Evaluation A, patient satisfaction might be measured on a scale of 1 to 100, with 1 corresponding to the very lowest satisfaction and 100 to the very highest. In Evaluation B, patient satisfaction might be measured through a count of the number of people who return each year for services; if the number equals a preset standard, then participants will be considered satisfied.

Independent variables are used to explain or predict a program's outcomes (or dependent variables). Typical independent variables in program evaluations include group membership (experimental and control), health status (excellent, very good, good, fair, poor), age, and other demographic and health characteristics. Typical dependent variables are "outcomes" such as health status (including physical, social, and psychological functioning), mortality, efficiency, quality of care, and learning.

Evaluators most often rely on three types of measurement scales, termed *nominal, ordinal,* and *numerical.* The data produced by these scales are called nominal, ordinal, and numerical (continuous or discrete) data or variables or observations.

Nominal Scales

Nominal scales produce data that fit into categories. Because of this, they are sometimes called *categorical.* For example:

1. What is the patient's gender?	**Check one**
Male	☐
Female	☐
2. Describe the type of lung cancer.	**Check one**
Small cell	☐
Large cell	☐
Oat cell	☐
Squamous cell	☐

Both of the questions above categorize the responses and require the respondent to "name" the category into which the data fit. When nominal data take on one of two values (e.g., the category of disease is present or absent), they are termed *dichotomous* (as in "divided in two").

Typically, nominal data are presented as percentages and proportions (e.g., 50 of 100 individuals in the sample, or 50%, were male). The measure used to describe the center of their distribution is the *mode,* or the number of observations that appears most frequently.

Ordinal Scales

If an inherent order exists among categories, the data come from an ordinal scale. For example:

How much education have you completed?	**Circle one**
Never finished high school	1
High school graduate, but no college	2
Some college	3
College graduate	4
Stage of tumor	**Circle one**
Duke's A	1
Duke's B	2
Duke's C	3
Duke's D	4

Table 8.1 Measurement Scales: Nominal, Ordinal, and Numerical Variables

Measurement Scale and Type of Data	*Examples*	*Comments*
Nominal	Type of disease (small cell, large cell, oat cell, squamous cell cancer), source of transfused blood (autologous donation, homologous donation); ethnicity; gender	Observations belong to categories. Observations have no inherent order of importance. Observations are sometimes called categorical. When data assume two values (yes the disease is present or no it is not), they are termed *dichotomous.* Percentages and proportions are used to describe nominal data, and the mode is used to measure the midpoint.
Ordinal	Staging of disease (carcinoma of the cervix is staged from 0 to IV, where stage 0 is in situ and stage IV represents carcinoma extending beyond the pelvis); socioeconomic status	Order exists among the categories; that is, one observation is greater than the other. Percentages and proportions are used to describe ordinal data; the measure of the center of the distribution of the data is often the median.
Numerical	Continuous numerical scales (scores on a test of health status); age; height; length of survival; laboratory values (serum glucose, sodium potassium) Discrete numerical scales (number of visits to a nurse practitioner, number of falls)	Differences between numbers have meaning on a numerical scale (e.g., higher scores mean better achievement than lower scores, and a difference between 12 and 13 has the same meaning as a difference between 99 and 100). Some statisticians distinguish between interval scales (arbitrary 0 point as in the Fahrenheit scale) and ratio scales (with an absolute 0 as in the Kelvin scale); in program evaluation, these measures are treated the same statistically, so they are combined here as numerical. Means and standard deviations are used to describe numerical data.

Ordinal scales produce data that can be used to classify diseases according to their severity. For example, colorectal tumors are classified in order, from Duke's A (in situ) to Duke's D (systemic disease). Ordinal scales typically are seen in questions that call for ratings of health (excellent, very good, good, fair, poor, very poor), agreement (strongly agree, agree, disagree, strongly disagree), and the probability that something is present (definitely present, probably present, probably not present, definitely not present).

Ordinal data are presented as percentages and proportions, and the center of the distribution is often expressed as the *median,* or the observation that divides the distribution into halves. The median is equal to the 50th percentile.

Numerical Scales

When differences between the numbers on a scale have a meaning, the scale is called *numerical.* For example, age is a numerical variable; weight, length of survival, birth weight, and many laboratory values are also numerical variables. Numerical data are amenable to precision; that is, the evaluator can obtain data on age, for example, to the nearest second.

Numerical data may be *continuous,* such as height, weight, and age. Or they may be *discrete,* such as numbers of visits to this clinic, numbers of previous pregnancies. Means and standard deviations are used to summarize the values of numerical measures.

Table 8.1 contrasts the three types of scales and data. Understanding the differences among them is essential to the evaluator in choosing methods of analysis.

Selecting a Method of Analysis

The evaluator's choice of the method to use in analyzing the data for each evaluation question is dependent on the following:

- Whether the independent variable is nominal, ordinal, or numerical
- The number of independent variables
- Whether the dependent variable is nominal, ordinal, or numerical
- The number of dependent variables
- Whether the design, sampling, and quality of the data meet the assumptions of the statistical method

Example 8.1 shows the relationships among evaluation questions, independent and dependent variables, research design and sample, types of measures, and data analysis.

Example 8.1 Analyzing Evaluation Data: Connections Among Questions, Designs, Samples, Measures, and Analysis

Evaluation question: Is quality of life satisfactory?

Standard: A statistically significant difference in quality of life favoring program versus control group participants

Independent variable: Group membership (program participants versus controls)

Design: An experimental design with concurrent controls

Sampling: Eligible participants are assigned at random to experimental or control group; 150 participants are in each group (a statistically derived sample size).

Dependent variable: Quality of life

Types of data: Group membership (nominal data), quality of life (continuous numerical data from the CARES Questionnaire, a 100-point survey in which higher scores mean better quality)

Analysis: A two-sample independent groups *t* test

Justification for the analysis: This *t* test is appropriate when the independent variable is measured on a nominal scale and the dependent variable is measured on a numerical scale. In this case, the assumptions of a *t* test are met. These assumptions are that each group has a sample size of at least 30, the sizes of both groups are about equal, the two groups are independent (an assumption that is met most easily with a strong evaluation design and a high-quality data collection effort), and the data are normally distributed. (If one of these assumptions is seriously violated, other rigorous analytic methods should be used, such as the Wilcoxon rank-sum test, also called the Mann-Whitney *U* test. This test makes no assumption about the normality of the distribution; whereas the *t* is termed *parametric,* this test is one of a number called *nonparametric.*)

The classification of data into nominal, ordinal, and numerical is a guide for the program evaluator. Individual evaluations and sets of data will vary. For the sake of simplicity, for example, evaluators sometimes treat independent variables that are measured on an ordinal scale as if they were nominal. Dependent variables that are measured on an ordinal scale are often treated as if they were numerical. Other exceptions exist as well. Example 8.2 illustrates some of these exceptions.

Example 8.2 Some Exceptions: Taking Liberties With Nominal, Ordinal, and Numerical Data

Evaluation A

Evaluation question: How do patients with differing severity of illness compare in their satisfaction with the nurse-run clinics?

Independent variable: Extent of illness

Measurement scale: Ordinal: severe, moderate, mild in choosing an analytic method; treat severe, moderate, and mild as nominal

Dependent variable: Satisfaction (with clinic)

Measurement scale: Numerical (continuous): scores on the Patient Satisfaction Survey

Analysis: One-way ANOVA (presuming the necessary assumptions are met)

Evaluation B

Evaluation question: How do people of differing ages compare in their satisfaction with their health care?

Independent variable: Age

Measurement scale: Numerical (continuous); in choosing an analytic method, treat as nominal (dichotomous) with only two values—under 55 years and over 55 years

Dependent variable: Numerical: scores on the Patient Satisfaction Survey

Analysis: t test (presuming the necessary assumptions are met)

Unfortunately, no definitive rules can be set for all evaluations and their data. Table 8.2, however, provides a general guide to the selection of 15 of the most commonly used data-analytic methods. To use this guide, the evaluator must identify the number and measurement characteristics of the independent and dependent variables. For simplicity, the guide omits ordinal variables. When independent variables are measured on an ordinal scale, they are often treated as if they were nominal. For example, in an evaluation that aims to predict the outcomes of participation in a program for patients with good, fair, and poor functional status, good, fair, and poor (ordinal, independent variables) may be regarded as nominal. When dependent variables are measured on an ordinal scale, they are habitually treated as if they were numerical. For example, if the dependent variable in a nutrition program is the length of time a weight-loss diet is maintained (less than 3 months, between 3 and 6 months, and more than 6 months) by men and women with differing motivations to diet, the dependent, ordinal variable can, for the sake of the analysis, be regarded as numerical.

The evaluator must remember to check the assumptions (in a statistics text or computer manual) before conducting any statistical analysis. If the evaluation's data do not meet the assumptions, the evaluator should look for other statistical methods to use. The fields of biostatistics and epidemiology are advancing constantly, and new methods may be emerging that could meet the needs of a particular program evaluation.

Hypothesis Testing and *p* Values: Statistical Significance

Evaluators often compare two or more groups to find out if differences in outcome exist that favor a program; if differences are present, the evaluators examine the magnitude of those differences for significance. Consider Example 8.3.

Table 8.2 A General Guide to Data-Analytic Methods in Program Evaluation

Sample Questions	*Type of Data: Independent Variable*	*Type of Data: Dependent Variable*	*Analytic Method*
For questions with one independent and one dependent variable			
Do experimental and control patients differ in their use or failure to use mental health services?	Nominal: group (experimental and control)	Nominal: use of mental health services (used services or did not)	Chi-square; Fisher's exact test; relative risk (risk ratio); odds ratio
How do the experimental and control groups compare in their attitudes (measured by their scores on the Attitude Survey)?	Nominal (dichotomous): group (experimental and control)	Numerical (attitude scores)	Independent samples, *t* test
How do teens in the U.S., Canada, and England compare in their attitudes (measured by their scores on the Attitude Survey)?	Nominal (more than two values: U.S., Canada, and England)	Numerical (attitude scores)	One-way ANOVA (uses the *F* test)
Do high scores on the Attitude Survey predict high scores on the Knowledge Test?	Numerical (attitude scores)	Numerical (knowledge scores)	Regression (when neither variable is independent or dependent, use correlation)
For questions with two or more independent variables			
Do men and women in the experimental and control programs differ in whether or not they adhered to a diet?	Nominal (gender, group)	Nominal (adhered or did not adhere to a diet)	Log-linear
Do men and women with differing scores on the Knowledge Test differ in whether or not they adhered to a diet?	Nominal (gender) and numerical (knowledge scores)	Nominal and dichotomous (adhered or did not adhere to a diet)	Logistic regression
How do men and women in the experimental and control programs compare in their attitudes (measured by their scores on the Attitude Survey)?	Nominal (gender and group)	Numerical (attitude scores)	Analysis of variance (ANOVA)

Sample Questions	*Type of Data: Independent Variable*	*Type of Data: Dependent Variable*	*Analytic Method*
How are age and income and years living in the community related to attitudes (measured by scores on the Attitude Survey)?	Numerical (age and income and years living in the community)	Numerical (attitude scores)	Multiple regression
How do men and women in the experimental and control programs compare in their attitudes (measured by their scores on the Attitude Survey) when their level of education is controlled for?	Nominal (gender and group) with confounding factors (such as education)	Numerical (attitude scores)	Analysis of covariance (ANCOVA)
For questions with two or more independent and dependent variables			
How do men and women in the experimental and control programs compare in their attitude and knowledge scores?	Nominal (gender and group)	Numerical (scores on two measures: attitudes and knowledge)	Multivariate analysis of variance (MANOVA)

Example 8.3 Comparing Two Groups

Evaluation question: Do participants improve in their knowledge of how to interpret food-label information in making dietary choices?

Standards:

1. A statistically significant difference in knowledge between participants and nonparticipants must be found. The difference in scores must be at least 15 points.
2. If a 15-point difference is found, participants will be studied for 2 years to determine the extent to which the knowledge is retained. The scores must be maintained (no significant differences) over the 2-year period.

Measurements: Knowledge is measured on the Dietary Choices Test, a 25-item self-administered test.

Analysis: A *t* test will be used to compare the two groups in their knowledge. Scores will be computed a second time, and a *t* test will be used to compare the average or mean differences over time.

In the evaluation described in Example 8.3, tests of statistical significance are called for twice: to compare participants and nonparticipants at one point in time and to compare the same participants' scores over time. In addition, the evaluators stipulate that for the scores to have practical meaning, a 15-point difference between participants and nonparticipants must be obtained and sustained. With experience, health program evaluators have found that, in a number of situations, statistical significance is sometimes insufficient evidence of a program's merit. With very large samples, for example, very small differences in numerical values (such as scores on an achievement test or laboratory values) can be statistically significant but have little practical, educational, or clinical meaning and may actually incur more costs than benefits.

In the evaluation presented in Example 8.3, the standard includes a 15-point difference in test scores. If the difference between scores is statistically significant but only 10 points, then the program will not be considered significant in a practical sense.

Statistical significance and the p *value.* A statistically significant program evaluation effect is one that is probably due to a planned intervention rather than to some chance occurrence. To determine statistical significance, the evaluator restates the evaluation question ("Does a difference exist?") as a null hypothesis ("No difference exists") and sets the level of significance and the value that the test statistic must obtain to be significant. After this is completed, the calculations are performed. The following guidelines describe the steps the evaluator takes in conducting a hypothesis test and in determining statistical significance.

Guidelines for Hypothesis Testing, Statistical Significance, and *p* Values

1. *State the evaluation question as a null hypothesis.* The null hypothesis (H_0) is a statement that no difference exists between the averages or means of two groups. The following are typical null hypotheses in program evaluations:

    - No difference exists between the experimental program's mean and the control program's mean.
    - No difference exists between the sample's (the evaluation's participants) mean and the population's (the population from which the participants were sampled) mean.

    When evaluators find that a difference does not exist between means, they use the following terminology: "We failed to reject the null hypothesis." They do not say, "We accepted the null hypothesis." Failing to reject the null suggests that a difference probably exists between the means, say, between Program A and Program B. Until the evaluators examine the data, however, they do not know if A is favored or B is. When the evaluators have no advance knowledge of which is better, they use a two-tailed hypothesis test. When they have an alternative hypothesis in mind—say, A is larger (better) than B—they use a one-tailed test. Before they can describe the properties of the test, other activities must take place.

2. *State the level of significance for the statistical test (for example, the* t *test) being used.* The level of significance, when chosen before the test is performed, is called the alpha value (denoted by the Greek letter alpha: α). The alpha gives the probability of rejecting the null hypothesis when it is actually true. Tradition keeps the alpha value small—.05, .01, or .001—because among the last things an evaluator needs is to reject a null hypothesis when, in fact, it is true and there is no difference between group means.

   The p value is the probability that an observed result (or result of a statistical test) is due to chance (and not to the program). It is calculated *after* the statistical test. If the p value is less than alpha, then the null hypothesis is rejected.

   Current practice requires the specification of exact p values. That is, if the obtained p is .03, the evaluator should report that $p = .03$ rather than $p < .05$. Reporting the approximate p was common practice before the widespread use of computers (when statistical tables were the primary source of probabilities). This practice has not been eradicated, however. The merit of using the exact values can be seen in that, without them, a finding of $p = .06$ may be viewed as not significant, whereas a finding of $p = .05$ will be.

3. *Determine the value that the test statistic must attain to be significant.* Such values can be found in statistical tables. For example, for the z distribution (a standard, normal distribution) with an alpha of .05 and a two-tailed test, tabular values (found in practically all statistics textbooks) show that the area of acceptance for the null hypothesis is the central 95% of the z distribution and that the areas of rejection are 2.5% of the area in each tail. The value of z (found in statistical tables) that defines these areas is –1.96 for the lower tail and +1.96 for the upper tail. If the test statistic is less than –1.96 or greater than +1.96, it will be rejected. Figure 8.1 illustrates the areas of acceptance and rejection in a standard normal distribution using $\alpha = .05$.

4. *Perform the calculation.* Numerous software packages are available for making statistical computations. To choose among them, the evaluator can consult computing software reviews in professional journals of statistics, epidemiology, and medicine or ask colleagues for recommendations. Each of the packages includes a manual (and/or tutorial) that contains instructions for how to enter data and perform the calculations.

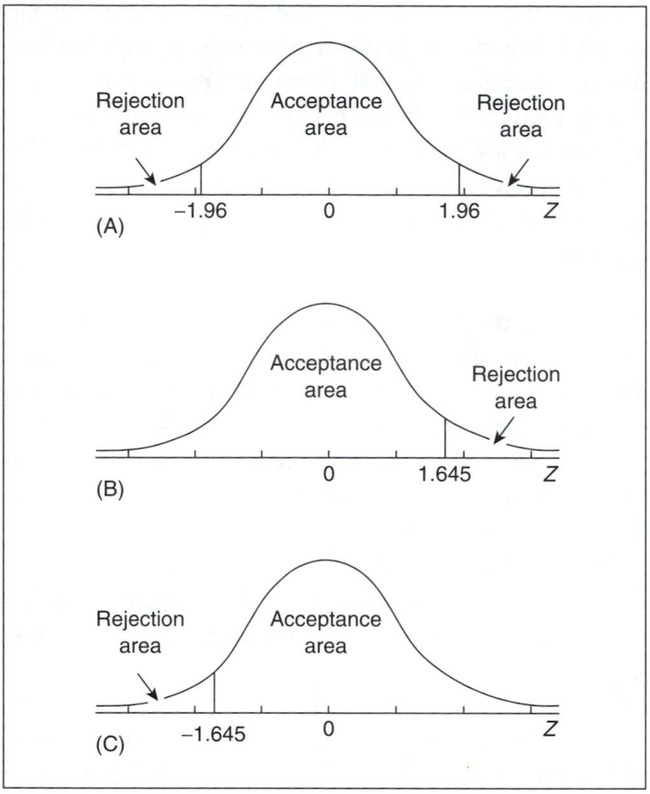

Figure 8.1. Defining Areas of Acceptance and Rejection in a Standard Normal Distribution Using $\alpha = .05$

SOURCE: B. Dawson-Saunders and R. Trapp. (1990). *Basic and clinical biostatistics* (New York: Appleton and Lange), p. 74; used by permission.

NOTE: (A) two-tailed or nondirectional, (B) one-tailed or directional upper tail, (C) one-tailed or directional lower tail.

Clinical or Practical Significance: Using Confidence Intervals

As noted above, the results of a statistical analysis may be significant, but not necessarily practical. In clinical research, this duality is called "statistical significance versus clinical significance." The following discussion is based on an editorial that appeared in the *Annals of Internal Medicine* in 1991 (for the complete reference, see the entry for Braitman in the "Suggested Readings" section of this chapter). Although that editorial refers to the clinical significance of a treatment for cancer, the issues addressed and the extreme clarity of the discussion make it especially useful for program evaluators.

Evaluation 1. Suppose that, in a large, multicenter evaluation of a program in pain management for cancer patients, 480 of 800 (60%) respond well to the new program, while 416 of the 800 (52%) do well in the traditional or standard program. Using a chi-square to assess the existence of a real difference between the two treatments, a p value of .001 is obtained. This value is the probability of obtaining by chance the 8-point (60% – 52%) difference between patients in the new and traditional programs or an even larger difference. The point estimate is 8 percentage points, but because of sampling and measurement errors (which always exist in evaluation research), the estimate is probably not identical to the true percentage difference between the two groups of patients. A confidence interval provides a plausible range for the true value. A confidence interval is computed from sample data that have a given probability that the unknown true value is located between them. Using a standard method, the 95% confidence interval (95% CI) of the 8-percentage-point difference comes out to be between 3% and 13%. A 95% CI means that about 95% of all such intervals would include the unknown true difference and 5% would not. Suppose, however, that given the side effects and other costs of the new program, the smallest practical and thus acceptable difference (determined during the standard-setting step of the evaluation process) is 15%; then the evaluator will conclude that the 8-percentage-point difference between interventions is not significant from a practical, health perspective although it is statistically significant.

Evaluation 2. Consider another evaluation with 15 of 25 patients (60%) responding to a new program in cancer pain management and 13 of 25 (52%) responding to a traditional program. The sample size is $\frac{1}{32}$ of that in the first example. The p value is .57 in this evaluation, in contrast to $p = .001$ in the larger evaluation. These ps correspond to the same observed 8-percentage-point difference. In this evaluation, the 95% CI extends from –19% to 35%; these values are statistically indistinguishable from the observed difference of 8 percentage points. The larger evaluation permits a more precise estimate of the true value. The greater width of the interval also shows the greater uncertainty that is produced in an estimate based on a smaller sample. Thus the use of a confidence interval enables the evaluator to assess statistical and practical significance.

Establishing Clinical or Practical Significance

A difference in outcome between two groups in a program evaluation is significant in a practical sense when its 95% confidence interval is completely above the smallest practical or clinically important difference, as shown in Figure 8.2. As this figure shows, the confidence interval (3% to 13%) obtained for Evaluation 1 falls below the desired 15-point difference; it is not practically significant. The difference between groups obtained in Evaluation 2 (–19% to 35%) contains the smallest difference, so no definite conclusion about practical and clinical significance is possible.

Eval.	% Responding to Treatment: New	% Responding to Treatment: Standard	*p* Value	Statistical Significance	Difference in % responding: Point Estimate	Difference in % responding: 95% CI	Clinical Significance
1	480/800 = 60%	416/800 = 52%	0.001	Yes	8%	3% to 13%	No
2	15/25 = 60%	13/25 = 52%	0.57	No	8%	–19% to 35%	Inconclusive
3	15/25 = 60%	9/25 = 36%	0.09	No	24%	–3% to 51%	Inconclusive
4	240/400 = 60%	144/400 = 36%	<0.0001	Yes	24%	17% to 31%	Yes

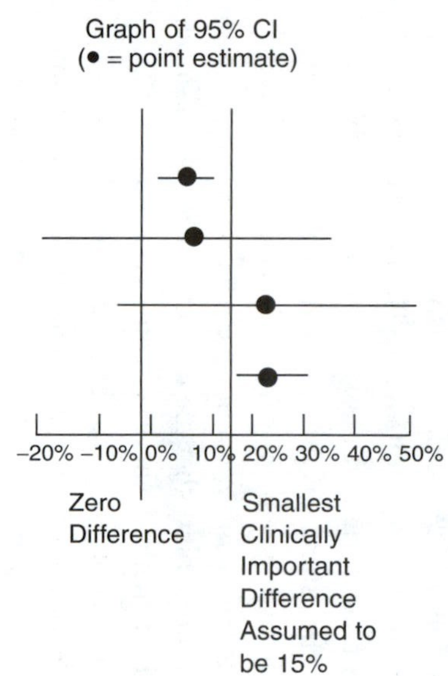

Figure 8.2. Statistical Significance and Clinical Significance Using 95% Confidence Intervals (CI) of Differences Between Patients in Two Programs

SOURCE: L. E. Braitman. (1991). Confidence intervals assess both clinical and statistical significance. *Annals of Internal Medicine*, *114*, 515–517; reproduced by permission.

Evaluation 3. In this evaluation, 15 of 25 (60%) and 9 of 25 (36%) of patients benefit from the new and traditional programs. The confidence interval for the difference (60% – 36% = 24%) is –3% to 51%. The *p* value (found in a table in a statistics text) is equal to or greater than .05, which is not statistically significant. The confidence interval and *p* are related; if the interval contains 0, then the *p* is not significant. In this case, 0% can be found in the –3% to 51% interval. But 0% is only one of many values inside the confidence interval. The evaluator cannot state, "No meaningful difference"; because much of the interval falls above the 15-point-difference cutoff, the results can be interpreted as practically or clinically inconclusive.

Evaluation 4. In this evaluation, 240 of 400 patients (60%) respond to the new program, while 144 of 400 (36%) respond to the traditional or standard one. The difference is 24% and the 95% CI is 17% to 31%. The difference is statistically ($p < .05$) and practically significant.

Proceed With Caution: Screening and Transforming Data

Before analyzing the data, the evaluator should review the entire data set. A first step is to screen for outliers and incorrect values. As noted in Chapter 7, outliers are observations that are not consistent with the rest of the data set. For example, an outlier might be a single clinic out of 15 clinics that has uncharacteristically low patient satisfaction scores. Including that clinic's data in the analysis might bias the results, but excluding it might do the same, and, in addition, the exclusion might be unethical. When outliers appear in the data set, the evaluator might run the main analysis twice: once with the outlier and once without it. In this way, the evaluator can determine the effects of the outlier and use that information in deciding how to handle it.

The evaluator should also screen the data for incorrect values—that is, erroneous statistics. For example, if an evaluator finds data on veterans who are 2 or 22 years of age in a study of a program to improve the health care of elderly veterans, it is likely that these ages represent errors in data entry.

Another issue that the evaluator should resolve before analysis is what do about *missing values*—that is, required data that have not been collected from an individual or other sampling unit. Suppose that you need information on nurses' attitudes toward their working conditions, but only 75 of 100 nurses in your sample respond to all questions on an attitude survey. If you require a complete set of information on all nurses for the analysis, then you must treat your evaluation's sample size as 75 and not 100 respondents. Missing values might also result from the failure of all or nearly all individuals in a sample to provide data on a variable. This can happen, for example, if nearly all nurses fail to respond to one or more items on the survey of their attitudes. In this situation, the evaluator should probably exclude the items from the analysis.

The evaluator may also need to transform some data—that is, change them from one type of scale to another. Linear transformations, which are made for convenience, involve changes in the means and in scaling factors. This occurs, for example, when the z transformation is used, and the mean of a distribution is expressed as 0 and its standard deviation (a measure of dispersion) is 1. A nonlinear transformation changes the shape of the distribution so that it becomes normal, allowing the evaluator to use statistical tests such as the t test. In rank transformations, the evaluator rank orders observations from lowest to highest. Such transformations are appropriate when observations are skewed.

Risk and Odds

Evaluators commonly assess risk and odds in evaluation studies. These are alternative ways of describing the likelihood that a particular outcome will occur. Suppose that you are conducting a survey to find out why a weight-loss program was not effective. You decide to survey the people in the program to find out the nature and characteristics of the problems they had with dieting. You find that out of every 100 people who have trouble dieting, 20 report frequent problems. To identify the risk of a person's having frequent problems, you divide the number of individuals reporting frequent problems by the number you are studying, or 20/100: The risk is 0.20. The odds of a person's having frequent problems are calculated differently. To get the odds, you subtract the number of persons with frequent problems (20) from the total (100) and use the result (80) as the denominator. Thus the odds of having frequent problems with dieting are 20/80, or 0.25. Table 8.3 shows the difference between risk and odds.

Table 8.3 Risk and Odds, Compared and Contrasted

Number of Persons With Outcome	*Risk*	*Odds*
20 of 100	20/100 = 0.20	20/80 = 0.25
40 of 100	40/100 = 0.40	40/60 = 0.66
50 of 100	50/100 = 0.50	50/50 = 1.00
90 of 100	90/100 = 0.90	90/10 = 9.00

Because assessing risk and calculating odds are really just different ways of talking about the same relationship, risk can be derived from odds, and vice versa. We can convert risk to odds by dividing it by 1 minus the risk, and we can convert odds to risk by dividing odds by 1 plus the odds:

$$\text{Odds} = \text{Risk}/(1 - \text{Risk}).$$

$$\text{Risk} = \text{Odds}/(1 + \text{Odds}).$$

When an outcome is infrequent, little difference exists in numerical values between odds and risk. When the outcome is frequent, however, differences emerge. If, for instance, 20 of 100 persons have frequent problems following a diet, the risk and odds are similar: 0.20 and 0.25, respectively. If 90 of 100 persons have frequent problems, then the risk is 0.90 and the odds are 9.00.

Odds Ratios and Relative Risk

Evaluators often use *odds ratios* to compare nominal dependent variables between groups. Odds ratios allow an evaluator to estimate the strength of the relationship between particular variables. For example, suppose that you have evidence that people who have trouble dieting also do not eat breakfast. (You have reason to believe that people who don't eat breakfast often decide to "snack" before lunchtime.) You want to check out the strength of the relationship between not eating breakfast and subsequent problems with keeping to a diet. You put together two groups of people: those who have problems adhering to a diet and those who do not. You ask them all, "Do you eat breakfast?" Their response choices are yes or no.

To analyze the responses, you might create a 2×2 table such as the following:

No Breakfast	Problems Adhering to a Weight-Loss Diet	
	Yes	No
Yes	A	B
No	C	D

This is a 2×2 table because it has two variables with two levels: breakfast (yes or no) and problems adhering (yes or no). Notice that the table has four cells for data entry. The two variables, "no breakfast" and "problems adhering," are nominal variables.

If you were interested only in whether statistical differences exist in the numbers of people in each of the cells, you could use the chi-square test. A chi-square test will not tell you about the strength of the relationship between the variables, however; it will only allow you to infer differences. An odds ratio, in contrast, will allow you to say something like this: "The odds of having problems adhering to a diet are greater (or lesser) among people who eat (or do not eat) breakfast."

The odds ratio is used in evaluations that are case control studies. In such studies, the researcher decides how many "cases" (e.g., people who have problems) and "controls" (e.g., people who do not have problems) to include in the sample. To calculate the odds ratio, the evaluator counts how many in each group have the "risk factor" (e.g., no breakfast) and divides the odds of having the risk factor among the cases by the odds of having the risk factor among the controls. (The use of terms such as *case control* and *risk factor* comes from studies of public health problems.)

Odds ratios are integral components of other statistical methods. Analytic software programs that do logistic regressions or interpret them automatically yield odds ratios. Example 8.4 gives the formula for the odds ratio.

Example 8.4 The Formula for the Odds Ratio

Risk Factor Present?	Case	Control	Total
Yes	A	B	a + b
No	C	D	c + d
Total	a + c	b + d	*n*

Example 8.5 illustrates of how this formula works.

Example 8.5 The Odds Ratio

Suppose that you are interested in the relationship between not eating breakfast (the risk factor) and trouble adhering to a diet. You ask this question: When compared with people who eat breakfast, what is the likelihood that people who do not will have trouble adhering to a weight-loss diet?

You identify 400 people who have trouble adhering to a diet and 400 who do not. You find that among all people with problems, 100 do not eat breakfast and 300 do. Among people without problems, 50 do not eat breakfast. To compare the odds of problems between the two groups, you put the data into a 2 × 2 table:

	Problems Keeping to a Diet		
No Breakfast	Case	Control	Total
Yes	100	50	150
No	300	400	700
Total	400	450	850

The odds ratio (OR) is calculated as follows:

$OR = ad/bc = 100 \times 400/50 \times 300 = 40{,}000/15{,}000 = 2.67.$

The odds of being exposed to the risk factor (no breakfast) are 2.67 higher for people in the sample who have problems adhering to a weight-loss diet than for people who do not have such problems. The answer to your question is that people who do not eat breakfast are 2.67 times more likely to encounter problems adhering to a diet than people who eat breakfast.

Evaluators also use *risk ratios* to examine the strength of the relationship between two nominal variables, but this method for studying the relationship is quite different from calculating odds ratios. Risk ratios are calculated through a cohort design (for more on cohort designs, see Chapter 3). Suppose that you want to determine how likely it is that people who do not eat breakfast have trouble adhering to a weigh-loss diet. First you pick the cohort—in this situation, people with problems adhering to a diet. Then you select a period of time to observe them, say, 12 months. At the end of the 12 months, you count the number of people who had adherence problems and the number of people who did not. Do these numbers differ? If so, was a greater risk likely for people who did not eat breakfast?

When you rely on cohort designs to calculate risk ratios (also called *relative risk* or *likelihood ratios*), you have no control over how many people are in each group. Obviously, you cannot control the number of people in the study group who develop problems, although you do have control over the number of people in your study group. The evaluator who uses a case control design has control over the numbers of people who have and who do not have the problem. He or she can say: I will have 100 cases and 100 controls. It may take the case control evaluator more or less than 12 months to identify enough cases for each group. In technical terms, the risk ratio is the ratio of the incidence of "disease" (e.g., problems adhering to a diet) among the "exposed" (people who do not eat breakfast) to the incidence of "disease" among the "nonexposed" (people who do eat breakfast). Incidence rates can be estimated only prospectively.

In a case control study, you cannot estimate the probability of having a problem because you, the evaluator, have determined in advance how many people are in the cases and how many are in the controls. All you can do is determine the probability of having the risk factor. This is unusual given that normally evaluators are concerned with finding out the probability of having the problem, not the risk for the problem. However, when you compare odds in an odds ratio, you will find that the ratio of the odds for having the risk factor is identical to the ratio of odds for having the disease or problem. Thus you can calculate the same odds ratio for a case control as for a cohort study or randomized controlled trial. It doesn't matter which variable is independent and which is dependent—the odds ratio will have exactly the same value. This is not true of risk ratios, and so researchers find odd ratios an excellent way to answer questions or test hypotheses involving nominal dependent variables between groups defined by nominal independent variables.

Qualitative Evaluation Data: Content Analysis

Content analysis is a set of procedures for analyzing qualitative information. The researcher may collect information directly from people, by asking them questions about their knowledge, attitudes, and behavior, or indirectly, through observations of their behavior. Perhaps the most familiar kinds of qualitative data are those that come from responses to open-ended survey items that invite respondents to provide their own answers (e.g., "Please feel free to comment on . . .").

Analyzing the data that result from open-ended items requires the researcher to pore over the respondents' written or verbal comments to look for ideas that appear repeatedly; such ideas are called *themes.* Once the themes are identified, they can be coded, which allows them to be counted and compared.

Another familiar type of qualitative data comes from observations of people. For example, two members of an evaluation team might spend a month observing patients as they arrive at a hospital's emergency department to determine what happens to them as they wait to be seen by health professionals. The observers would then compare notes and summarize their findings.

Evaluators might also obtain qualitative data from documents and from various forms of media that were produced for other purposes. For instance, suppose that you are part of a program planning and evaluation team that wants to start an antismoking media campaign in a particular community. A first step is to examine how stories about smoking and health have been handled in the mass media, specifically in news coverage. Of the several types of news media, you decide to restrict your review of stories about smoking and health to local and national newspapers. As in any analysis, you also have to be concerned with research design, sampling, and analysis. What time period should your review cover? The past 10 years of news? The past 20 years? How many articles should you survey? All of them? A sample? How should you define and code each type of story? Which data-analytic methods are appropriate for comparing the number and types of stories over time? You might hypothesize that the number of newspaper stories about the harmful effects of smoking increased significantly from 1990 to 2000, but that the number of stories has remained relatively constant since that time. You can use content analysis methods to test these hypotheses and to answer your research questions.

There are five main activities involved in conducting a content analysis:

1. Assembling the data from all sources
2. Learning the contents of the data
3. Producing a codebook
4. Entering and cleaning the data
5. Doing the analysis

Assembling the Data

Qualitative data often take the form of a great many pages of notes and interview transcripts. The unsorted data are the foundation of a qualitative database. They are not the same as the database, and, on their own, they are not interpretable or amenable to analysis.

In addition to transcripts of individual and group interviews and field notes from observations, qualitative data include participants' responses to open-ended survey questions and reviews of written, spoken, and filmed materials.

Transcripts are written, printed, or typed accounts of every word spoken in interviews or by observed individuals during data collection. Producing a transcript can take a great deal of time. For example, a verbatim report of a typical discussion among eight people during a 90-minute group interview may result in 50 or more pages of transcript text.

Of course, not all data in a complete transcript are necessarily relevant, and so producing complete transcripts may be unnecessary. Sometimes people get sidetracked during a discussion—they tell jokes, change the subject, and so on—and all of these digressions are included in a complete transcript. Because producing complete transcripts is so time-consuming, and because such transcripts often contain many data that are irrelevant to the research topic, some evaluators rely on abridged transcripts, which include all pertinent discussion and omit irrelevant remarks. It should be noted, however, that by using abridged transcripts an evaluator may run the risk of excluding important information.

Written transcripts do not capture the expressions on people's faces during a discussion, nor do they adequately describe the passion with which some people state their positions. Because of this, transcripts are often supplemented by audio and visual documentation. Evaluators sometimes use portions of the visual and audio records from their studies in their evaluation reports to illustrate the findings and lend a "human" touch to the reports' words and statistics. Evaluators should be aware, however, that any use of participants' words, voices, or visual images to justify or explain the research findings or recommendations may raise legal and ethical questions. Participants must be given the opportunity to consent to the use of their words and visual images in advance of data collection. They should be told where and under what circumstances the information will be used and what the risks and benefits of use are.

Field notes are the notes taken by observers or interviewers "in the field"—that is, while they are conducting observations or interviews. Transcribing and sorting through field notes is an onerous process. The evaluator must review the notes and fill in any missing information, which requires remembering what was said or done, when, and by whom. Some people have great memories; others are less fortunate. Some observers and interviewers take better notes than others. It is preferable to have two or more observers taking notes in any given setting, so that the evaluator can compare their findings in order to estimate interrater reliability (for more on interrater reliability, see Chapter 6). Having two note takers or observers may also reduce the amount of recall needed to assemble a complete set of data, because if one observer forgets who did what to whom, the other may have recorded the information in great detail. Using two or more observers in a setting can, however, increase a study's personnel costs. Also, with two or more observers, disagreement is inevitable. The need for a third person to arbitrate when disagreements occur also increases personnel costs, as well as the time needed to organize notes and observations.

Focus groups are targeted discussion groups. To be effective, a focus group must be led by a skilled moderator, an individual who is able to focus the group's attention on a specific topic. Note takers are often employed to record focus group discussions because the moderators are too busy keeping group members on track to take notes as well. However, even skilled note takers may leave out a great deal of information due to the difficulty of capturing every speaker's point. Because of the fear of losing vital information, evaluators usually record focus group discussions on audiotape or, when possible, videotape. In recent years, voice recognition software has become available that may become part of the focus group leader's toolbox. Such technology would eliminate some of the difficulties of transcribing and interpreting notes.

Learning the Contents of the Data

The evaluator's second step in content analysis is to become extremely familiar with the data that have been collected. The evaluator must understand the data thoroughly before he or she can assign them codes in anticipation of data entry and analysis. Learning the contents of the data can mean reading through hundreds of recorded pages of text, watching videotapes, and listening to audiotapes for days or even weeks. Becoming reacquainted with the discussion in a single group interview, for example, may require a full day of the evaluator's time, and transcribing 1 hour's worth of audiotape may take 4 to 8 hours.

Creating a Codebook

Surveys with closed (or closed-ended) questions assign code or values in advance of data collection. Surveys with open-ended questions assign them after the data are collected. This is illustrated in Example 8.6.

Example 8.6 Coding Closed and Open-Ended Questions

Closed Questions

The following are excerpts from a survey of visits to a clinic made by new mothers as part of an evaluation of the effectiveness of a program to prevent postpartum depression.

Question 5. Did the mother visit the clinic within 2 weeks of delivery? (postpartum)

Yes	❑ (1)
No	❑ (0)
No data	❑ (.a)

Question 7. Did the mother visit the clinic within 6 weeks of delivery? (well visit)

Yes	❑ (1)
No	❑ (0)
No data	❑ (.a)

A corresponding portion of a codebook for this survey appears as follows:

Variable Number	Variable Label	Description and Comments
1	PROJID	A five-digit ID project code
2	INDIVID	A four-digit ID individual code
3	DLIVDATE	Enter month/day/year using 2 digits for each segment. Example: May 20, 2002 = 052002
4	FOLLDATE	Use same procedure as for DLIVDATE.
5	POSPARVIS	No = 0; Yes = 1; use .a if missing
6	VISTDATE	Follow DLIVDATE procedure. If POSPARVIS = No, use 0; use .a if missing
7	WELVISIT	No = 0; Yes = 1; use .a if missing

Open-Ended Questions

The following are excerpts from a summarized transcript of a group interview discussion among participants in an evaluation of a program to prevent postpartum depression in new mothers.

Theme	Code
Identified common depressive symptoms but did not always conceptualize them as an illness (depression)	*1*
Acknowledged role of environmental stress (environment)	*2*
Pointed to need for new knowledge about counseling (knowledge)	*3*
Wanted to help themselves but felt impaired by depression and lack of information (depression; knowledge)	*1 and 3*
Felt that having someone to talk to in a confidential manner, to be able to "unburden oneself," would be helpful (counseling)	*4*
Believed counselor might be able to help them solve their own problems, change their negative thoughts and behaviors, have a more positive outlook (counseling)	*4*

Entering and Cleaning the Data

In content analysis, data entry involves organizing and storing the contents of transcripts and notes. Data may be entered and organized by person, place, observation, quotation, or some other feature. If you are conducting a very small program evaluation, you might be tempted to organize such data on index cards. However, better options for storage include spreadsheets, database management programs, and word processing programs. Special software designed specifically for qualitative analysis is also available.

Cleaning the data may mean deciding on which data to discard. Why would anyone discard data? Sometimes evaluators have to discard data because they are indecipherable (e.g., incomplete or unreadable notes; broken audiotape) or irrelevant. If the evaluator elects to discard data, he or she must create rules regarding what to do about lost or missing data. How will the lost data be handled? How much will the absence of particular data influence the conclusions that can be drawn? When data are missing, the evaluator must be sure to discuss the implications of this fact in the evaluation report.

Once the data are cleaned and their strengths and weaknesses are understood, they can be organized into a database. Only a clean database stands a chance of producing reliable information. Inconsistent and incomprehensible information is invalid. Obtaining a clean database is an objective shared by all evaluators, whether their data collection methods are qualitative or statistical. Accomplishing this objective is extremely time-consuming, and evaluators using qualitative data collection should plan adequate time for this major task regardless of the size of the evaluation.

Doing the Analysis

The final step is actually doing the analysis. One approach to the analysis involves asking respondents to give their views without prompting, whereas another approach involves prompting in the form of mentioning specific topics or themes. Example 8.7 shows how a content analysis with prompting might work.

Example 8.7 Barriers to Attendance at Depression Therapy Classes

Evaluation data collection: Structured interview with 200 new mothers

Purpose: To discover barriers to attendance at depression therapy classes

Premise: Barriers include lack of transportation, lack of child care for older children, inability to get off from work, lack of motivation (don't think they need the classes)

Question: Which of the following [the barriers are listed] is the most important reason why you or other mothers might not be able to attend parenting classes?

Analysis: Count each time a particular barrier (e.g., lack of transportation) is chosen as the most important reason

Results:

Barriers	50 Mothers 25 Years of Age and Younger	150 Mothers 26 Years of Age and Older
Lack of transportation	15*	86
Lack of child care	20	81
Inability to get off from work	5	17
Doesn't need classes	40	16

*The number in each cell represents the number of times that barrier is mentioned.

Conclusions: Overall, lack of child care is the most frequently mentioned reason for not attending classes. Older and younger women differed in their barriers, with younger women believing strongly that they don't need classes. A greater number of older women than younger women cited lack of transportation as a barrier. Inability to get off from work was not cited frequently by either age group.

Prompting to collect evaluation information means identifying preselected themes. The evaluator must derive such themes from the research literature and from past experience. If you were to prompt the mothers in Example 8.7 with preselected themes, you might ask them to come together in a group interview or focus group to answer questions like these: How important is lack of transportation (child care, inability to get off work, need for classes) as a reason for your coming or not coming to classes? What other reasons can you think of that might help us understand why women might choose to stay away from classes? After the group session, you would analyze the data by reviewing the transcript of the interview and counting the number of times the participants cited each of the barriers.

Meta-Analysis: A Superanalysis of Evaluation Data

Meta-analysis is a method for combining and analyzing the findings of studies that address the same research questions. The idea is that the larger numbers obtained from contributing studies have greater statistical power and generalizability together than any of the individual studies. Meta-analysis provides a quantitative alternative to the traditional review article in which experts use judgment and intuition to reach conclusions about the merits of a treatment or program or, alternatively, base their conclusions on a count of the number of positive versus negative and inconclusive studies.

Suppose that you are conducting a meta-analysis to answer the question, Do programs to educate adolescents about health care result in improved decisions among adolescents about their own health care? (See Figure 8.3.) You would answer the question by completing these seven tasks:

1. State the problem (in this case, whether programs to educate adolescents improve their decisions about their own health care).
2. Identify all studies that address the problem.
3. Prepare a scale to rate the quality of the studies.
4. Have at least two people review and rate the quality of the studies.
5. Include all studies that meet the criteria for quality, according to the reviewers' ratings of quality.
6. Calculate the difference in improvement between adolescents who were educated and those who were not and plot the difference as a point on a chart.
7. Calculate the chances that each study can be repeated and produce the same results; show the statistical range as a line on the chart.

The hypothetical meta-analysis of three evaluations illustrated in Figure 8.3 shows that the weight of the results suggests that programs to educate adolescents have no advantage over the controls.

Although meta-analysis has its origins in psychology and education, it has become associated with research in epidemiology and medicine. Meta-analyses have been used to summarize a number of diverse investigations, including studies of the care of pregnant women, the effects of estrogen replacement therapy on breast cancer, the influence of oat bran on lipid levels, and the treatment of heart attack.

Meta-analysis methods are continually advancing. Techniques for cumulative meta-analyses, for example, permit the identification of the year when the combined results of multiple studies first achieved a given level of statistical significance. The technique also reveals whether the temporal trend seems to be toward superiority of one program or intervention or another, and it allows assessment of the impact of each new study on the pooled estimate of the treatment effect.

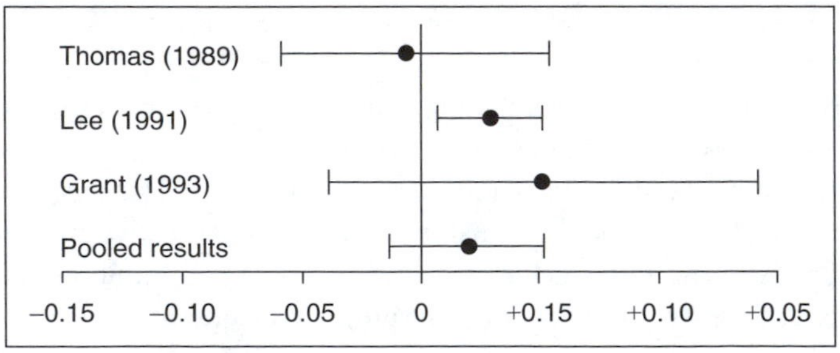

Figure 8.3. Meta-Analysis of Three Educational Programs for Adolescent Health Care

Meta-analyses have not been used to combine the results of program evaluations because too few scientifically appropriate studies have been conducted on any single topic to make the effort worthwhile. Nevertheless, evaluators should be familiar with the tasks included in a meta-analysis because they need to perform many, if not all, of them and to review and use the results. Every meta-analysis requires a review of the literature to identify eligible studies, the preparation and use of a measure of the quality of the literature, a review of the literature to select studies for the meta-analysis, and the analysis and interpretation of the results. At a minimum, evaluators must be able to review the literature in a systematic fashion (because they use data from published and unpublished sources in setting standards of program performance); determine sample size; provide paradigms of research design, measurement, data analysis, and presentation; explain the context in which the current evaluation is conducted; and demonstrate how the current evaluation's findings will add to current knowledge.

Summary and Transition to the Next Chapter on Evaluation Reports

This chapter has discussed the types of analysis that are particularly useful in program evaluations. Before choosing a method of analysis, the evaluator should determine the number of variables and the characteristics of the data describing or measuring each: nominal, ordinal, or numerical. When using tests of significance, the evaluator should decide on clinical or practical as well as statistical meaning.

The next chapter discusses written and oral evaluation reports. It addresses the contents of written reports, including objectives, methods, results, conclusions, discussion, and recommendations. Special emphasis is placed on the use of tables and figures to present data. The chapter also explains the contents of an abstract. Because much of evaluation reporting is oral, the chapter provides guidelines for the preparation of computer presentations.

Exercises

EXERCISE 1

Directions

For each of the following situations, describe the independent and dependent variables and determine whether they will be described with nominal, ordinal, or numerical data.

Situation	Describe the independent and dependent variables	Are the data nominal, ordinal, or numerical (interval/ratio)?
Patients in the experimental and control groups tell whether painkillers give complete, moderate, or very little relief.		
Participants in the program are grouped according to whether they are severely, moderately, or marginally depressed and are given a survey of anxiety that is scored from 1 to 9.		
Children are chosen for the evaluation according to whether or not they have had all recommended vaccinations; they are followed for 5 years and their health status is monitored.		
Men and women with stage 1, 2, and 3 of a disease are compared in quality of life as measured by scores ranging from 1 to 50 that are obtained from standardized observations.		
RNs and LVNs are surveyed, and their average proficiency scores are compared.		

EXERCISE 2

Directions

Use the following information to select and justify a method of data analysis.

> *Evaluation question:* After program participation, is domestic violence decreased?
>
> *Standard:* A statistically significant difference in domestic violence is found between families who have participated in the experimental program and families in the control program.
>
> *Independent variable:* Group membership (experimental versus control)
>
> *Design:* An experimental design with concurrent controls
>
> *Sampling:* Eligible participants are assigned at random to either an experimental group or a control group; 100 participants are in each group (a statistically derived sample size).
>
> *Dependent variable:* Domestic violence
>
> *Types of data:* Data on domestic violence will come from the DONT Survey, a 50-point measure in which lower scores mean less violence.

EXERCISE 3

Directions

Suppose that the evaluation of the program to reduce domestic violence described in Exercise 2 is concerned with finding out how younger and older persons compare in the experimental and control groups. Assuming the use of the DONT Survey, which produces numerical scores, which statistical method would be appropriate? Explain.

Suggested Readings

Afifi, A. A., Clark, V. A., & May, S. J. (2004). *Computer-aided multivariate analysis* (4th ed.). New York: Chapman & Hall.

This textbook on multivariate analysis takes a practical approach. The authors discuss data entry, data screening, data reduction, and data analysis, and also explain the options available in different statistical packages.

Antman, E. M., Lau, J., Kupelnick, B., Mosteller, F., & Chalmers, T. C. (1992). A comparison of the results of meta-analyses of randomized controlled trials and recommendations of clinical experts. *Journal of the American Medical Association, 268,* 240–248.

This article provides details on how to conduct a literature review and a meta-analysis. It also includes an excellent set of references.

Braitman, L. E. (1991). Confidence intervals assess both clinical and statistical significance. *Annals of Internal Medicine, 114,* 515–517.

This brief article contains one of the clearest explanations anywhere of the use of confidence intervals and is highly recommended.

Davey Smith, G., & Egger, M. (1998). Meta-analysis: Unresolved issues and future developments. *British Medical Journal, 316,* 221–225.

This article is from two of the leading experts in meta-analysis. It contains basic information on this technique and raises concerns about current and future developments.

Dawson, B., & Trapp, R. G. (2001). *Basic and clinical biostatistics* (3rd ed.). East Norwalk, CT: Appleton & Lange.

This book is an essential primer on the use of statistics in medicine and medical care settings. The authors explain study designs, how to summarize and present data, sampling, and the main statistical methods used in analyzing data.

Greenhalgh, P. (1997). How to read a paper: Statistics for the non-statistician. I: Different types of data need different statistical tests. *British Medical Journal, 315,* 364–366.

This article provides basic information on how to understand the uses of statistical testing.

Lau, J., Antman, E. M., Jimenez-Silva, J., Kupelnick, B., Mosteller, F., & Chalmers, T. C. (1992). Cumulative meta-analysis of therapeutic trials for myocardial infarction. *New England Journal of Medicine, 327,* 248–254.

This article describes and demonstrates the technique of cumulative meta-analysis.

Mays, N., & Pope, C. (1995). Qualitative rigour and qualitative research. *British Medical Journal, 311,* 109–112.

This article is important reading for evaluators who use qualitative research methods and want to be sure that they apply these methods rigorously and understand their limitations (and potential advantages).

Sacks, H. S., Berrier, J., Reitman, D., Anconca-Berk, V. A., & Chalmers, T. C. (1987). Meta-analyses of randomized, controlled trials. *New England Journal of Medicine, 316,* 450–455.

This article provides a basic, but technical, explanation of the principles of issues related to meta-analyses in medicine.

Steinberg, K. K., Thacker, S. B., Smith, S. J., Stroup, D. F., Zack, M. M., Flanders, W. D., & Berkelman, R. L. (1991). A meta-analysis of the effect of estrogen replacement therapy on the risk of breast cancer. *Journal of the American Medical Association, 265*, 1985–1990.

This article gives excellent examples of how to conduct a literature review, how to rate studies according to their quality, and how to conduct a meta-analysis.

Thompson, K. M., & Haninger, K. (2001). Violence in e-rated video games. *Journal of the American Medical Association, 286*, 591–598.

This article is an excellent example of a content analysis in action for an important public health problem.

See also the StatSoft Web site at http://statsoftinc.com for an online statistics textbook that covers everything a good statistics text covers and then some. This volume, which includes an excellent glossary, is highly recommended for those interested in learning *about* statistics as well as those who want to learn statistics. StatSoft, the publisher of STATISTICA analysis and graphic software, offers this textbook as a public service.

Purpose of This Chapter

This chapter focuses on the evaluation report, which answers the evaluation questions, describes how the answers were obtained, and translates the findings into conclusions and recommendations regarding program evaluation, health care, and health policy. Evaluation reports can be written, presented orally, or both. The chapter first discusses how to prepare a written report of an evaluation and provides a scoring sheet for use in assessing the quality of an evaluation report. The chapter also addresses the use of figures and tables to present evaluation results. Finally, the oral presentation of an evaluation report is examined, and specific recommendations are given for the preparation of computer "slide" presentations.

9 Evaluation Reports

A Reader's Guide to Chapter 9

The Written Evaluation Report

Elements: introduction, methods, results, recommendations, the abstract, the executive summary

Reviewing the Quality of the Report

Precision of and justification for the objectives and standards, need for the evaluation, description of the intervention, evaluation design and sampling, justification for and validity of the data sources, appropriateness of the data analysis, completeness and accuracy of reporting, boundaries of the evaluation

Oral Presentations

The Written Evaluation Report

Nearly all evaluations result in written reports. A useful evaluation report provides enough information so that at least two interested individuals who read it can agree on the evaluation's purposes, methods, and conclusions. If an evaluation report is to be submitted to a funding organization, such as a health foundation or a government agency, the composition and format of the report may be set by that organization. In most cases, however, evaluators are on their own in deciding on the length and content of their reports.

Most health program evaluation reports are somewhere between 2,500 and 15,000 words in length, or from 15 to 60 double-spaced printed pages (using common fonts such as Arial and Times New Roman, 11- to 12-point type, and 1-inch margins). In addition to the text, evaluation reports include lists of relevant bibliographic references as well as tables and figures (e.g., photographs, graphs) to illustrate evaluation findings; usually, no more than 10 tables and 10 figures are needed. In addition, an abstract of approximately 250 words and a summary of up to 15 pages are often helpful. Very long reports are rarely read. Evaluators who produce long reports should always make sure that their executive summaries are well done, because most people will focus on those.

Evaluators may also include working documents such as résumés, project worksheets, survey response frequencies, complex mathematical calculations, copies of measures (such as questionnaires or medical record review forms), organizational charts, memorandums, training materials, and project planning documents in appendixes attached to their reports.

Example 9.1 displays the table of contents for an evaluation report on an 18-month program combining diet and exercise to improve health status and quality of life for persons 75 years of age or older.

Example 9.1 Sample Table of Contents for a Report: An Evaluation of the Living-at-Home Program for Elders

Abstract: 250 words

Summary: 8 pages

Text of report: 41 pages

I. Introduction: The Health Problem, the Program, and the Evaluation Questions (6 pages)

II. Methods (10 pages)
   A. Evaluation Design
   B. Objectives and Activities of the Intervention and Control Programs
   C. Sample
      1. Inclusion and exclusion criteria
      2. Justification of sample sizes
      3. How sample was selected and assigned to groups

D. Outcome Measures
   1. Reliability and validity of measures of quality of life, health, and cost-effectiveness
   2. Quality assurance system for the data collection

E. Analysis

(In this section, the evaluators cite and justify the specific method used to test each hypothesis or answer each evaluation question. For example: "To compare men and women in their health, we used a *t* test, and to predict who benefited most from participation in the experimental program, we relied on stepwise multiple regression.")

III. Results (15 pages)

A. Response rates (such as how many eligible men and women agreed to participate in the evaluation; how many completed the entire program; how many individuals completed all data collection requirements)

B. Demographic and other descriptive characteristics (for the experimental and control groups: numbers and percentages of men and women; numbers and percentages under 65 to 75 years of age, 76 to 85, and 85 and older; numbers and percentages choosing each of the two health care staffing models)

C. Effectiveness: Quality of Life and Health Status

D. Cost-Effectiveness of Two Staffing Models of Care

V. Conclusions (8 pages)

V. Recommendations (2 pages)

VI. Tables and Figure

A. Table 1. Demographic Characteristics of Participants

B. Table 2. Health Outcomes and Quality of Life for Men and Women With Varying Levels of Illness

C. Table 3. Costs of Three Clinic Staffing Models

D. Figure 1. Flowchart: How Participants Were Assigned to Groups by "Cluster"

VII. Appendixes

A. Copies of all measures

B. Calculations linking costs and effectiveness

C. Final calculations of sample size

D. Testimony from program participants regarding their satisfaction with participation in the experimental program

E. Informed consent statements

F. List of panel participants and affiliations

G. Training materials for all data collection

H. Data collection quality assurance plan

Suppose that the fictional program and evaluation presented in Example 9.1 work this way:

- *Program:* The members of an experimental group of elderly people who still live at home receive the diet and exercise program, whereas elderly individuals in another living-at-home group do not. Participants in the evaluation who need medical services choose freely between two clinics offering differing models of care, one staffed primarily by physicians and the other staffed primarily by nurses.
- *Assignment to study groups:* Participants are randomly assigned to the experimental or control groups according to the streets on which they live. That is, participants living on Street A are randomly assigned, as are participants living on Streets B, C, and so on.
- *Main outcomes:* (a) Whether program participation makes a difference in the health and quality of life of elderly men and women and the role of patient mix in making those differences and (b) the cost-effectiveness of the two models of health care delivery.

Elements of the Report

Introduction

The introduction to a health program evaluation report has three components: (a) a description of the health problem, (b) an explanation of the means by which the experimental program is to solve the health problem, and (c) a list of questions that the evaluation answers about the merits of the program's solution to the problem. Example 9.2 illustrates the contents of the introduction to a written report.

Example 9.2 What to Include in the Introduction to a Written Report

Your written evaluation report's introduction should include information on the following:

1. *The health problem:* Describe the problem that the program and its evaluation are designed to solve. In the description, tell how many people are affected by the problem and what its human and financial costs are. Cite the literature to defend your estimates of the importance and costs of the problem.

2. *The program:* Give an overview of the program's objectives and activities and any unique features (such as its size, location, and number and types of participants). If the program is modeled on some other intervention, describe the similarities and differences and cite supporting references.

3. *The evaluation:* State the objectives of the evaluation, the questions, and the standards. If you used an evaluation framework to guide planning and evaluation, describe it and its use in the evaluation. Establish the connections among the general health problem, the objectives of the program, and the evaluation. That is, tell how the evaluation will provide knowledge about this particular program and also provide new knowledge about the health problem, as in the following example.

Sample Introduction

The purpose of this experimental evaluation is to identify whether community-dwelling elderly who participated in a home health care program improved in their health and quality of life. Participants were randomly assigned to an experimental or a control group. Because evidence exists that home health care can improve social, emotional, and physical functioning in the elderly [references regarding the potential benefits of home health care should have been cited in the first part of the introduction], we asked about the effectiveness of the program for men and women of differing ages and levels of medical and social problems and the nature, characteristics, and costs of effective home health services. We based standards of effectiveness on the comparative performance of the experimental and control groups.

Methods

The methods section of the report should define terms and describe the program or interventions, design, participants, outcomes and their measures, and analysis. Some specific recommendations are as follows:

- *The program:* Describe the experimental and comparison programs, carefully distinguishing between them. How long did each participate in the evaluation? If you prepared protocols to standardize the implementation of the programs, describe them and any training in the use of the protocols that took place.
- *Definitions:* Define all potentially misleading terms, such as quality of life, health status, high risk, accessible care, high quality of care, and efficiency.
- *Design:* Tell whether the evaluation used an experimental or observational design. If the design was experimental, specify the type (e.g., concurrent controls, in which participants are randomly assigned to experimental and control groups).
- *Setting:* Report on where the evaluation data were collected. You might include the geography (e.g., name of city and state or country), the locale (e.g., urban versus rural), and the site (e.g., clinic, academic medical center, community-based group practice).
- *Participants:* Give the inclusion and exclusion criteria for participation in the evaluation. Tell whether the participants were randomly selected and randomly assigned. Explain how the sample sizes were determined.
- *Outcomes and measures:* Describe each outcome and the characteristics of the data collection measures for the main evaluation questions. Who administered the measure? Was training required? Is the measure reliable? It is valid? How much time is required to complete the measure? How many questions does it contain? How were they selected? If appropriate, cite the theory behind the choice of questions or the other measures on which they were based. How is the measure scored?
- *Analysis:* Check each evaluation question for the main variables. Then, for the main variables, describe and justify the analytic method. Have you used any

unusual methods in the analysis? If so, you should describe them. Name the statistical package used in case other evaluators want to perform a similar analysis using the same setup. If you have used a relatively new or complex data-analytic method, provide a reference for it.

Results

The results section of the report presents the results of the process or implementation evaluation and the statistical analyses. All response rates should appear in this section, along with descriptions of the evaluation participants' characteristics. When appropriate, this section should include a comparison of the individuals who agreed to participate with those who refused or did not complete the entire program or provide complete data. The results for each major evaluation question and its subquestions also appear in this section. For example, if one of your main questions asks whether patients' quality of life improves, you should present the results for that question. You might also provide data on the types of individuals (e.g., older men, sicker patients) for whom the program was most and least effective in terms of quality of life.

Tables and figures (graphs or other illustrations) are useful for summarizing results in this section. Example 9.3 displays a table that is typical of the kind that often appears first in most reports.

Example 9.3 A Table to Describe the Characteristics of an Evaluation's Participants

	Experimental		*Control*			*Confidence*
Characteristic	*n*	*(%)*	*n*	*(%)*	*Difference*	*Interval*
Age (years)						
65–75						
76–85						
86 or more						
Health						
Excellent						
Good						
Fair						
Poor						
Choice of clinic						
Primarily nurse-run						
Primarily physician-run						

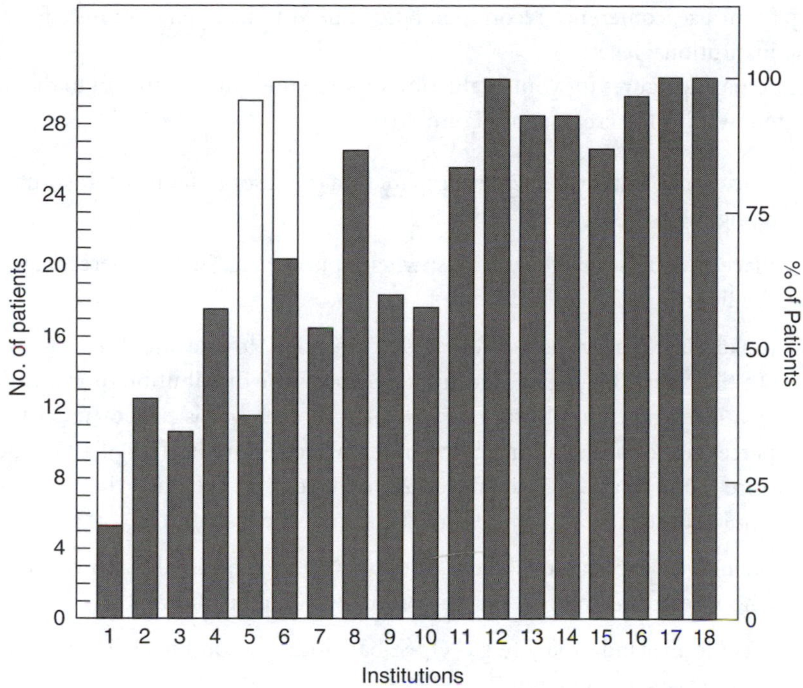

Figure 9.1. Variability in Transfusion Practice During Coronary Artery Bypass Surgery

SOURCE: L. T. Goodnough, M. F. M. Johnston, P. T. C. Y. Toy, and the Transfusion Medicine Academic Award Group. (1991). The variability of transfusion practice in coronary artery bypass graft surgery. *Journal of the American Medical Association, 265,* 286–290. Copyright 1991, 1992, American Medical Association; reprinted by permission.

NOTE: Number (percentage) of patients transfused with red blood cells among 30 first-time coronary artery bypass graft patients at each institution. The distribution of institutions is expressed as a histogram, indicating the number of institutions each transfusing zero to 30 patients. The distribution of patients who received red blood cells was variable among institutions. Open bars indicate autologous blood; shaded bars indicate homologous blood.

The results section is *not* the place for an interpretation of the data. Statements such as "These results contradict the findings of previous . . ." belong in the discussion section.

Some specific recommendations for the use of figures and tables in reporting evaluation results follow.

Using figures. Figure 9.1 provides an example of one kind of figure that is useful for reporting results. This figure comes from a study concerned with describing variability in transfusion practice during coronary bypass surgery. Based on the data presented in the figure, the study reported that the variation in the percentage of patients receiving red blood cells among institutions differed significantly (range, 17% to 100%; $p < .001$). Among the study's conclusions was that, in view of the NIH's Consensus Conference programs that addressed perisurgical blood component use, conference recommendations need to be applied more effectively at the institutional level.

In preparing figures for your evaluation report, you should conform to the same rules followed by the creators of Figure 9.1:

1. Place variables that are being compared (in the case of Figure 9.1, institutions) along the *x*-axis.
2. Place numbers along the *y*-axis; when appropriate, include percentages on the figure.
3. Make sure that visual differences correspond to meaningful differences. (In the case of Figure 9.1, the authors express the distribution of institutions as a histogram. In a histogram, the area of each bar is proportional to the percentage of observations in that interval. For example, if 11 of 100 patients were found in an interval labeled 20 to 50 years of age, then the 11 patients would constitute $^{11}/_{100}$, or 11%, of the area of the histogram.)
4. Include an explanation of the findings (e.g., "The distribution of patients who received red blood cells was variable among institutions.")
5. Include a legend or key (e.g., "Open bars indicate autologous blood; shaded bars indicate homologous blood.").

Using tables. When you create a table for an evaluation report, you should keep three main rules in mind. First, the most important values to be compared should appear in the table columns. For example, if you are describing the characteristics (such as age or educational level) of users and nonusers of smokeless tobacco (see Figure 9.2), the values (such as numbers and percentages of persons with the differing characteristics) go in the columns.

Characteristics	**Users *N* (%)**	**Nonusers *N* (%)**
Age (years)		
Under 18		
18–25		
26–35		
36–45		
46 and over		
Sex		
Male		
Female		
Years using		
Less than 1		
1–3		
4–6		
More than 6		

Figure 9.2. The Columns: Users and Nonusers of Smokeless Tobacco

Second, if appropriate and possible, the statistical values should appear in ascending (largest values) to descending order. Suppose that the table depicted in Figure 9.3 displays the results of a nationwide survey of 734 people who were asked whether or not they preferred fish or meat for dinner. Note that, in this table, the preferences for meat are in descending order. The choice of which values to place first depends on the points being emphasized. If the focus of the evaluation in this case were on preferences for fish instead of for meat, then the first cell of the table under the column head "Region" would be West.

	Number of People Choosing		
Region	*Meat*	*Fish*	*Total*
Northeast	140	124	264
South	100	52*	152
West	89	138**	227
North-Central	45	46	91
Total	374	360	734

Figure 9.3. Example of a Table With Statistical Values in Order: The National Dietary Preferences Survey (hypothetical)

NOTE: Survey administered by the Center for Nutrition and Health, Washington, DC
*P = .003.
**P = .002.

Third, you should use a standardized method for calling the reader's attention to key aspects of the table, such as statistical significance. One typical hierarchy of symbols used for this purpose is as follows: *, ?, §, and ¶. Figure 9.4 shows the use of such symbols in a table that compares the effectiveness of an extensive ethics education intervention, a limited intervention, and a control. In this table, the investigators report that the rate of documentation of an appropriate consent conversation with the patient or surrogate, although not significantly different among the groups at baseline, rose from 75% to 100% in the extensive intervention group. Moreover, the postintervention rate was significantly higher for the extensive intervention group than for the controls and the limited intervention groups ($p < .05$).

Conclusions or Discussion

The conclusions or discussion section of the evaluation report should tell readers what the results mean by answering questions such as the following:

- Taking the broadest perspective, what can one conclude from the evaluation? Is the program any good? For whom? Under what circumstances?

	Controls		Limited Intervention		Extensive Intervention	
	Before	After	Before	After	Before	After
No.	18	22	4	25	16	9
% Appropriate	78	77	50	52	75†	100‡

Figure 9.4. Percentage of Charts Documenting Appropriate Consent Conversation: Effects of Education*

NOTES: *"Appropriate" is defined as speaking to patient if patient is competent, or to surrogate if patient is incompetent.

† Not significantly different from Controls + Limited before the intervention.

‡ Significantly greater than Controls + Limited after the intervention ($P < .95$).

SOURCE: D. P. Sulmasy, G. Geller, R. Faden, and D. M. Levine. (1992). The quality of mercy: Caring for patients with "do not resuscitate" orders. *Journal of the American Medical Association*, *267,* 682–686. Copyright 1981, 1991, 1992, American Medical Association; reprinted by permission.

Example 9.4 presents an illustration of one answer to these questions from the first sentences in the "Comments" section of a report on an evaluation of an ethics education intervention for physicians.

Example 9.4 Conclusions of an Evaluation of an Ethics Education Intervention

"This study has examined the quality of care for patients with DNR [do not resuscitate] orders as it is reflected in the documentation of attention to such important considerations as informed consent and the appropriateness of a variety of other CCCs [concurrent care concerns; e.g., intubation, dialysis, blood product support] that are not specified by the DNR order itself. We conclude that the quality of such care can be improved by an extensive ethics education intervention for medical house officers and that quality varies systematically according to the patient's diagnosis."

SOURCE: D. P. Sulmasy, G. Geller, R. Faden, and D. M. Levine. (1992). The quality of mercy: Caring for patients with "do not resuscitate" orders. *Journal of the American Medical Association, 267,* 682–686. Copyright 1981, 1991, 1992, American Medical Association; reprinted by permission.

In addition to explaining the evaluation results, this part of the report might answer the following kinds of questions:

- Did the program achieve its goals and objectives?
- For which participants was the program most effective?
- For which participants was the program least effective?
- Which components of the program were most/least effective?
- How do the results of this evaluation compare in whole or in part with the findings of other studies?
- What new knowledge about health, health program evaluation, health care policy, and the health care system do the evaluation results contribute?
- What gaps in knowledge have been revealed by this evaluation?
- What are the limitations of this evaluation (due to imperfections in the design, sample, measurement, and analysis), and how do these affect the conclusions?

Recommendations

In the recommendations section of the evaluation report, the evaluator might consider answering questions such as these:

1. Without changing its basic goals and objectives, if the program were to be redone to remove its flaws, what are the top five changes or additions that should be considered?
2. If the program were to be applied to another setting or group of participants, who would be likely to benefit most?
3. If the program were to be instituted in the same or some other setting, what costs could be expected?
4. What objectives should be changed or added to the program to expand its scope and effectiveness?

The Abstract

The abstract of an evaluation report is usually quite brief: between 200 and 300 words. Its purpose is to present the evaluation's main objectives, methods, and findings. The following topics are usually addressed in the abstract, although the amount of detail about each topic varies:

Objective: In one or two sentences, tell the purpose of the evaluation.

Design: Using standard terminology, name the design (e.g., *randomized controlled trial* or *true experiment; nonrandomized trial* or *quasi-experiment; survey*). Describe any unique feature of the design, such as the use of blinding.

Participants: Describe the characteristics of the participants, including the numbers of participants in the experimental and control groups, demographics (such as age, income, and health status), region of the country, and size of facility (such as hospital, clinic, school). Describe any unique features of the participants, such as their location or special health characteristics.

Main outcome measures: Describe the main outcomes and how were they measured. Describe any unique features of the measures, use their proper names if appropriate, and include any special notes on reliability or validity.

Results: For each major dependent variable, give the results.

Conclusions: In one or two sentences, explain what the results mean. Did the program work? Is it applicable to other participants?

Figure 9.5 provides an illustration of an annotated abstract used in an evaluation report. It comes from an evaluation of the impact of ethics education on the knowledge, confidence, and practices of house officers regarding ethical issues.

Objective. — To assess (1) the effect of an ethics education intervention for medical house officers on practices surrounding "Do Not Resuscitate" (DNR) orders and (2) the association of DNR care with patient diagnosis and demographic variables.

Design. — A 1-year randomized, controlled trial.
Setting. — An urban, university teaching hospital.
Participants. — Eighty-eight internal medicine house officers.
Intervention. — House officers were arbitrarily assigned to four "firms."

One firm was randomized to an extensive ethics education intervention (EI), one to a limited intervention, and two served as controls.

Main Outcome Measures. — Charts of patients with DNR orders were reviewed for compliance with the hospital's DNR policy, which instructs that when DNR orders are written there should be (1) an attending signature, (2) document of reasons, (3) appropriate consent, and (4) attention to 11 concurrent care concerns (CCCs) (e.g., the appropriateness of intubation, tube feedings, hospice).

Results. — Thirty-nine charts were reviewed before the intervention and 57 after. The number of CCCs per DNR order fell among patients cared for by controls (1.9 to 1.0, $p < .05$) and rose among patients cared for by the EI group (0.9 to 3.8, $p < .05$). Compliance with the DNR policy varied among patients with differing diagnoses. "Do Not Resuscitate" orders were signed less frequently ($p = .01$) for patients with the acquired immunodeficiency syndrome (AIDS) (65%) compared with patients who had other diagnoses (85%) or malignancy (91%). Similarly, appropriate consent was recorded for 59% of patients with AIDS, 83% of others, and 85% of those with malignancy ($p < .05$). The number of CCCs per DNR was 0.7 for AIDS, 1.4 for others, and 2.4 for malignancy ($p < .05$). In multivariate regression analysis, house officer ethics education and patient diagnosis, but not patient gender, age, race, or insurance status, were predictors of the number of CCCs per DNR.

Conclusions. — (1) An extensive ethics education intervention can improve care for DNR patients, especially with respect to CCCs. (2) In this setting, quality of care for DNR patients varied systematically with diagnosis. These results have implications for the design and implementation of ethics education programs.

Figure 9.5. An Example of an Illustrative Annotated Abstract

SOURCE: D. P. Sulmasy, G. Geller, R. Faden, and D. M. Levine. (1992). The quality of mercy: Caring for patients with "do not resuscitate" orders. *Journal of the American Medical Association, 267,* 682–686. Copyright 1981, 1991, 1992, American Medical Association; reprinted by permission.

The Executive Summary

The evaluation report's executive summary provides all potential users with an easy-to-read summarization of the evaluation's major purposes, methods, findings, and recommendations. Executive summaries are relatively brief, usually from 3 to 15 pages in length. Evaluation funders nearly always require that reports include such summaries, and they frequently specify the number of pages expected.

Three rules should govern your preparation of an executive summary for your evaluation report:

1. Include the important purposes, methods, findings, and recommendations.
2. Avoid the use of jargon. For example:
   Poor:
   We used a *cluster sampling strategy* in which hospitals were assigned at random . . .
   Better:
   We assigned hospitals at random . . .

   Poor:
   We established *concurrent validity by correlating scores* on Measure A with those on Measure B.
   Better:
   We examined the relationship between scores on Measures A and B.
3. Use active verbs.
   Poor:
   The use of health care services *was found* by the evaluation to be more frequent in people under 45 years of age.
   Better:
   The evaluation found more frequent use of services by people under 45 years of age.

   Poor:
   It is recommended that the prevention of prematurity be the focus of prenatal care education.
   Better:
   We recommend that the prevention of prematurity be the focus of prenatal care education.

As you prepare the executive summary, you should be guided by the following topics:

The program or intervention: Describe the intervention or program's purposes and objectives, settings, and unique features. Consider answering questions like these:

- During which years did the intervention take place?
- Who were the funders?
- How did the intervention differ from others that have similar purposes?
- How great was the need for the intervention?

The evaluation: Present an overview of the purposes of the evaluation, describe the evaluation framework, describe the questions and standards, review the design and sample, discuss the outcomes and how they were measured, and explain the main analytic methods. Consider answering questions like these:

- How was the evaluation defined?
- Were the evaluation methods unique in any way?
- For whom are the evaluation's findings and recommendations most applicable?
- Who performed the evaluation?
- During which years did the evaluation take place?

The findings: Give the answers to the evaluation questions and note whether the program or intervention was effective. Did it achieve agreed-upon standards of merit? Consider answering questions like these:

- Is the intervention likely to be sustained over time?
- Who benefited most (and least) from participation?

Conclusions: Tell whether the intervention solved the problem it was designed to solve. Were the findings consistent with those of evaluations of similar interventions? What is the bottom line? Did the intervention succeed? If so, explain the reasons for success. If the intervention did not succeed, explain the reasons for failure.

Recommendations: Tell other evaluators, researchers, and policy makers about the implications of the evaluation. Explain what changes to the program or intervention could make it more effective. Describe the participants who are most likely to be in need of the intervention in the future. Describe ways to improve future interventions and evaluations.

Reviewing Your Report

After you have written your evaluation report, you should review it to determine the extent to which it conforms to acceptable standards. The "scoring" sheet provided in Figure 9.6 can serve as a guide for your review. This guide can also be useful for reviewing a variety of evaluation manuscripts and reports.

Scale: 4 = definitely yes
3 = probably yes
2 = probably no
1 = definitely no
0 = no data; uncertain
NA = not applicable

CRITERIA: PRECISION OF OBJECTIVES/JUSTIFICATION OF STANDARDS	**RATING SCALE**					
	4	**3**	**2**	**1**	**0**	**NA**
Are the evaluation's objectives/ questions/hypotheses stated precisely?						
Are the standards clear?						
Are practical standards justified?						
Are statistical standards justified?						
Other?						

CRITERIA: NEED FOR THE EVALUATION	**RATING SCALE**					
	4	**3**	**2**	**1**	**0**	**NA**
Is the need for the evaluation justified?						
Is the current evaluation placed within the context of previous work?						
Are criteria given for any literature that is reviewed?						
Is the quality of the reviewed literature assessed?						
Does the current evaluation continue the work of others?						
Does the current evaluation build on the previous work of others?						
Does the current evaluation fill in gaps in knowledge?						
Other?						

Figure 9.6. Reviewing Evaluations: A Scoring Guide *(Continued)*

Figure 9.6. (Continued)

CRITERIA: DESCRIPTION OF THE INTERVENTION	RATING SCALE					
	4	3	2	1	0	NA
Is the importance of the health problem to be solved by the program justified?						
Are experimental program goals and objectives specified?						
Are descriptions given of the special features of the experimental program?						
Are quality assurance systems in place for monitoring the implementation of the experimental program?						
Is the experimental program standardized within sites?						
Is the experimental program standardized across sites?						
Are the resources of the experimental program described?						
Are the settings in which the experimental program takes place described?						
Are control group program goals and objectives specified?						
Are descriptions given of the implementation of the control group program?						
Are quality assurance systems in place for monitoring the implementation of the control group program?						
Is the control group program standardized within sites?						
Is the control group program standardized across sites?						
Are the resources of the control program described?						
Are the settings in which the control program takes place described?						
Are the effects on the evaluation's generalizability given for failure to have uniform program goals, objectives, protocols, settings, or resources?						
Other?						

CRITERIA: EVALUATION DESIGN AND SAMPLING	**RATING SCALE**					
	4	**3**	**2**	**1**	**0**	**NA**
Is the entire population included?						
If a sample, are sampling methods adequately described?						
If a sample, are the evaluation's participants randomly selected?						
If more than one group, are the evaluation's participants randomly assigned?						
If the unit that is sampled (e.g., patients) is not the population of main concern (e.g., physicians), is this properly addressed in the analysis or discussion?						
If a sample and a nonrandom sampling method are used, is evidence given regarding the similarity of the groups at baseline?						
If groups are not equivalent at baseline, is this problem adequately addressed in analysis or interpretation?						
Are criteria given for including all evaluation units (e.g., patients, physicians, and whoever else is studied)?						
Are criteria given for excluding evaluation units?						
Is the sample size justified (say, with a power calculation)?						
Is information given on the number of participants in the source population?						
Is information given on the number of participants eligible to participate?						
Is information given on the number who agreed to participate?						
Is information given on the number who refused to participate?						
Is information given on the number who dropped out or were lost to follow-up before completing all elements of data collection?						
Is information given on the number who completed all elements of data collection?						
Is information given on the number for whom some data are missing?						

(Continued)

Figure 9.6. (Continued)

CRITERIA: EVALUATION DESIGN AND SAMPLING (continued)	RATING SCALE					
	4	3	2	1	0	NA
Are participants measured over time?						
If observations or measures are made over time, is the time period justified?						
Are participants blinded?						
Are reasons given for individuals or groups who dropped out?						
Are reasons given for missing data?						
Are the effects on generalizability of choice, equivalence, and participation of the resultant sample explained?						
Are the effects on internal validity of choice, equivalence, and participation of the resultant sample explained?						
Other?						

CRITERIA: JUSTIFICATION AND VALIDITY OF DATA SOURCES AND DATA COLLECTION	RATING SCALE					
	4	3	2	1	0	NA
Are the independent variables defined?						
Are the dependent variables defined?						
Are data provided on the reliability of data sources for the main variables?						
Are data provided on the validity of data sources for the main variables?						
Is the reliability of each data source adequate?						
Is the validity of each data source adequate?						
Are the data collection methods adequately described?						
Is information provided on methods for ensuring the quality of data collection?						
Is the length of the data collection period justified?						
Is the length of the data collection period sufficient for the evaluation's objectives?						
Are the effects on the research's generalizability of the selection, reliability, validity of data sources, and the length of data collection explained?						
Other?						

CRITERIA: APPROPRIATENESS OF DATA ANALYSIS	RATING SCALE					
	4	3	2	1	0	NA
Are the statistical methods adequately described?						
Are the statistical methods justified?						
Is the purpose of the analysis clear?						
Are scoring systems described?						
Are potential confounders adequately controlled for in the analysis?						
Are analytic specifications of the independent and dependent variables consistent with the evaluation questions or hypotheses under study?						
Is the unit of analysis specified clearly?						
Is a sensitivity analysis performed to account for imprecise measurements or uncertain outcomes?						
Other?						

CRITERIA: COMPLETENESS AND ACCURACY OF REPORTING	RATING SCALE					
	4	3	2	1	0	NA
Are references given for complex statistical methods?						
Are complex statistical methods described in an appendix?						
Are exact *p* values given?						
Are confidence intervals given?						
Are the results of the analysis clearly described?						
Are the evaluation's results clearly described?						
Do the conclusions follow from the study's results?						
Other?						

(Continued)

Figure 9.6. (Continued)

CRITERIA: BOUNDARIES OF THE EVALUATION	RATING SCALE					
	4	3	2	1	0	NA
Are the evaluation's biases explained?						
Are the results practical?						
Are the uses of the evaluation's findings clear?						
Are directives given for future evaluations?						
Are directives given for policy decisions?						
Are ethical considerations included?						
Other?						

NOTE: Scale: 4 = definitely yes; 3 = probably yes; 2 = probably no; 1 = definitely no; 0 = no data, uncertain; NA = not applicable.

Oral Presentations

An oral presentation of a program evaluation may consist of an account of some or all of the evaluation objectives, methods, and findings. Most commonly, oral evaluation reports take the form of computer "slide" presentations, although sometimes evaluators use overhead projectors to display transparencies or filmed slides. If you need to prepare an oral presentation, whether 10 minutes or an hour in length, the following recommendations can be helpful.

Recommendations for the Preparation of Computer "Slide" Presentations

1. Do the talking and explaining and let the audience listen. Use slides to focus the audience's attention on the key points of your talk. Do not require audience members to read and listen at the same time.

Poor:

> **Reliability**
>
> A reliable measure is one that is relatively free from measurement error. Because of this error, individuals' obtained scores are different from their true scores. In some cases, the error results from the measure itself: It may be difficult to understand or poorly administered.

Better:

Reliable Measures
• Reliable measures are relatively free of error.
• Two causes of error are common:
  – Measure is hard to understand.
  – Measure is poorly administered.

The second of the two slides above is better than the first because the listener can more easily keep the main points in view without being distracted by a lot of reading requirements. If your objective is to have the audience read something, a handout (and the time to read it) is more appropriate than a slide.

2. Make sure that each slide has a title.

3. During the talk, address the talk's purposes and the evaluation's purposes, main methods, main results, conclusions, and recommendations. A typical oral presentation covers the following:

A. Title of the talk and names and affiliations of the evaluators

Children and Prevention (CAP): **What the Evaluation Found** Prepared by Jane Austen, PhD Louis Pasteur, MD Michael Jackson, RN *The Center for Program Evaluation* *in the Health Professions*

B. What the evaluation is about

Goal of the Evaluation of CAP • To appraise impact • To determine costs • To estimate benefits

C. A description of the purpose of the report

> **Purpose**
>
> - Describe and compare children in CAP with other children in the following areas:
> - Knowledge of selected health promotion activities
> - Health status

D. A description of the program

> **The Children and Prevention (CAP) Program**
>
> - Goal is to improve children's health prevention knowledge and behavior.
> - Duration of program is 3 years.
> - Cost of program is 3 million.
> - Program is sponsored by the Education Trustees, a nonprofit health promotion group.

E. A description of the participants

> **Who Was in CAP?**
>
> - 500 children between the ages of 4 and 7 years
> - Six public schools: three in the experimental group and three in the control group
> - Random assignment of schools to groups
> - Control schools: No special health promotion activities ("Usual care")

F. A description and explanation of the main outcome measures (The description and explanation can include information on reliability and validity and samples of the content of the measures.)

> **How Was Information Collected?**
>
> - Tests of students' knowledge
> - Interviews with students
> - Interviews with parents
> - Review of attendance records
> - Medical records review

G. An accounting of the main results, as in the following hypothetical table

Knowledge: How the CAPs and the Control Compare

Age	Experimental Scores	Control Scores
4	45	22*
5	46	20**
6	33	29
7	35	32

HIGHER SCORES ARE BETTER
STATISTICAL SIGNIFICANCE: *$p = .03$; **$p = .001$

Notice that no decimals are used in the table above; numbers should be rounded to the nearest whole number.

H. Conclusions

Conclusion

- Younger children benefit more than older children.

I. Alternative explanations, limitations, problems

Do the Results Fit?

- Few valid evaluations of the effects of preventive programs on young children exist.
- We could not find other programs on prevention during period of evaluation.
  - Checked content of health education classes
  - Checked movie and television listings

J. Recommendations

> **Recommendations**
>
> - Adopt CAP for 4- and 5-year-olds.
> - Revise the program and evaluate again for 6- and 7-year-olds.

4. *Keep tables and figures simple.* Explain the meaning of each table and figure, the title, the column and row headings, and the statistics. For the table above headed "Knowledge: How the CAPs and the Control Compare," you could say something like this:

> The next slide compares the knowledge of children in CAP with those in the controls. We used the CAP Test, in which higher scores are better, and the highest score is 50 points.
>
> As you can see [if possible, point to the appropriate place on the screen], children who are 4 and 5 did significantly better in CAP. We found no differences in children who were 6 and 7.

5. *Check all slides carefully for typographical errors.*

6. *Avoid the use of abbreviations and acronyms unless you are certain that your audience members will know what they mean.* In these examples, the acronym CAP was explained in the first slide. If necessary, you should explain and define each abbreviation and acronym.

7. *Outline or write out what you plan to say.*

8. *Rehearse the presentation before you create the final copies of the slides.* Then rehearse again. The purpose of the first rehearsal is to make sure that the talk is logical, that the spelling on all slides is correct, and that the arrangement of words, figures, and tables is meaningful.

9. *Ensure that the slides are easy to see.* Horizontal placement is better than vertical. All potential audience members should be able to see the slides. In advance of the talk, check the room, the seating plan, and the place where you will stand.

10. *Use humor and rhetorical questions to engage listeners.* Typical rhetorical questions are given in three of the slides above: Who was in CAP? How was information collected? Do the results fit?

11. *Allow the audience 1 to 2 minutes to view each slide.*

12. *Be consistent in using complete sentences or sentence fragments or parts of speech within a given slide.*

Poor:

> **Implementation Evaluation**
>
> - Teachers were given a one-week in-service course.
> - Random observation of their classes
> - There were two observers.
> - 10% of all classes
> - Kappa = .80, which is high

Better:

> **Implementation Evaluation**
>
> - Teachers participated in a one-week in-service course.
> - Two researchers monitored 10% of classes at random for adherence to the protocol.
> - Agreement between observers was excellent (kappa = .80).

The first of these two slides mixes sentence fragments ("random observation of classes") and full sentences, whereas the second uses only full sentences.

13. If you have "downtime" with no appropriate slides, use fillers. These are often opaque, blank slides or slides showing only the title of the presentation. Do not use cartoons as fillers because they are distracting in the middle of a talk. (If you use cartoons to lighten your presentation, make sure all audience members can see the captions.)

14. Use handouts to summarize information and provide technical details and references. Make sure that your name, the name of the presentation, and the date are on each page of every handout. Do not distribute handouts until you are finished speaking unless you plan to refer to them during your presentation.

15. When you create your slides, use upper- and lowercase letters in the text; in general, this is easier to read than text that is all uppercase.

16. Make sure that you discuss in your talk all information that is displayed on the screen.

17. Be careful not to overwhelm your audience with animation, graphics, and sound. Also, **do not assume** that you can routinely use graphics or other materials downloaded from the Internet. A great deal of the information accessible there is protected by copyright.

18. Use no more than four colors per slide. If you are unsure about which colors to use, consider using the slide presentation colors that are preselected by the software you use to create the slides. Yellow or white letters on royal blue are easy to see and read.

Exercises

EXERCISE 1

Directions

Review the following slide prepared as a visual aid for an oral evaluation presentation and, if necessary, improve it.

> A **stratified random sample** is one in which the population is divided into subgroups or "strata," and a random sample is then selected from each group. For example, in a program to teach women about options for treatment for breast cancer, the evaluator can sample from a number of subgroups including women of differing ages (under 19 years, 20 to 30, 31 to 35, over 35) and income (high, medium, low).

EXERCISE 2

Directions

Write the text to accompany the following table of data. These data were obtained in an evaluation of audit and feedback and local opinion leader education as methods of encouraging compliance among physicians with guidelines for the management of women patients who had had a previous cesarean section.

Table: Delivery Outcomes by Study Group

	% of Eligible Cases by Group*			Difference Between Opinion Leader Education Group and Control and Audit and Feedback Groups Combined		
	Control	Audit and Feedback	Opinion Leader Education	%	*F* Test†	*p*
Offered a trial of labor	51.3 (43.5–59.2)	56.3 (45.2–67.4)	74.2 (63.1–85.2)	+ 40	10.13	.002
Underwent a trial of labor	28.3 (23.0–33.7)	21.4 (13.9–29.0)	38.2 (30.6–45.7)	+ 46	7.86	.007
Vaginal birth	14.5 (10.3–18.7)	11.8 (5.8–17.7)	25.3 (19.3–31.2)	+ 85	9.74	.003
Elective cesarean section	66.8 (61.7–72.0)	69.7 (62.4–77.0)	53.7 (46.5–61.0)	− 21	11.37	.001
Unscheduled cesarean section	18.7 (15.4–22.1)	18.6 (13.9–23.2)	21.4 (16.8–26.1)	+ 14	1.96	.166
Before labor	1.7	3.5	1.7	. . .	. . .	. . .
Latent labor‡	11.7	7.5	11.8	. . .	. . .	. . .
Active labor‡	5.3	7.6	7.9	. . .	. . .	. . .

SOURCE: J. Lomas, M. Enkin, G. M. Anderson, W. J. Hannah, E. Vayda, and J. Singer. (1991). Opinion leaders vs. audit and feedback to implement practice guidelines. *Journal of the American Medical Association, 265,* 2022–2207.

NOTES: *Numbers in parentheses are 95% confidence limits.

†For each *F* test, *df* = 1.74.

‡Latent labor defined as dilatation less than 3 cm; active labor as dilatation of 3 cm or greater.

Suggested Readings

Bailar, J. C., & Mosteller, F. (1988). Guidelines for statistical reporting in articles for medical journals. *Annals of Internal Medicine, 108,* 266–273.

The title of this article suggests that the information it provides is primarily appropriate for writers of articles for medical journals. People with other interests, however, can benefit from the discussion on figures and tables and on the merits of confidence intervals and exact *p* values.

Bates, E. S., & Abemayor, E. (1991). Slide presentation graphics using a personal computer. *Archives of Otolaryngology and Head and Neck Surgery, 117,* 1026–1030.

This article presents an evaluation of four graphics programs for making slides. Although the information is out-of-date in terms of technology and costs, the criteria the authors use are still relevant.

Hendricks, M. (1994). Making a splash: Reporting evaluation results effectively. In J. S. Wholey, H. P. Hatry, & K. E. Newcomer (Eds.), *Handbook of practical program evaluation.* San Francisco: Jossey-Bass

This chapter provides some handy tips on evaluation reporting.

Lin, Y.-C. (1989). Practical approaches to scientific presentation. *Chinese Journal of Physiology, 32,* 71–78.

This article describes the purposes, language, and style of oral presentation, with particular emphasis on using slides in scientific presentations.

Pfeiffer, W. S. (1991). *Technical writing.* New York: Macmillan.

This book provides useful tips on the details of putting together formal reports. The author discusses the cover and title page, table of contents, and executive summary and also presents rules for preparing charts and giving oral presentations. Although this volume is oriented toward business, many of the lessons can be adapted to program evaluation.

Spinler, S. (1991). How to prepare and deliver pharmacy presentations. *American Journal of Hospital Pharmacy, 48,* 1730–1738.

This article provides extremely useful tips on the preparation and use of slides for oral presentations. It discusses how to rehearse and then deliver an oral presentation.

Answers to Exercises

Chapter 1

Exercise 1

1. The evaluation questions:
    - To what extent have key curriculum objectives been achieved?
    - How enduring are the effects? (For example, did quality of care improve?)
    - For which groups was the program most effective? (For example, do differences exist in knowledge between faculty and residents?)

2. The standards:
    - Although not explicitly stated, the standards are probably improvements over time.

3. The design:
    - Observations over time and possibly comparisons of performance among groups (e.g., this year's third- and fourth-year students versus the next two years' third- and fourth-year students).

4. The data collection measures used:
    - The measures are achievement tests, medical record reviews, and surveys.

5. Additional information needed:
    - An explicit statement of the standards: For example, if changes are observed in quality of care, how will the adequacy of those changes be assessed?
    - An explanation and justification of the numbers and types of individuals who will participate in the evaluation: For example, how many residents and faculty will be included? Are the samples large enough to allow the evaluators to discern true differences?
    - A description of the number of observations and when they will be made.
    - A description of the data-analytic methods to be used.

Exercise 2

1. *Telling eligible subjects that participation is voluntary, they can leave whenever they choose, and their health care will not be affected:*

   You can choose to take part in this study or not. If you volunteer to take part in this study, you may stop taking part in the study at any time. This will have no effect of any kind on the health care you receive through the Diabetes Self-Care Program.

2. *Telling participants that the program will use their answers (and answers from others) to find out about the appropriateness of services and any needed changes:*

   The Diabetes Self-Care Program will use your answers and the answers from other program participants to find out if the program is providing the right services to its participants and to find out if any changes need to be made to the program.

3. *Telling respondents that the surveys may include questions about their physical or emotional health or their experience with the program that they may feel sensitive about answering, and that they do not have to answer questions that bother them:*

   You may be sensitive about answering questions that ask about your physical and emotional health or your experiences with the Diabetes Self-Care Program. However, you do not have to answer any question with which you are uncomfortable.

4. *Telling participants that they will not be paid for their time:*

   No payment will be given to you for completing the telephone interviews or self-administered questionnaires.

5. *Telling participants that it is up to them whether or not they want to take part and that, if they do, they can stop at any time and their health care will not be affected:*

   You can choose whether to take part in this study or not. If you decide to take part in the telephone interviews and self-administered questionnaires, you may stop taking part at any time. This will have no effect of any kind on the health care you receive through the Diabetes Self-Care Program.

Chapter 2

Exercise 1

1. Have physicians learned the guidelines for transfusing red blood cells, fresh frozen plasma, platelets, and cryoprecipitated AHF?

2. Have appropriate transfusion practices been ensured?

3. To what extent are the guidelines associated with improved quality of care at the institution?

4. Have all physicians benefited equally?

Exercise 2

Question: Did nonphysician staff become knowledgeable about privacy issues pertaining to infectious diseases such as hepatitis and tuberculosis?

Standards:
- Of the staff, 80% become knowledgeable about privacy issues.
- An improvement in knowledge is observed before and after the program (for up to 5 years) for each group of nonphysician staff.
- A difference in knowledge is found between current and future staff in their knowledge.

Independent variable: Staff

Dependent variable: Knowledge

Chapter 3

Evaluation question 1: Has the center's quality of care improved?

Standard: The appropriateness of pain management practices improves over the 3-year program period.

Independent variables: Participation in the program

Design: An experimental evaluation with self-controls

Potential biases: During the 3-year period, a number of external events having nothing to do with the program may influence practice. For example, the World

Health Organization or a charitable foundation might provide additional or new funds for pain management, or refugees may move on or drop out of the program. Use of a control group can guard against the influence of outside variables.

Evaluation question 2: How do patients and health care providers perceive the quality of care pertaining to the management of pain?

Standard: No judgment can be made regarding the answers to this question because it is solely for descriptive information.

Design: Survey

Potential biases: This design will provide a cross section of opinions. It cannot produce data on the extent to which the views of the responding individuals have been affected by the program or how the views compare with those held by nonparticipants.

Chapter 4

Situation 1: C

Situation 2: B

Situation 3: A

Chapter 5

Exercise 1

Description 1, measure C

Description 2, measure G

Description 3, measure A

Description 4, measure F

Description 5, measure B

Description 6, measure D

Description 7, measure E

Exercise 2

Directions: This form is to be completed upon each project participant's delivery.

WHAT IS THE MOTHER'S EVALUATION ID?

1. Baby's birth date:__/__/__
2. Birth weight: __ __ __ __ __ grams *OR* __ __ lbs __ __ ozs
3. Baby's sex: Male ☐ Female ☐ Unknown/Could not get ☐
4. Gestational age assessed by clinician at birth: ______ weeks
5. Was drug toxicology performed at birth on the **mother** at delivery?

   Yes ☐

   No ☐

   Unknown/Not reported ☐

5a. If **yes,** what were the results?

   negative ☐

   positive for alcohol ☐

   positive for amphetamines ☐

   positive for opiates ☐

   positive for barbiturates ☐

   positive for cannabinoids ☐

   positive for cocaine or metabolites ☐

   positive, other, specify: ____________________ ☐

   unknown/not reported ☐

6. Was a drug toxicology screen performed at birth on the **baby?**

   Yes ☐

   No ☐

   Unknown/Not reported ☐

6a. If **yes,** what were the results?

   negative ☐

   positive for alcohol ☐

positive for amphetamines ☐

positive for opiates ☐

positive for barbiturates ☐

positive for cannabinoids ☐

positive for cocaine or metabolites ☐

positive, other, specify: ______________________ ☐

7. What was the total number of clinical prenatal visits attended by the patient during this pregnancy?

   total prenatal care visits ☐ ☐

8. Was the baby: stillborn ☐ live birth ☐

Chapter 6

Exercise 1

Excerpt A: The concept is content validity because the instrument is based on a number of theoretical constructs (e.g., the health beliefs model and social learning theory).

Excerpt B: The concept is interrater reliability because agreement is correlated between scorers. If we also assume that each expert's ratings are true, then we have concurrent validity; κ (kappa) is a statistic that is used to adjust for agreements that could have arisen by chance alone.

Excerpt C: The concept is test-retest reliability because each test is scored twice.

Exercise 2

This information collection plan has several serious flaws. First, it anticipates collecting data only on student knowledge and skill despite the fact that the objectives also encompass attitude. Second, even if the evaluators are expert test constructors, they must pilot-test and evaluate the tests to determine their reliability and validity. Finally, the evaluators do not plan to monitor the use of the educational materials. If faculty cannot or will not use these materials, then any results may be spurious. The 5-year period planned for testing is, however, probably of sufficient duration to allow the evaluators to observe changes.

Chapter 7

Exercise 1

- The "T" stands for "telephone" and the "_9" stands for the "ninth question."
- "All of the time" is coded 100; "most of the time," 75; "some of the time," 50; "a little of the time," 25; "none of the time," 0; "don't know," 8; and "refused," 9.
- The codes of 100, 75, 50, and 25 allow the data analyst to compute a "score."

Exercise 2

[T_1] My illness has strengthened my faith. Would you say this statement is very much, quite a bit, somewhat, a little bit, or not at all true?

Very much	☐	(4)
Quite a bit	☐	(3)
Somewhat	☐	(2)
A little bit	☐	(1)
Not at all	☐	(0)
DON'T KNOW	☐	(8)
REFUSED	☐	(9)

[T_2] How much of the time during the LAST 4 WEEKS have you wished that you could change your mind about the kind of treatment you chose for prostate cancer? Would you say all of the time, most of the time, a good bit of the time, some of the time, a little of the time, or none of the time?

Very much	☐	(4)
Quite a bit	☐	(3)
Somewhat	☐	(2)
A little bit	☐	(1)
Not at all	☐	(0)
DON'T KNOW	☐	(8)
REFUSED	☐	(9)

Note that because 8 and 9 are used as codes in the first question, these codes are repeated in the answers to the second. It is always a good idea to keep codes consistent in all evaluation data collection measures.

Chapter 8

Exercise 1

Situation	Describe the independent and dependent variables	Are the data nominal, ordinal, or numerical?
Patients in the experimental and control group tell whether painkillers give complete, moderate, or very little relief.	Independent variable: group Dependent variable: pain relief	Independent variable: nominal Dependent variable: ordinal
Participants in the program are grouped according to whether they are severely, moderately, or marginally depressed and are given a survey of anxiety that is scored from 1 to 9.	Independent variable: depressed patients in the program Dependent variable: anxiety	Independent variable: ordinal Dependent variable: numerical
Children are chosen for the evaluation according to whether or not they have had all recommended vaccinations; they are followed for 5 years and their health status is monitored.	Independent variable: having or not having recommended vaccinations Dependent variable: health status	Independent variable: nominal Dependent variable: not enough information to tell
Men and women with stage 1, 2, and 3 of a disease are compared in quality of life as measured by scores ranging from 1 to 50 that are obtained from standardized observations.	Independent variable: gender and stage of disease Dependent variable: quality of life	Independent variables: nominal and ordinal Dependent variable: numerical
RNs and LVNs are surveyed, and their average proficiency scores are compared.	Independent variable: type of nurse Dependent variable: proficiency	Independent variable: nominal Dependent variable: numerical

Exercise 2

Analysis: A two-sample independent groups *t* test

Justification for the analysis: This *t* test is appropriate when the independent variable is measured on a nominal scale and the dependent variable is measured on a numerical scale. In this case, the assumptions of a *t* test are met. These assumptions are that each group has a sample size of at least 30, the two groups are about equal in size, and the two groups are independent (an assumption that is met most easily with a strong evaluation design and a high-quality data collection effort).

Exercise 3

If the evaluation aims to find out how younger and older persons in the experimental and control groups compare in amount of domestic violence, and presuming that the statistical assumptions are met, then analysis of variance is an appropriate technique.

Chapter 9

Exercise 1

This slide requires the audience to do too much reading. Also, the title should be more informative. The text suggests the following two slides:

A. Stratified Random Sampling

- Population is divided into subgroups or strata.
- Random sample is selected from each stratum.

B. Stratified Random Sampling: Blueprint

Income

Age (years)

Under 19

20–30

31–35

Over 35

High

Medium

Low

Exercise 2

Report on the table: The table shows that, in the Opinion Leader Education group (OLE), about half the women eligible for a trial of labor still underwent an elective cesarean section. Nevertheless, the rate was 21% lower than in the other groups and was significantly different ($p = .001$). The larger proportion of women undergoing the trial of labor in the OLE group did not result in significantly higher rates of unscheduled cesarean section ($p = .166$). This implies that physicians were appropriately selecting candidates for the trial of labor. Finally, slightly more than one-half of the women eligible for a trial of labor were actually offered one by their physicians in the control and in the audit and feedback groups, whereas significantly more (74.2%) received the offer from physicians in OLE hospitals ($p = .002$). [*Note:* This text is reprinted from J. Lomas, M. Enkin, G. M. Anderson, W. J. Hannah, E. Vayda, and J. Singer. (1991). Opinion leaders vs. audit and feedback to implement practice guidelines. *Journal of the American Medical Association, 265,* 2202–2207. Copyright 1981, 1991, 1992, American Medical Association; reprinted by permission.]

Index

About the Author

Arlene Fink, PhD, is Professor of Medicine and Public Health at the University of California, Los Angeles. She is an evaluation and policy advisor to UCLA's Robert Wood Johnson Clinical Scholars Program and president of Arlene Fink Associates. She has conducted evaluations throughout the United States and abroad and has trained thousands of health professionals, social scientists, and educators in program evaluation. In addition, she has published more than 100 articles related to evaluation methods and health services research.

About the Author